Sexuality & Ageing

Across the globe, both in developed and developing countries, the population is rapidly ageing. In the fields of sexual and relationship therapy and sexual health, ageing has not been an issue of priority. Too often, ageing is thought of as a process that relates to problems, deficits, and taboos, and less to pleasure, change, growth, and diversity. It is treated as a separate life stage and not a process throughout the lifecycle. Sexuality and sexual health are important parts of the lives of older people, as they have a significant impact on quality of life, psychological well-being and physical health, as well as social and family life.

This book brings together contributions from those currently writing on and researching ageing as it relates, in a therapeutic context, to gender identity, to sex and sexuality, and to intimate relationships.

This book was originally published as a special issue of *Sexual and Relationship Therapy*.

Walter Pierre Bouman is a consultant psychiatrist-sexologist at the Nottingham Centre for Gender Dysphoria, UK, and an accredited psychotherapist and supervisor. His work and therapeutic practice both focus on the areas of gender, sex and relationships, with a particular interest on the ageing population. Dr Bouman is deputy editor of *Sexual and Relationship Therapy – International Perspectives on Theory, Research and Practice*.

Peggy J. Kleinplatz is professor of medicine and clinical professor of psychology at the University of Ottawa, Canada. Her book, *New Directions in Sex Therapy*, was winner of the AASECT 2013 Book Award. Her clinical work focuses on eroticism and transformation. Her current research focuses on optimal sexual experience, with a particular interest in sexual health in the elderly, disabled and marginalized populations.

Sexuality & Ageing

Edited by
**Walter Pierre Bouman and
Peggy J. Kleinplatz**

Routledge
Taylor & Francis Group

LONDON AND NEW YORK

College of Sexual and Relationship Therapists

First published 2016
by Routledge
2 Park Square, Milton Park, Abingdon, Oxon, OX14 4RN, UK

and by Routledge
711 Third Avenue, New York, NY 10017, USA

Routledge is an imprint of the Taylor & Francis Group, an informa business

British Library Cataloguing in Publication Data
A catalogue record for this book is available from the British Library

ISBN 13: 978-1-138-93263-0

Typeset in Times New Roman
by RefineCatch Limited, Bungay, Suffolk

Publisher's Note
The publisher accepts responsibility for any inconsistencies that may have
arisen during the conversion of this book from journal articles to book chapters,
namely the possible inclusion of journal terminology.

Disclaimer
Every effort has been made to contact copyright holders for their permission to
reprint material in this book. The publishers would be grateful to hear from any
copyright holder who is not here acknowledged and will undertake to rectify
any errors or omissions in future editions of this book.

Contents

CONTENTS

Citation Information

The chapters in this book were originally published in *Sexual and Relationship Therapy*, volume 30, issue 1 (February 2015). When citing this material, please use the original page numbering for each article, as follows:

For any permission-related enquiries please visit:
http://www.tandfonline.com/page/help/permissions

Notes on Contributors

Martyn Baker is a principal lecturer in the Department of Psychology at University of East London, UK.

Catherine Barrett is the chief investigator and coordinator of the Sexual Health and Ageing Program at The Australian Research Centre in Sex, Health and Society, La Trobe University, Melbourne, Australia. The program includes research to document models for promoting sexual health and well-being; understanding sexual and gender diversity; and preventing sexual assault.

Jean Bégin is a research officer in the Department of Psychology, Université du Québec à Montréal, Canada.

Walter Pierre Bouman is a consultant psychiatrist-sexologist at the Nottingham Centre for Gender Dysphoria, UK, and an accredited psychotherapist and supervisor. His work and therapeutic practice both focus on the areas of gender, sex and relationships, with a particular interest on the ageing population. Dr Bouman is deputy editor of *Sexual and Relationship Therapy – International Perspectives on Theory, Research and Practice*.

Richard Boyer is a full professor in the Department of Psychiatry, Université de Montréal, Canada, and a researcher at the Centre de Recherche Fernand Séguin (Institut en Santé Mentale de Montréal).

Meghan Campbell is a clinical psychologist with an independent practice in Ottawa, Canada.

Jude Comfort worked in public health for over 20 years before moving to an academic appointment in the School of Public Health at Curtin University, Perth, Australia. As well as lecturing in health promotion, she undertakes research within Curtin University's WA Centre for Health Promotion Research. Her research interests include the health of diverse sexualities and gendered communities, and legal drug interventions.

Derrell W. Cox II holds a master's degree in anthropology and is currently a doctoral candidate in medical anthropology at the University of Oklahoma, Norman, Oklahoma, USA. His areas of research include sexual and reproductive health in minority or historically colonized communities, sexual decolonization, health disparities and socio-economic inequality, ageing and sexual health, elder mistreatment, public policy and health, and structural violence.

Pauline Crameri is a research officer with the Sexual Health and Ageing Program at the Australian Research Centre in Sex, Health and Society at La Trobe University, Melbourne, Australia. Her current research includes LGBTI people's experiences of dementia, LGBTI inclusive aged care services, workforce diversity, and the care of older LGBTI people and sexual boundaries in home care services.

Luc Dargis is a doctoral student in the Department of Psychology, Université du Québec à Montréal, Canada. Her PhD research concerns the relation between marital functioning and psychological distress in older people.

John DeLamater is Conway-Bascom professor of sociology at the University of Wisconsin-Madison, WI, USA. The focus of his research is sexuality across the life course. He teaches on human sexuality and is the co-author of *Understanding Human Sexuality* (12th ed., 2014).

Tinashe Dune is a lecturer in interprofessional health sciences at the University of Western Sydney, Australia. Her research and publications focus on sexuality, marginalisation and health inequities. She explores the phenomenological experiences of sex work, physical disability, women's health, GLBTI people and sexual agency.

Bianca Fileborn is a research officer at the Australian Research Centre in Sex, Health and Society, School of Public Health and Human Biosciences, La Trobe University, Melbourne, Australia.

Margaret Flaget-Greener is a clinical psychologist in the Mental Health Clinic at Park Nicollet Health Services in Minneapolis, MN, USA. Her research and clinical interests include older adult sexuality, transgender healthcare and women's health.

James R. Fleckenstein maintains a relationship education and coaching practice in Manassas, Virginia, USA. He is a also a student in the master of public health degree program at the Institute for Advanced Study of Human Sexuality in San Francisco, California, USA, and a co-investigator on the largest survey of self-identified polyamorous persons ever conducted.

Cesar A. Gonzalez is an assistant professor and primary care psychologist with a joint appointment in the Department of Psychiatry and Psychology, and the Department of Family Medicine, at Mayo Clinic in Rochester, MN, USA. He is on the editorial boards of the *International Journal of Transgenderism* and the *International Journal of Sexual Health*.

Gail Hawkes is an associate professor in sociology at the University of New England, Armidale, Australia.

Jonathan D. Huber is an obstetrician/gynaecologist with specialization in female sexuality, practising at the Queensway Carleton Hospital in Ottawa, Canada.

Peggy J. Kleinplatz is professor of medicine and clinical professor of psychology at the University of Ottawa, Canada. Her book, *New Directions in Sex Therapy*, was winner of the AASECT 2013 Book Award. Her clinical work focuses on eroticism and transformation. Her current research focuses on optimal sexual experience, with a particular interest in sexual health in the elderly, disabled and marginalized populations.

Erica Koepsel is a master's candidate in gender and women's studies at the University of Wisconsin-Madison, WI, USA. Her research focus is on pleasure and sex education, and healthy sexual expression throughout life.

Shannon Lawless is a couple and family therapist with specialization in sexuality. She has a private practice in Ottawa, Canada.

Roy J. Levin was reader in physiology in the Department of Biomedical Science, University of Sheffield, UK, from 1977 until his retirement in 2000. He is presently honorary research associate at the Sexual Physiology Laboratory, Porterbrook Clinic, Sheffield, UK. In 2005, he was awarded the Gold Medal of the World Association of Sexology (now the World Association for Sexual Health) for his work in sexology and sexual health and in June 2011, he was given the honour of the fellowship of the Sheffield Society for the Study of Sex and Relationships for his studies on the physiological mechanisms of human sexual arousal. In 2014, he became the vice chair of the Gold Medal Awards Committee of the World Association of Sexual Health (WAS).

Lih-Mei Liao is the professional lead for psychological services to women's health at University College London Hospitals NHSFT, UK.

Sarah Lunn is a clinical health psychologist at Camden & Islington Mental Health & Social Care NHSFT, UK.

Anthony Lyons is a senior research fellow at the Australian Research Centre in Sex, Health and Society, School of Public Health and Human Biosciences, La Trobe University, Melbourne, Australia. His research focuses on the health and well-being of marginalised or stigmatised populations, including gay men, lesbians and other sexual minorities.

A. Dana Ménard recently completed her doctorate in clinical psychology and is working in private practice and at the First Episode Mood and Anxiety Program in London, Ontario, Canada.

Victor Minichiello is a sociologist and public health researcher, an emeritus professor at the University of New England, Armidale, Australia, and adjunct professor at the Australian Research Centre in Sex, Health and Society, School of Public Health and Human Biosciences, La Trobe University, Melbourne, Australia. He has published widely on the topic of sexuality in later life and health ageing.

Nicholas Paradis is a professional counsellor with the Student Academic Success Service, and counsels students living in residence at the University of Ottawa, Ottawa, Canada.

Marian Pitts is emeritus professor and ex-director at the Australian Research Centre in Sex, Health and Society, School of Public Health and Human Biosciences, La Trobe University, Melbourne, Australia.

Michel Préville is a full professor in the Department of Community Health Sciences, and a researcher at the Centre de Recherche de l'Hôpital Charles LeMoyne, at the Université de Sherbrooke, Montreal, Canada.

Lianne Rosen is a PhD candidate in clinical psychology at the University of Victoria, Victoria, British Columbia, Canada.

Eric Sprankle is an assistant professor, clinical psychologist, and AASECT-certified sex therapist in the Department of Psychology at Minnesota State University, Mankato, MN, USA. His research interests include older adult sexuality, sexual compulsivity, and the intersection of genital piercings and sexual health.

Lyba Spring has been a sexual health educator for 32 years, 30 years of which she spent working for Toronto Public Health in English, French and Spanish. Now retired, she works independently, writing curricula, speaking at conferences and workshops, writing articles as well as a regular blog for the Canadian Women's Health Network. She is concerned with a broad range of issues, from publicly funded programmes for human papillomavirus (HPV) vaccine (which she opposes), to the underpinnings of rape culture.

Yiu Tung Suen is an assistant professor of sociology at the Chinese University of Hong Kong. His research interests include sexualities, ageing and life course, and qualitative research methods.

Rachel Thorpe is a research fellow and PhD candidate at the Australian Centre in Sex, Health and Society, School of Public Health and Human Biosciences, La Trobe University, Melbourne, Australia.

Gilles Trudel is a full professor in the Department of Psychology, Université du Québec à Montréal, Canada, and a researcher at the Centre de Recherche Fernand Séguin (Institut en Santé Mentale de Montréal). He has published more than 150 scientific papers, chapters and books.

Laurence Villeneuve is a doctoral student in the Department of Psychology, Université du Québec à Montréal, Canada. Her thesis concerns marital functioning, physical health and psychological distress in older couples.

Carolyn Whyte is the coordinator of Val's Café, a national programme established to promote the health and well-being of older Australians. Carolyn's current research includes the needs of older LGBTI carers, older LGBTI people's mental health and sexuality after stroke.

INTRODUCTION

Moving towards understanding greater diversity and fluidity of sexual expression of older people

Much of the literature on sexuality in older people focuses on sexual problems, leaving clinicians with the impression that older adults have either dismal or non-existent sex lives. Sex is assumed to be for the young, beautiful, able-bodied, and heterosexual. Older people are often perceived and portrayed as post-sexual. Unfortunately, the result of these negative perceptions is that older people themselves often hold similar self-stereotypes. Few data are available on "normal" sexuality in older people, let alone the entire spectrum of sexual expression including optimal sexuality (Kleinplatz, 2008; Kleinplatz et al., 2013). Few empirical studies have been conducted on the subjective sexual experiences of older people.

Many older people continue to engage in and enjoy a wide range of sexual activities, whilst others do not for a variety of reasons. Older people adapt and reprioritize sex when faced with barriers to remaining sexually active, such as not having sexual partners, having poor health status, the impact of polypharmacy on sexuality and sometimes, lack of privacy. If older people are not sexually active, sex is *not necessarily not important* to them (Gott & Hinchliff, 2003). Age, sex, gender, the availability of a partner, living conditions, social context and physical as well as mental health are important factors in influencing sexual interest and activity.

One needs to consider a number of methodological issues when evaluating *sexuality & ageing*. They include issues of sampling, research strategies and the scope of sexual measures and assessment procedures. A pertinent question is to which extent disease contributes to the sexual changes noted in studies of older people. Most people live longer without significant morbidity. The relationship between ageing and disease, and the extent to which they are considered as separable rather than inseparable constructs, have important implications for research strategy. The view that illness is an *intrinsic* component of ageing leads to design studies where individuals are included without regard to health status or to the assessment of age-related changes on a healthy-unhealthy continuum. In contrast, the view that ageing and disease are *distinct* constructs leads to studies where individuals are screened for all identifiable medical illnesses, with the expectation that age-related differences or changes then identified represent 'normal' or non-pathological ageing. The study of such a specific group of older people provides valuable information but is not necessarily applicable to the general population. Studies of sexual behaviour and ageing are largely cross-sectional in design, sampling different age cohorts and interpreting any differences across age-groups as a longitudinal trend. This approach confounds the effects of the widely divergent individual, cultural and developmental experiences of younger and older cohorts with the effects of ageing. Similarly, older adults are frequently considered as a single older cohort, ignoring the bio-psycho-social, cultural and religious heterogeneity within this group. Longitudinal studies, in which serial assessments are carried out on a given group of individuals at specified intervals, have their own limitations, because they confound the effect of ageing and the temporal changes in societal attitudes concerning sexuality.

Two major problems in sex research regarding *sexuality & ageing* are the inadequate characterization of the sample populations and the drawing of conclusions from small, non-representative and non-random samples. There is controversy as to the magnitude and direction of participation bias in studies which explore sensitive issues such as sexual attitudes and behaviour. In general, people who volunteer to participate in sex research have higher levels of education and less conservative sexual attitudes than non-participants. The extent to which the results of studies of *sexuality & ageing* are influenced by a differential, age-dependent participation bias is unknown. Moreover, most studies of *sexuality & ageing* focus predominantly on coital activity – or lack thereof – and erectile capacity. They tend to be uni-dimensional and orientated towards sexual performance, neglecting the importance of motivational, cognitive, affective and interpersonal factors. Phenomenologically relevant aspects of the sexuality of older people such as sexual interest, sexual expectations and beliefs, satisfaction, and optimal sexual experience are frequently ignored. There is a need for operational definition and measurement of these constructs, as they evolve and influence the sexual experiences of those who are growing older (Bouman, 2013).

The idea for this special issue on *Sexuality & Ageing* arose in June 2011 at an Editorial Board meeting for *Sexual and Relationship Therapy* during the World Association for Sexual Health (WAS) in Glasgow, Scotland. The following year one author contacted the other in Canada by telephone to agree on a timeline for this project. Intercontinental time differences can be confusing, and calling your co-editor at 5AM is perhaps not the best start for a project, which requires close and intense collaboration. Notwithstanding this little blip we agreed on a Call for Papers in 2013, and a subsequent timeline for submission and a period for review and editing the year after. During this process we got to know each other well through regular phone calls and e-mails. We discovered that our opinions regarding submitted manuscripts were very similar, as are our work ethics. Very rarely did we disagree. We both have a close affinity with and deep interest in all aspects of clinical sexology, and particularly in people whose sexuality is often marginalized in society. We look forward to celebrating our warm and productive friendship face-to-face at the *International Academy of Sex Research* Meeting in Toronto in August this year.

This special issue consists of 12 papers on topics related to *sexuality & ageing*. There is a combination of empirical and review papers. Many authors have endeavoured to move away from reductionist or limited views about *sexuality & ageing*. There is greater emphasis upon exploring and understanding greater diversity and fluidity of sexual expression of older people. There is a welcome emphasis on the agency of older adults with regard to their own sexual decision-making. Some of the research findings challenge assumptions of monogamy and heterosexuality as the norm. European and North American sex scripts suggest that men and women are expected to feel, think, and behave in different but complementary ways. These scripts suggest that women, more than men, should be having sex in committed (heterosexual) relationships. They also suggest that men should be interested in frequent sex, where sex is typically defined as intercourse. The belief that women want romance in a committed (heterosexual) relationship and men engage in more sexual behaviours with higher levels of desire continues to be held in the predominant understanding of gender differences. Research questions and hypotheses are often framed accordingly, but clearly do not always reflect reality (Kleinplatz et al., 2013). This is in keeping with our clinical practice, where we come across older adults, particularly older women, who eschew sexual identity/labels but quietly begin having sex with same-sex partners.

Clinicians are not immune to ageism when regarding sexual matters with their older clients and patients. Nor are clinicians immune to heteronormativity or regarding monogamy as the norm. We should be sensitive to this mindset when probing into clients' and patients' concerns over sexual desire, initiation, frequency, satisfaction, relations and their meanings to all parties — in an open and non-judgmental manner. Many clinicians (and particularly physicians), who are not trained sexologists or sex therapists are known to be uncomfortable about asking clients and patients questions about their sex lives, let alone clearly and without euphemisms. This is particularly so when the clients' and patients' personal characteristics differ from their own (for example, their sex, gender, age, sexual orientation). This may be especially disadvantageous when dealing with older patients who are already assumed to be invisible and post-sexual by society. Being an older adult in non-monogamous, non-heterosexual relationships further compounds this disadvantage. Given that sex plays an increasingly valuable role in the lives of older people we are well placed to affirm the value of fulfilling sexual relations for the wellbeing of all clients and patients, independent of age, sex, gender, sexual orientation or relationship status.

Walter Pierre Bouman, MD, FRCPsych
Nottingham National Centre for Gender Dysphoria, Nottingham, United Kingdom

Peggy J. Kleinplatz, PhD
University of Ottawa, Ottawa, Canada

References

Bouman, W.P. (2013). Sexuality in later life. In T. Dening & A. Thomas (Eds.), *The Oxford Textbook of Old Age Psychiatry* (pp.703–723). Oxford: Oxford University Press.

Gott, M., & Hinchliff, S. (2003). How important is sex in later life? The views of older people. *Social Science & Medicine, 56*, 1617–1628.

Kleinplatz, P. (2008). Sexuality and older people. *British Medical Journal, 337*, a239.

Kleinplatz, P.J., Ménard, A., Paradis, N., Campbell, M., & Dalgleish, T.L. (2013). Beyond sexual stereotypes: Revealing group similarities and differences in optimal sexuality. *Canadian Journal of Behavioural Science/Revue Canadienne des Sciences du Comportement, 45*(3), 250–258.

Older women and sexuality – are we still just talking lube?

Lyba Spring

Independent Sexual Health Educator, Toronto, Canada

There is little practical information for older women about their changing sexuality. As they age, women are likely to continue to seek ways of expressing their sexuality, but there are issues to consider that both their family doctors and therapists may overlook. Physical conditions or disabilities may hamper their ability to enjoy sex. Pharmaceutical interventions only attempt to improve desire and sexual response. If an older woman begins a new sexual relationship, ignorance of sexually transmitted infections (STIs) puts her at risk. There is good evidence that the incidence of STIs is rising amongst older people. Older women's lack of knowledge about safer sex and poor communication skills may increase their risk of developing sexually acquired infection. Older women who live in long-term care facilities face additional challenges. Their right to be sexually active, along with their right to privacy, may not be realised. Such problems also present challenges for caregivers. In addition, comprehensive assessment criteria are needed to ensure that women in long-term care facilities have the capacity and knowledge to give informed consent to sexual activity and to avoid sexual exploitation. Older gay women may find themselves dealing with an additional problem: Do they feel obliged to conceal their sexual orientation? Older transgender people, who have "passed" for years and find themselves in the physical care of untrained staff, may risk prejudice and humiliation. More evidence is required to determine ways that older women may be helped to live a healthy sexual life and to augment both their knowledge and skills. Professionals working with older women would benefit from more training.

You have been seeing an older female client over the past few months. She had separated from her long-term partner a few months earlier, ostensibly because of low desire, which had a devastating effect on the relationship. One day, she appears radiant, eyes sparkling, with a girlish laugh you have never heard from her before. She tells you that she has met someone. She compares the sex to riding a bicycle. Her body remembered exactly what it was supposed to do. She did not even need lubricant. After congratulating her on this new development in her life, you consider asking her if they have been using condoms or getting tested for sexually transmitted infections (STIs). Or do you even consider asking these questions?

When a version of this article first appeared online in the Canadian Women's Health Network Magazine (Spring, 2012), it received more hits than any article they had ever published. The thirst for information about older women's sexuality was very apparent.

Over the past few decades, with women's sexual pleasure front and centre (in women's magazines at least), where do older women fit into the equation? Typing "older women and sex" into a Google search yielded 139,000,000 results in 0.22 seconds, most being links to porn sites. Clearly, older women maintain an interest in sexual activity, yet there is little information available to them about how to adjust to their changing bodies and situations beyond "communicate with your partner" and "use lube".

We cannot assume that older women have regular sex partners, or that single older women even want to find partners. The search "dating sites for seniors Canada" gives us 1,890,000 results in 0.32 seconds, suggesting that older women, newly single, separated, divorced or bereaved, have the same needs for intimacy, emotional connection, physical affection and sensual pleasure as other women. While dating sites are not the forum of choice for all, single, older women figure prominently on these sites, including those exclusively designed for older people.

There is a body of research stretching from Masters and Johnson up until the present day which supports evidence that sexual activity continues well into the later years. As early as 1966, Masters and Johnson investigated 34 women and 39 men over the age of 50 for a period of four years. In view of the small sample size, they said that they were only able to "suggest clinical impression rather than to establish biological fact" (Masters & Johnson, 1966). But perhaps the most important clinical impression they offer is that physiological ageing processes do not preclude sexual activity in later life, and that ageing may even bring potential benefits to sexual response – an idea as radical today as it was at the time.

Desire in women is maintained until quite late in the aging process. Thompson et al. (2011) reported that "self-rated successful aging, quality of life and sexual satisfaction appear to be stable in the face of declines in physical health, some cognitive abilities, and sexual activity and function [. . ...] from age 60 – 89". Many other studies in older women have corroborated these findings (e.g., Heiman et al., 2011; Trompeter, Bettencourt, & Barrett-Connor, 2012).

What do practitioners have to offer their older female clients beyond the above-mentioned advice to use lube? Unfortunately, advice that does not generally include disabilities associated with ageing, for example, arthritis and body image concerns similar to those experienced following mastectomy. Certainly, lubricant can be helpful to the postmenopausal woman. However, in addition to vaginal dryness, some postmenopausal women may have thinning or even atrophy of the vaginal walls. Bachmann and Nevadunsky (2000) found that up to 40% of postmenopausal women have symptoms of atrophic vaginitis.

Postmenopausal women are also at greater risk of developing a condition called lichen sclerosis. The condition usually presents as white, itchy, sore patches on the skin of the genital area and sometimes around the anus. Treatment is required to reduce symptoms and prevent complications such as persistent symptomatic labial adhesions.

Although the treatment of conditions such as lichen sclerosis is not lucrative, pharmaceutical companies have developed an interest in "sexier" conditions experienced by this group of women. The pharmaceutical industry has identified potential markets for the medical treatment of diminished desire, reduced frequency of orgasm and vaginal dryness. Kuzmarov and Bain (2008) discussed female sexual arousal and response, but moved quickly to recommend hormone therapy to correct low levels of desire. After devoting a few pages to testosterone therapy, they allow two short paragraphs to an alternative vision: there might be psychosocial issues that play a larger role in defining the female sexual response; and secondly, that serum and androgen levels do not necessarily correlate with the degree of sexual interest or arousal.

In keeping with the medicalisation of female sexual dysfunction, pharmaceutical companies have been seeking the elusive magic treatment equivalent to those little blue pills for men. Given Tiefer's analysis which served as the basis of the New View Campaign, Challenging the Medicalisation of Sex, one wonders if they have missed something crucial, namely those psychosexual issues (Tiefer, 2001).

Those fortunate newly single, older women who find a new partner may be pleasantly surprised at their physical response. A woman who was in a loveless relationship, with the lack of desire (and lubrication) that went along with it, may find herself feeling like a teenager, lubricating effortlessly with the right new partner. She may throw away the lube and the Replens, but forget to reach for the condom, if her new partner is male.

Here is the "rub": Fang, Oliver, Jayaraman, and Wong (2010) reported that between 1997 and 2007, rates of STIs in Canada had increased with higher rates reported amongst 40–59 year olds compared with those aged 15–29. This suggests that women entering new sexual relationships may be at a greater risk of developing STIs because they lack sufficient awareness about safer sex or are unable to assert themselves in the relationship. As a result, older women may fail to ask a male partner to use a condom.

Looking at the older cohort, Von Simson and Kulasegaram (2012) cite studies showing an increase in the cases of syphilis, chlamydia and gonorrhea in the UK, USA and Canada in 45–64 year olds. They reported (Von Simson & Kulasegaram, 2012, p. e688), "there has also been an increase in cases of HIV with those aged 50 and over accounting for 20% of adults accessing HIV care, an 82% increase in figures from 2001…" and "new diagnoses of HIV in the over 50s have doubled between 2000 and 2009". Similarly, Bodley-Tickell et al.'s (2008) study found that in less than 10 years, the rate of STIs in those over the age of 45 will be doubled.

Researchers at the Center for Sexual Health Promotion, National Survey of Sexual Health and Behavior Indiana University found that (Reece et al., 2010, pp. 266–276) "one in five sexually active singles reported using a condom regularly and only 12 percent of the men and 32 percent of women said they used one every time". Those over the age of 45 had the lowest rate of condom use (Reece et al., 2010). In the same year Jena, Goldman, Kamdar, Lakdawalla, and Yang (2010) revealed that men using phosphodiesterase type 5 (PDE5 inhibitors such as Viagra) had higher rates of STIs in the years before and after they used these drugs.

It is not surprising that older, single people are not using barrier methods of protection. When these women were younger and they were sexually active, human immunodeficiency virus/acquired immuno deficiency syndrome (HIV/AIDS) and barrier protection to prevent STIs were not widely promoted by health professionals. The combined oral contraceptive was the method of choice for most women at that time with some using an intrauterine device or the diaphragm. Older women may establish sexual relationships with men who have also been in long-term relationships. It would be erroneous to assume that their previous relationships had been monogamous. But how many partners have they each had since then? Have they been getting tested and using STI protection with each new partner?

What is the likelihood of older patients getting tested for the common STIs, let alone HIV? Physicians and therapists may make assumptions about their patients in the same way that patients make assumptions about their partners. Practitioners may be reluctant to raise sexual health issues with older people or encourage routine testing for STIs. Women who continue to have their Pap tests until the age of 70 are not likely to be tested for Chlamydia, which is generally considered a young person's STI. Women in the age group of 15–24 years, who are at the highest risk for chlamydia and gonorrhea may assume that their physicians are checking them for "everything" when they are having their annual internal exams. They may just have a Pap test without getting any STI swabs. For that reason, they should be asking their physicians to check for STIs if they have been engaging in risk-taking sexual behaviours. Women who request STI testing will get a swab during an internal examination, which may reveal gonorrhea or chlamydia. A vaginal smear can detect trichomonas, yeast or bacterial vaginosis. Depending on her history and clinical relevance, a doctor may also order a blood test for syphilis, Hepatitis B, C or HIV.

Regardless of their age, women find it difficult to raise issues of protection and to negotiate safer sexual practices and STI screening with their new partners. It is difficult for some people to tell a new partner what pleases them. Imagine the scenario when it comes to safer sex:

> Did you use protection with all of your partners until you got tested? How often did you get tested? When was the last time you got tested and for which STIs? Of course I trust you. No I don't think you're promiscuous...

Take the example of Canadian "snowbirds". At an HIV conference in 2009, gerontology researcher, Kathleen Mairs, reported that she had surveyed 299 Canadians over the age of 50, who took vacations during the winter months in Florida, USA (Mairs, 2009). She found most were sexually active, and almost half had dated at least one Floridian. New cases of STIs amongst this age group are growing faster than in people under 40. But only 47 of those surveyed – 17.7% – had ever been tested for HIV. Less than a quarter of men and almost none of the women used condoms. According to the "Senior HIV Intervention Project" in Fort Lauderdale, FL, women over the age of 60 are one of the fastest growing risk groups (Agate, Mullins, Prudent, & Liberti, 2003).

The US Centres for Disease Control and Prevention track the age of first HIV diagnosis. In 2003, they reported 865 new diagnoses of HIV in people aged between 60 and 64 years. By 2007, this figure had increased to 980 new HIV diagnoses in the same age group (available at: http://www.cdc.gov/hiv/topics/surveillance/resources/reports/2007report/pdf/2007surveillancereport.pdf).

Vaginal dryness increases the risk of acquiring STIs. A case in point is HIV, which attacks white blood cells. With increased white blood cells at the site of infection, a woman's irritated, inflamed vagina facilitates direct access of the virus to her bloodstream.

Try to imagine a conversation about safer sex between older adults who have met online, or even through friends. People make assumptions about their own health, but "I feel fine" is not a medical diagnosis. Most people are unaware when they have an infection. For example, 75% of the women with chlamydial infection are asymptomatic. This suggests that asking prospective partners if they are "clean" or "have anything" is unhelpful. Those who are asked about their own sexual health may be suspicious about their partner's sexual history.

The difficulties faced by older women living independently are significant, but such problems are compounded when individuals live in long-term care facilities. Caregivers often receive insufficient or inadequate training about older people's sexual health. Requests for training are often motivated by the caregivers' fear that, although following "routine practice" (also known as "universal precautions") to control the spread of infection, they remain at the risk of infection from residents' body fluids. As the population ages, increasing numbers of older people with Hepatitis B and HIV/AIDS will enter long-term care facilities. This suggests that the need for education and training of caregivers about sexual health will also increase. Initial training should focus on health and safety issues. Training should then concentrate on developing caregivers' communication skills to enable them to feel comfortable when discussing sexuality with older clients.

Training professional caregivers raises a number of issues. Caregivers have to appreciate that residents and their partners will expect their need for privacy to be respected.

It may also be difficult to establish whether a woman with cognitive impairment has the capacity to give informed consent to sexual activity with her partner. It is important for caregivers to understand that consent must be voluntary. There must be no coercion so that unwanted advances can be effectively rejected. If someone is unable to recognise potentially abusive situations, she does not have the capacity to give informed consent. Where mental capacity is in doubt, caregivers should be clear about who has the authority to determine capacity.

Older peoples' advocates have reported that attitudes to sexuality and capacity to consent in some long-term care facilities are laissez-faire. Advocates report that caregivers believe that as residents are adults, they are autonomous. This attitude results in failure to acknowledge and report abuse. The Advocacy Centre for the Elderly in Canada has uncovered more than one cases where women with dementia were being sexually assaulted, including assault by a spouse.

Some facilities medicate older people to eradicate their sexual drives. Such a practice is, *prima facie*, unlawful because it fails to adhere to the doctrine of informed consent to medical intervention. Is there a role for staff in assisting seniors in practising safer sex, for example, putting on a condom in the face of a disability? There are also equity issues. Does a woman who was an "out" lesbian in her entire adult life feel that she needs to go back for the closet? What about someone assigned as a male at birth who transitioned to a female as an adult? What she had chosen not to undergo genital reconstructive surgery? There are little caregivers who do not know about one's body. What was private is no longer so. Thankfully, a lesbian, gay, bisexual, transgender (LGBT) toolkit was created in Toronto, Canada to assist care providers in these situations (available at: http://www.toronto.ca/ltc/lgbt_toolkit.htm).

So, although a little lube may go a long way, it is clear that the needs of older women require a good deal more study — and a great big reality check.

References

Agate, L.L., Mullins, J.M., Prudent, E.S., & Liberti, T.M. (2003). Strategies for reaching retirement communities and aging social networks: HIV/AIDS prevention activities among seniors in South Florida. *Journal of Acquired Immunodeficiency Syndrome, 33*(Suppl. 2), 238–242.

Bachmann, G., & Nevadunsky, N.S. (2000). Diagnosis and treatment of atrophic vaginitis. *American Family Physician, 61*(10), 3090–3096.

Bodley-Tickell, A.T., Olowokure, B., Bhaduri, S., White, D.J., Ward, D., Ross, J.D.C., . . . Goold, P. (2008). Trends in sexually transmitted infections (other than HIV) in older people: Analysis of data from an enhanced surveillance system. *Sexually Transmitted Infections, 84*, 312–317.

Fang, L., Oliver, A., Jayaraman, G.C., & Wong, T. (2010). Trends in age disparities between younger and middle-age adults among reported rates of chlamydia, gonorrhea, and infectious syphilis infections in Canada: Findings from 1997 to 2007. *Sexually Transmitted Diseases, 37*(1), 18–25.

Heiman, J.R., Scott Long, J., Smith, S.N., Fisher, W.A., Sand, M.S., & Rosen, R.C. (2011). Sexual satisfaction and relationship happiness in midlife and older couples in five countries. *Archives of Sexual Behavior, 40*, 741–753.

Jena, A.B., Goldman D.P., Kamdar A., Lakdawalla, D.N., & Yang L. (2010). Sexually transmitted diseases among users of erectile dysfunction drugs: Analysis of claims data. *Annals of Internal Medicine, 153*(1), 1–7.

Kuzmarov, I.W., & Bain, J. (2008). Sexuality in the aging couple, part 1: The aging woman. *Geriatrics & Aging, 11*(10), 589–594.

Mairs, K. (2009). *The lifestyles and Sexual Health of Canadian Snowbirds* (Unpublished master's thesis). University of Waterloo, Waterloo, Ontario, Canada. Retrieved from https://uwspace. uwaterloo.ca/bitstream/handle/10012/4922/Mairs_Kathleen.pdf?sequence=1

Masters, W.H., & Johnson, V.E. (1966). *Human sexual response*. Boston, MA: Little, Brown.

Reece, M., Herbenick, D., Schick, V., Sanders, S.A., Dodge, B., & Fortenberry, J.D. (2010). Condom use rates in a national probability sample of males and females ages 14 to 94 in the United States. *Journal of Sexual Medicine, 7* (suppl 5), 266–276.

Spring, L. (2012, July 17). Older women and sexuality . . . are we still just talking lube? *Canadian Women's Health Network Magazine.* Retrieved from http://www.cwhn.ca/en/networkmagazine/ olderwomenandsexuality.

Thompson, W.K., Charo, L., Vahia, I.V., Depp, C., Allison, M., & Jeste, D.V. (2011). Association between higher levels of sexual function, activity, and satisfaction and self-Rated successful aging in older postmenopausal women. *Journal American Geriatric Research Society, 58*(8), 1503–1508.

Tiefer, L. (2001). A new view of women's sexual problems: Why new? Why now? *Journal of Sex Research, 38*, 89–96.

Trompeter, S.E., Bettencourt, R., & Barrett-Connor, E. (2012). Sexual activity and satisfaction in healthy community-dwelling older women. *American Journal of Medicine, 125*(1), 37–43.

Von Simson, R., & Kulasegaram, R. (2012). Sexual health and the older adult. *Student British Medical Journal, 20*, e688.

Are sociodemographic characteristics, education and training, and attitudes toward older adults' sexuality predictive of willingness to assess sexual health in a sample of US psychologists?

Margaret Flaget-Greener[a], Cesar A. Gonzalez[b] and Eric Sprankle[c]

[a]Park Nicollet Health Services, Mental Health, St. Louis Park, MN, USA; [b]Department of Psychiatry and Psychology, and Department of Family Medicine, Mayo Clinic, Rochester, MN, USA; [c]Department of Psychology, Minnesota State University, Mankato, MN, USA

Studies suggest an association between older adults' sexual health and quality of life. Despite this, previous research suggests a lack of assessment of older adults' sexual health. To understand this gap, we examined predictors of practicing psychologists' attitudes to and assessment of the sexual health of older adults. This study utilized purposive online sampling to recruit 119 US practicing psychologists (median years licensed = 11). Participants completed questionnaires on sociodemographics, education and training, and were randomized to a vignette condition depicting a middle-aged or older adult with mood and sexual health concerns. Following the vignette, participants completed a survey on attitudes and their willingness to assess patients' sexual health. Participants' vignette condition, sociodemographics, clinical education, experience, and specialty did not predict attitudes toward older adults' sexuality. However, results indicated that negative attitudes toward older adults' sexuality ($p = .01$) and sexuality education and training ($p = .001$) predicted psychologists' willingness to assess sexual health. Results indicate that in order to increase psychologists' assessments of older adults' sexual health, interventions should focus on changing attitudes toward older adults' sexuality, and increasing psychologists' sexuality education and training.

Introduction

Internationally, it is estimated that the number of adults aged 65 or older will outnumber children under the age of 5 by the year 2016 (United Nations Department of Economic and Social Affairs, Population Division, 2013). Between 2012 and 2050, the number of adults aged 65 and older in the United States (US) will increase by over 100% from approximately 40.3 to 88.5 million people, representing 20% of the US population (United States Census Bureau, 2012). Despite the projected upsurge, there is a gap amongst healthcare providers about how to meet the needs of older adults (Campos, Brasfield, & Kelly, 1989; Kane, 2004; Karel, Knight, Duffy, Hinrichsen, & Zeiss, 2010; Qualls, Segal, Norman, Niederehe, & Gallagher-Thompson, 2002; Wiederman & Sansone, 1999). Moreover, research indicates that as the proportion of older adults increases, advancements in healthcare are contributing to healthy aging and improvements in quality of life (Centers for Disease Control and Prevention

[CDC], 2013). Research suggests that indicators of quality of life include sexual activity (Group, 1998) and this association has also been found among older adults (Robinson & Molzahn, 2007).

Sexual activity among older adults continues well into their 80s and is associated with higher quality of life among older adults (Lindau et al., 2007; Robinson & Molzahn, 2007; Schick et al., 2010). However, in the US, sexual health among older adults has been dismissed due to sociocultural values that associate youth and beauty with sexuality (Hillman, 2000; Huffstetler, 2006). The corollary being that the older adult is widely believed to be stereotypically non-sexual (Pangman & Seguire, 2000) and may explain the frequency with which the sexual health of older adults is ignored or only partially addressed by health providers (Bouman & Arcelus, 2001; Bouman, Arcelus, & Benbow, 2006; Gott, Hinchliff, & Galena, 2004; Hillman, 2012; Kane, 2008; Robinson & Molzahn, 2007). Given these findings, there is a need to understand the barriers that prevent older adults gaining access to sexual health assessments.

Older adults and sexual health in clinical settings

Research findings suggest that beliefs regarding patients' social and behavioral characteristics may directly influence providers' clinical decisions (Dowrick, Gask, Perry, Dixon, & Usherwood, 2000; Van Ryn, 2002). Social cognitive theory (Duncan, 1976), when applied to a clinical setting, suggests providers' interpret older patients' clinical presentation through a framework of beliefs associated with stereotypes of older adults. For example, among psychologists, older adults are perceived as more rigid, poorer learners, less energetic, and as poorer candidates for psychological interventions compared to their younger counterparts (Meeks, 1990). However, the majority of the research on attitudes toward sexual health care in older adults focuses on the attitudes of physicians, nurses, and nursing home staff (Bouman et al., 2006; Gott et al., 2004; Lewis & Bor, 1994). The existing body of literature shows that medical and nursing professionals appear to have greater negative attitudes toward later-life sexuality, compared to younger adults, despite the implementation of professional guidelines to counter ageism (Bouman et al., 2006).

Research indicates that attitudes and biases toward sexual health are often moderated by sex, age, and clinical experience, and extend into providers' clinical interactions. For instance, Schover (1981) found that attitudes and beliefs were predictive of male providers either over- or under-emphasizing patients' sexual health concerns. Furthermore, among male providers, liberal sexual attitudes and beliefs were associated with non-therapeutic sexualized inquiry, while conservative sexual attitudes were associated with increased anxiety and avoidance of sexual health topics. In contrast, female providers were found to be more comfortable with patients' sexual health concerns. Similarly, Bowers and Bieschke (2005) found female providers to hold more positive attitudes and anticipate positive treatment outcomes for patients with diverse sexual orientations than male providers. Similar to the moderating effects of sex/gender in other studies (Bowers & Bieschke, 2005; Schover, 1981), in a probability sample of psychologists in Norway, older age and greater clinical experience among providers was associated with assessing sexual health and satisfaction (Træen & Schaller, 2013). The most recent study confirmed an association between increased age of practitioners and provision of sexual health assessments (Ports, Barnack-Tavlaris, Syme, Perera, & Lafata, 2014).

Sexual health education and training among health providers

Education and training in sexual health is found to increase the frequency with which providers ask patients about sexual health (Miller & Byers, 2009, 2010; Reissing & Di Giulio, 2010). In a study of Canadian psychologists, the majority of psychologists did not ask about sexual health and indicated a lack of education and training in concerns related to sexual health care (Reissing & Di Giulio, 2010). Furthermore, Miller and Byers' (2009) study of practicing psychologists found that less than half of psychologists failed to ask patients about sexual issues when completing a diagnostic assessment, despite patients presenting with sexual concerns. In addition, Miller and Byers found that psychologists with less sex education are more likely to make unnecessary or inappropriate referrals to specialists (i.e., sex therapists) rather than provide treatment.

In further examining the impact of sexuality education and training, Miller and Byers (2010) also found that most psychologists had some sexuality education during their training. However, the depth and breadth of the training was limited to sexual disorders rather than to including a broad spectrum of sexual health. In addition, Miller and Byers found that specific sexual health training was more predictive of subsequent integration of sexual health into the providers' clinical practice than were their characteristics or cognitive-affective factors.

Despite the benefits of sexuality training and education for health providers, there continues to be a lack of graduate training programs integrating sexual health into the curricula (Campos et al., 1989; Miller & Byers, 2008; Ng, 2007; Reissing & Di Giulio, 2010; Wiederman & Sansone, 1999). This gap creates an opportunity for clinical researchers and educators to investigate and address barriers preventing integration of sexual health provision into clinical practice, particularly among older adult patients.

Current study

To address the gap in providers' knowledge and to increase the quality of life of older adult patients, there is a need to investigate the characteristics that facilitate the integration of sexual health into health providers' clinical practice. Previous studies on the characteristics of health care providers that influence clinical decision making with underserved and stigmatized groups suggest significant differences across health disciplines (Bouman & Arcelus, 2001; Burgess, Fu, & Van Ryn, 2004; Kane, 2008) and clinical settings (Bouman et al., 2006; Gott et al., 2004). Our study is guided by the absence of research that focuses on mental health professionals and their attitudes toward the sexual health care of older adults. Furthermore, our study contributes to the literature by exploring how attitudes affect the relationship between mental health care providers' demographic and professional characteristics and the assessment of sexual health, particularly among older adults.

In this study, we examine the role of psychologists' demographic and education and training characteristics on attitudes toward older adults' sexuality. Furthermore, we examine how these characteristics and attitudes predict psychologists' willingness to assess sexual health of older adults. Based on previous research, we hypothesized that among our sample of psychologists: (1) female participants and older age would be associated with permissive attitudes toward older adults' sexuality and willingness to assess sexual health and (2) geropsychology/gerontopsychology education and training, and sexuality-specific education and training would be associated with permissive attitudes toward older adults' sexuality and willingness to assess sexual health. Even when accounting for significant demographic characteristics, geropsychology, and sexuality education and training, we hypothesize that the willingness of psychologists to assess sexual health is influenced by permissive attitudes toward older adults' sexuality.

Method

Participants

A demographic questionnaire asked participants to report their age, sex, and completed educational level. One hundred and eighty-nine participants began the survey. We received 13 partial responses and 51 participants abandoned the survey before answering any questions. Overall, 66% of participants who consented to participate in the study completed the survey. Six participants were removed from subsequent analysis because they were not doctoral level psychologists. The final sample included 119 doctoral level psychologists licensed in the US, who reported to be the members of the American Psychological Association (APA). The majority of the participants were female (61.3%; $n = 73$) and ranged in age from 24 to 76 years ($M = 48.31$, SD $= 12.81$; Mdn $= 48$). Doctoral degree type reported by participants included Ph.D (56.3%), PsyD (42.9%), and EdD (0.8%). The duration since obtaining licensure ranged from 2 months to 38 years ($M = 12.47$ years, SD $= 9.86$; Mdn $= 11$).

In order to ensure that participants in the study were practicing psychologists and to increase the heterogeneity of participants, this study utilized online purposive sampling. Participants were invited to participate through email listservs for the US licensed psychologists, including the APA's division listservs (e.g. the Society of Clinical Psychology, Psychoanalysis, and the Society for the Study of Lesbian, Gay, Bisexual, and Transgender [LGBT] Issues). These listservs were chosen in order to contact psychologists working in a clinical role. A recruitment announcement was sent to each listserv and the link remained active for approximately four months. The email included a statement that the study involved research and provided information about the study's purpose, duration, procedures, foreseeable risks or discomforts, benefits, and confidentiality of information. The email also contained a link to the website that hosted the survey. Individuals were informed that by clicking the link, they were agreeing to participate in the study. Participation in the study was voluntary and no incentives were provided.

Measures

Geropsychology and sexuality education and training

Participants were asked to rate the amount of training they had received and their perceived level of competency (based on the training/education) to treat sexual and older adult-related health concerns. Examples of questions included, "How much education/training have you received in treating older adults?" and "Based on your training/education of treating clients with sexuality issues, how prepared do you feel you are to treat this type of client?" This measure included four questions (two for gerontology; two for sexual health) and used a Likert-type scale, with possible responses ranging from 1 (none; not prepared) to 5 (specialized; very prepared). Scores were summed to create a composite indicating the amount of education and training in gerontology and sexual health participants had received. Higher scores indicated a greater amount of education and training. Cronbach's α for the gerontology items was .85, 95% confidence interval (CI) [.79, .90], and .86, 95% CI [.80, .90] for the sexual health items.

Attitudes toward the sexual health of older adults

The Aging Sexual Knowledge and Attitudes Scale (ASKAS; White, 1982) guided our measure of attitudes toward older adults' sexual health. The ASKAS is designed to assess the participant's knowledge and attitudes related to sexuality among older adults residing in long-term care facilities (Bouman, Arcelus, & Benbow, 2007). Responses to the ASKAS are on a Likert-type scale, with response options ranging from 1 (disagree) to 7 (agree). The ASKAS includes two subscales that assess knowledge and attitudes regarding older adults' sexuality; it has been found to be reliable and valid across diverse samples and settings (Allen, Petro, & Phillips, 2009; Bouman et al., 2007; Steinke, 1994; White, 1982).

Our study used a modified attitudinal subscale of the ASKAS; of the 26 original items measuring attitudes toward older adults' sexuality, 10 items were not included because of their emphasis on long-term care facilities and due to the concern that these items measured attitudes toward nursing homes rather than older adults' sexuality. Of the attitudinal items that were included, six items were modified to make them more general and less specific to nursing homes. For example, "If I knew that a particular nursing home permitted and supported sexual activity in residents who desired it, I would not place a relative in that nursing home" was revised to "If I knew that a colleague of mine supported sexual activity in older adults who desired it, I would not refer a relative to that colleague." Finally, six additional items were included in our measure of attitudes toward older adults' sexuality. These additional six items were items that have been previously used by Hillman and Stricker (1996) in conjunction with the attitude scale of the ASKAS and included such statements as, "I would feel very comfortable having a conversation about elderly sexuality."

Our final measure of attitudes toward older adults' sexual health included 22 items. Responses to the items were on a 7-point Likert-type scale, with response options ranging from 1 (disagree) to 7 (agree). A total score was calculated by summing all items; higher scores on this measure indicated more negative and restrictive attitudes, while lower scores indicated more positive and permissive attitudes. Cronbach's α for our measure of attitudes toward older adults' sexual health was .70, 95% CI [.62, .78].

Willingness to assess sexual health

Participants were asked to rate how likely they were to ask their patients questions related to sexual health through six items. Examples of questions used include, "How frequently do you engage in sexual activities?" and "Have you had any previous problems in your ability to have and enjoy sexual relationships?" Responses to the items were on a 7-point Likert-type scale, ranging from 1 (not likely) to 7 (very likely). Cronbach's α for this measure was .91, 95% CI [.88, .93].

Materials

Clinical vignettes

The study included two vignettes modeled after Bouman and Arcelus' (2001) study and included a written description and an age congruent photograph. In our study, one vignette described a 75-year-old woman with no previous psychiatric history and without any cognitive impairment, complaining of low mood and difficulty becoming sexually aroused. The other vignette described a 40-year-old woman with the same concerns.

Except for the manipulation of the photographs and the description of age in the vignettes, both vignettes were identical.

Procedures

Participants were directed to a website containing the questionnaire. The order of the measures and materials were as follows: (1) sociodemographics and education and training questionnaire; (2) randomization/allocation into vignette condition; and (3) attitudes measure. The approximate completion time for the survey was 15 minutes. An ethics review board at Widener University in the US approved the study in March 2010 and data collection began in April 2010.

Data analysis

Descriptive statistics for the sample are provided in Table 1 and include the study variables' coding descriptions, means, standard deviations, and bootstrapped CIs of the means, median, observed and theoretical ranges, and bivariate correlations with bootstrapped CIs. Pearson's correlation coefficients were used to determine the associations between the study's variables. To test the study's hypotheses, a hierarchical linear regression (using forced entry) was conducted; violations of statistical assumptions were evaluated and not found to be significant. The regressions' unstandardized regression coefficients (b), standard errors, and the coefficients of determination (R^2) and the changes in R^2 (noted as ΔR^2) are reported for each model (see Tables 2 and 3). Pearson's correlation and the hierarchical regressions included 10,000 samples and used bias-corrected and accelerated (BCa) 95% CIs. In utilizing bootstrapped BCa CIs into our statistical analyses, we adjusted for bias and skewness (Visalakshi & Jeyaseelan, 2013) in the bootstrap distribution and provide adequate coverage for adjusting for correlation attenuation (Padilla & Veprinsky, 2012). Furthermore, by using bootstrapping, we are likely to increase the precision and point approximation of our statistical results (Preacher & Hayes, 2004, 2008). Interpretation of the bootstrapping procedures for the correlation and regression-based analyses involved assessing the bootstrapped 95% BCa CIs bounds and determining whether the CIs of the coefficients included zero. Statistical significance was determined if the 95% BCa CIs included zero. All tests used two-tailed p-values; p-values less than .05 were noted as statistically significant.

Results

Attitudes toward older adults' sexuality

To examine whether vignette condition, providers' characteristics, and geropsychology and sexuality education and training, predicted attitudes toward older adults' sexuality, a forced-entry hierarchical regression was conducted. Step 1 included the condition of the vignette (middle age versus older age). Results indicated that the condition of the vignette did not significantly predict attitudes toward older adults' sexuality, $F(1, 114) = 0.14, p = .71, R^2 = .001$. In step 2, providers' characteristics were entered. Providers' characteristics did not significantly add to increasing the model's strength to explain the variance in scores on attitudes toward adults' sexuality, $F_{change}(3, 111) = 0.85, p = .47, \Delta R^2 = .02$. Moreover, age ($b = .01, p = .18$), sex ($b = .04, p = .56$), and years licensed ($b = -.03, p = .51$) did not independently predict attitudes toward older adults' sexuality. In step 3,

Table 1. Study variable means, standard deviations, confidence intervals, medians, ranges, and bivariate correlations with confidence intervals.

Variable	M (SD)	BCa 95% CI	Mdn	Observed range	Theoretical range	1	2	3	4	5	6	7
1. Age (years)	48.41 (12.91)	[46.09, 50.80]	48.00	24–68	18–∞	—						
2. Gender	1.60 (.49)	[1.52, 1.69]	2.00	1–2	1–2	−.12 [−.29, −.07]	—					
3. Years licensed	12.54 (9.87)	[10.78, 14.31]	11.00	0–38	0–∞	.68*** [.57, .78]	−.30** [−.47, −.12]	—				
4. Attitudes toward older adults' sexuality	6.53 (.35)	[6.46, 6.60]	6.59	5.05–7.00	1–7	.06 [−.12, .27]	.08 [−.10, .27]	.02 [−.20, .17]	—			
5. Geropsychology education and training	2.34 (.87)	[2.19, 2.51]	2.00	1–5	1–5	.07 [−.10, .22]	−.04 [.22, .15]	−.04 [−.19, .12]	.01 [−.29, .27]	—		
6. Sexuality education and training	2.49 (.85)	[2.34, 2.64]	2.50	1–5	1–5	−.10 [−.09, .28]	−.16 [−.09, .28]	.12 [−.06, .30]	.12 [−.04, .27]	.17 [.00, .34]	—	
7. Willingness to assess sexual health	5.32 (1.51)	[5.03, 5.59]	5.80	1–7	1–7	.03 [−.14, .21]	.03 [−.14, .21]	.01 [−.17, .18]	.27** [.05, .45]	.01 [−.20, .22]	.32** [.19, .44]	—

Note: Coding for gender variable: 1 = male; 2 = female.
CIs are based on 10,000 bootstrapped samples (bias corrected and accelerated).
** $p < .01$; *** $p < .001$.

Table 2. Summary of hierarchical regression analysis for vignette condition, provider characteristics, and education and training on predicting attitudes toward older adults' sexuality.

Step and variables	b	SE b	95% CI of b	R^2	ΔR^2
Step 1: Study manipulation				.00	—
Vignette condition	0.02	0.07	[−0.10, 0.15]		
Step 2: Provider characteristics				.02	0.02
Vignette condition	0.00	0.07	[−0.11, 0.15]		
Age	0.00	0.00	[−0.38, 0.84]		
Gender	0.04	0.07	[−0.10, 0.18]		
Years licensed	0.00	0.01	[−0.01, 0.01]		
Step 3: Geropsychology education and training				.02	.00
Vignette condition	0.02	0.07	[−0.11, 0.15]		
Age	0.01	0.00	[0.00, 0.12]		
Gender	0.04	0.07	[−0.09, 0.18]		
Years licensed	0.00	0.01	[−0.01, 0.01]		
Geropsychology education and training	0ᵣ.00	0.04	[−0.08, .08]		
Step 4: Sexuality education and training				.05	.02
Vignette condition	0.03	0.07	[−0.10, 0.16]		
Age	0.00	0.00	[0.00, 0.01]		
Gender	0.06	0.70	[−0.08, 0.20]		
Years licensed	0.00	0.01	[−0.01, 0.01]		
Geropsychology education and training	−0.01	0.04	[−0.09, 0.07]		
Sexuality education and training	−0.06	0.04	[−0.02, 0.14]		

Note: 95% CIs are based on 10,000 bootstrapped samples (bias corrected and accelerated).
Coding for vignette condition: 0 = middle age; 1 = older age.
Coding for gender variable: 1 = male; 2 = female.
$^*p \leq .05$; $^{**}p \leq .01$; $^{***}p \leq .001$.
Step 1: $df = (1, 114)$; Step 2: $df = (3, 111)$; Step 3: $df = (1, 110)$; Step 4: $(1, 109)$.

geropsychology education and training was added to the model. Results suggested that adding geropsychology education and training did not significantly increase the model's power to predict attitudes toward older adults' sexuality, $F_{change}(1, 110) = 0.00$, $p = .99$, $\Delta R^2 = .00$. Sexuality education and training was entered in step 4 and results indicated that sexuality education and training did not significantly increase the explained variance on the scores of attitudes toward older adults' sexuality, $F_{change}(1, 109) = 2.50$, $p = .12$, $\Delta R^2 = .02$; the final model was not significant in predicting attitudes toward older adults' sexuality, $F(6, 115) = 0.87$, $p = .52$, $R^2 = .04$.

Predictors of willingness to assess sexual health

A forced-entry hierarchical regression was utilized to examine whether vignette condition, providers' characteristics, attitudes toward older adults' sexuality, geropsychology education and training, and sexuality education and training would significantly predict psychologists' willingness to assess sexual health. In step 1, the condition of the vignette

Table 3. Summary of hierarchical regression analysis for vignette condition, provider characteristics, attitudes toward older adults' sexuality, and education and training on willingness to assess sexual health.

Step and variables	b	$SE\ b$	95% CI of b	R^2	ΔR^2
Step 1: Study manipulation				.00	–
Vignette condition	0.16	0.28	[−0.40, 0.71]		
Step 2: Provider characteristics				.01	0.01
Vignette condition	0.16	0.28	[−0.41, 0.72]		
Age	0.01	0.31	[−0.38, 0.84]		
Gender	0.23	0.02	[−0.02, 0.04]		
Years licensed	0.00	0.02	[−0.04, 0.04]		
Step 3: Attitudes toward older adults' sexuality				.08	.07**
Vignette condition	0.13	0.28	[−0.42, 0.68]		
Age	0.00	0.02	[−0.03, 0.03]		
Gender	0.18	0.30	[−0.41, 0.77]		
Years licensed	0.01	0.02	[−0.04, 0.05]		
Attitudes toward older adults' sexuality	0.05**	0.02	[0.02, 0.09]		
Step 4: Geropsychology education and training				.08	.00
Vignette condition	0.13	0.28	[−0.42, 0.68]		
Age	0.00	0.02	[−0.03, 0.03]		
Gender	0.18	0.30	[−0.41, 0.78]		
Years licensed	0.01	0.02	[−0.03, 0.03]		
Attitudes toward older adults' sexuality	0.05**	0.02	[0.02, 0.09]		
Geropsychology education and training	0.02	0.16	[−0.30, 0.34]		
Step 5: Sexuality education and training				.18**	.10***
Vignette condition	0.20	0.26	[−0.32, 0.72]		
Age	−0.02	0.01	[−0.03, 0.03]		
Gender	0.33	0.29	[−0.23, 0.91]		
Years licensed	0.00	0.02	[−0.04, 0.04]		
Attitudes toward older adults' sexuality	0.04**	0.02	[0.01, 0.08]		
Geropsychology education and training	−0.07	0.15	[−0.38, 0.23]		
Sexuality education and training	0.58***	0.16	[0.26, 0.90]		

Note: 95% CIs are based on 10,000 bootstrapped samples (bias corrected and accelerated).
Coding for vignette condition: 0 = middle age; 1 = older age.
Coding for gender variable: 1 = male; 2 = female.
**$p \leq .01$; ***$p \leq .001$.
Step 1: df = (1, 114); Step 2: df = (3, 111); Step 3: df = (1, 110); Step 4: df = (1, 109); Step 5: df = (1, 108).

was not predictive of providers asking sex assessment questions, $F(1, 114) = .31$, $p = .58$, $R^2 = .00$. Adding providers' characteristics (step 2) did not significantly increase the model's ability to explain the variance in scores on willingness to assess sexual health, $F_{change}(3, 111) = 0.30$, $p = .83$, $\Delta R^2 = .01$. Moreover, age ($b = .01$, $p = .69$), sex ($b = .23$, $p = .46$), and years licensed ($b = .00$, $p = .94$) did not independently predict willingness to assess sexual health. In step 3, providers' attitudes toward older adults' sexuality was entered into the model. Results indicated that permissive attitudes toward older adults' sexuality significantly increased the model's ability to explain the variance in scores on willingness to assess sexual health, $F_{change}(1, 110) = 8.53, p = .004, \Delta R^2 = .07$. In step 4, geropsychology education and training was entered into the model and indicated that geropsychology education and training did not significantly increase the model's strength to predict willingness to assess sexual health, $F_{change}(1, 109) = 0.01$, $p = .91, \Delta R^2 = .01$. Sexuality education and training was entered in step 5 and significantly increased the model's predictive power, $F_{change}(1, 108) = 12.72, p = .001$, $\Delta R^2 = .10$. The final model was significant in predicting willingness to assess sexual health, $F(7, 115) = 3.36, p = .003, R^2 = .18$. Furthermore, holding all the entered variables constant in the final model, permissive attitudes toward older adults' sexuality ($b = .04, p = .01$) and greater sex education and training ($b = .58, p = .001$) were independently predictive of psychologists' willingness to assess sexual health.

Discussion

This study aimed to examine whether psychologists' characteristics (age, sex/gender, geropsychology and sexuality education and training) predicted attitudes toward older adults' sexuality. Moreover, we examined whether psychologists' characteristics and attitudes predicted providers' willingness to assess sexual health in older patients. In order to control for social desirability of psychologist's responses, a randomized clinical vignette, with two conditions (middle-aged versus older-aged patient) was implemented. Our findings suggested that manipulating the age of the patient in the clinical vignette conditions did not influence psychologists to express significant differences on sexual attitudes or willingness to assess older adults' sexual health. This suggests that there were no response difference based on patients' age.

Our first hypothesis posited that female and older participants, who had received education and training in geropsychology and sexuality, would express more permissive attitudes toward older adults' sexuality, than younger male participants, who had less education and training in geropsychology and sexuality. In testing this hypothesis, we found that age, sex, education and training in geropsychology and sexuality in either vignette condition were not predictive of attitudes toward older adults' sexuality. This lack of association may be explained by the homogeneity of our participants' level of education (i.e., all holding doctorates). For example, results from Fischtein, Herold, and Desmarais (2007) demonstrated a correlation between increased levels of education and more liberal, permissive attitudes toward sexuality in a sample of individuals with heterogeneous education levels. Interestingly, our findings deviate from the literature that has found associations between older providers, greater clinical experience, and increased likelihood of assessing sexual health (Bowers & Bieschke, 2005; Ports et al., 2014; Schover, 1981; Træen & Schaller, 2013). However, our findings are in line with previous research that demonstrates a lack of association between sexual health knowledge and attitudes toward older adults' sexual health (Hillman, 2012; Snyder & Zweig, 2010).

Our second hypothesis posited that more permissive attitudes and training and education in geropsychology, and sexuality are predictive of psychologists' willingness to assess older adults' sexual health. Results of our study indicated that attitudes toward older adults' sexuality and sexual education and training were predictive of psychologists' willingness to assess older adults' sexual health, despite participants' demographic characteristics. Our results support findings from Miller and Byers' (2009, 2010) studies of clinical psychology programs and sexuality training. Miller and Byers did not find a correlation between individual characteristics such as sex, religiosity, sexual conservatism, or comfort with sexual communication and students' sex therapy experience. Furthermore, a study examining psychologists' sexual intervention, self-efficacy, and willingness to treat sexual issues found that psychologists who received more graduate education in sexual health sought more continuing education in sexuality. More education and training was associated with higher sexual intervention and self-efficacy that was, in turn, associated with more intervention behaviors (Miller & Byers, 2008). Our findings also support the idea that psychologists' attitudes may directly influence their clinical decisions (Dowrick et al., 2000; Van Ryn, 2002).

Implications and recommendations

The characteristics of participants were not found to be predictive of attitudes toward older adults' sexuality. Our data suggest that regardless of sex and age, therapists generally hold similar attitudes toward older adults' sexuality, and do not appear to differ significantly with respect to willingness to assess sexual health.

In our study, attitudes toward older adults' sexuality and sexuality education and training were found to be predictive of psychologists' willingness to assess sexual health. These results suggest that concentrating on attitudes toward older adults' sexuality, and sexuality education and training may increase the likelihood that psychologists will assess sexual health, regardless of the age of the patient. Future studies should investigate whether these patterns hold for psychologists with a patient who is perceived to be a young adult compared to an older adult.

With the anticipation of a dramatic increase in ageing of the global population, identifying factors that can increase the potential for quality of life in older age is vital. Improvement in quality of life is associated with better management of older people's medical issues and long-term cost savings for overburdened health-care systems (Carlson & Bultz, 2003). Research findings have recognized the link between sexual health and quality of life in older adults (Robinson & Molzahn, 2007). Ensuring that providers are assessing and addressing sexual health needs of older adults is essential to improving their quality of life, particularly given that mental health is increasingly being integrated with primary care in the US and beyond (Harris et al., 2012; Zivin et al., 2010).

A key finding of this study is that attitudes toward sexuality education and training are significant predictors of psychologists' willingness to assess sexual health. Our results support the burgeoning literature about the importance of including sexuality education and training in doctoral clinical psychology training programs (Miller & Byers, 2010; Wiederman & Sansone, 1999). Incorporating sexuality education specifically related to older adults in training programs, clinical rotations, as well as post-graduate education or training opportunities may begin to fill this need. Future research should focus on identifying core competencies in the area of sexual health needs across the lifespan. Programs should standardize training so they may properly integrate this education into curricula and clinical experiences. In addition, assessing to what extent this education improves sexual health related clinical skills would be beneficial.

Several researchers have proposed and developed solutions to improve the education and training of psychologists in both of the areas of sexual health and aging (Hinrichsen & McMeniman, 2002; Hinrichsen, Zeiss, Karel, & Molinari, 2010; Koder & Helmes, 2008; Miller & Byers, 2008, 2010). There are limitations to the depth and breadth of education and training that can be expected of programs, but many proposed solutions suggest streamlining the concepts into existing curricula rather than trying to make room for more courses. The key elements to these solutions are the assessment of attitudes and affective learning, which focuses on the way in which we learn through emotions, including feelings, values, appreciation, enthusiasms, motivations, and attitudes. The solutions are focused on attitude change and increased self-efficacy regarding clinical interventions. This can be accomplished through didactic learning, experiential learning, and high-quality interactions with the target population (i.e., older adults). In addition, using educational tools that increase self-reflection and self-awareness, such as journaling, may encourage changes on an affective level.

Limitations

Despite this study's experimental design, there are several limitations to consider in respect to the validity of our findings.

Regarding the internal validity of our study there were two limitations: (a) due to the specific research questions, significant modifications were made to the ASKAS. Although the measure retained an acceptable range of internal consistency, the range of the reliability coefficient was not optimal and may influence the precision of our assessment of attitudes toward older adults' sexuality; (b) another was the unintentional differences of the individuals portrayed in the clinical vignette pictures. For example, while the age of the patients in the vignette was independently rated as significantly differentiating between middle and older age, other physical characteristics were not systematically evaluated (e.g. skin tone, hair type) and may have confounded our findings by introducing implicit and explicit racial/ethnic biases (Wittenbrink, Judd, & Park, 1997). With respect to the external validity of the study, three major limitations were identified. (1) This study utilized a purposive online sample without incentives, thus limiting the generalizability of our finding only to psychologists that were self-selected. However, the strength of this sampling method is that without incentives, there is a greater assurance that the participant pool comprises solely psychologists. (2) Furthermore, the study utilized self-reporting methods, which are susceptible to social desirability biases. However, research has demonstrated that Internet-based methodology (as opposed to offline, paper and pencil methods) decreases social desirability biases due to perceived anonymity (Gosling, Vazire, Srivastava, & John, 2004). (3) The study's clinical vignettes depicted only female patients, thus limiting the generalizability to other women only. Portraying only a female patient may be more consistent with what psychologists are likely to experience in their clinical practice (Crowther, Shurgot, Perkins, & Rodriguez, 2006), given that women have greater longevity and health utilization than men, thus depicting only female patients in the clinical vignettes is a minor threat to external validity.

Conclusion

Our study's primary aim was to investigate whether providers' sociodemographics, attitudes, and education and training influence psychologists' willingness to assess sexual health among older adults whilst controlling for bias related to ageism. To achieve our aim, US psychologists were randomized into one of the two clinical vignettes depicting either a middle-aged or older-aged woman. Our findings indicated no significant differences in psychologists' with permissive sexual attitudes toward older adults or willingness to assess the sexual health of older adults. Furthermore, we found no significant predictors of attitudes toward older adults' sexual health, including sex, years licensed as a provider, training in geropsychology and sexuality training. Our results suggested that attitudes toward older adults' sexuality, and education and training in sexuality, predict psychologists' willingness to assess sexual health among older adults. Based on our study's findings, we encourage graduate programs to provide more sexuality-specific education and training in order to facilitate psychologists' willingness to assess older adults' sexual health.

References

Allen, R., Petro, K., & Phillips, L. (2009). Factors influencing young adults' attitudes and knowledge of late-life sexuality among older women. *Aging & Mental Health, 13*(2), 238–245.

Bouman, W.P., & Arcelus, J. (2001). Are psychiatrists guilty of 'ageism' when it comes to taking a sexual history? *International Journal of Geriatric Psychiatry, 16*, 27–31.

Bouman, W.P., Arcelus, J., & Benbow, S.M. (2006). Nottingham study of sexuality & ageing (NoSSA I). Attitudes regarding sexuality and older people: A review of the literature. *Sexual and Relationship Therapy, 21*(2), 149–161.

Bouman, W.P., Arcelus, J., & Benbow, S.M. (2007). Nottingham study of sexuality and ageing (NoSSA II). Attitudes of care staff regarding sexuality and residents: A study in residential and nursing homes. *Sexual and Relationship Therapy, 22*(1), 46–61.

Bowers, A.M., & Bieschke, K.J. (2005). Psychologists' clinical evaluations and attitudes: An examination of the influence of gender and sexual orientation. *Professional Psychology: Research and Practice, 36*(1), 97–103.

Burgess, D.J., Fu, S.S., & Van Ryn, M. (2004). Why do providers contribute to disparities and what can be done about it? *Journal of General Internal Medicine, 19*(11), 1154–1159.

Campos, P., Brasfield, T., & Kelly, J. (1989). Psychology training related to AIDS: Survey of doctoral graduate programs and predoctoral internship programs. *Professional Psychology: Research and Practice, 20*(4), 214–220.

Carlson, L.E., & Bultz, B.D. (2003). Benefits of psychosocial oncology care: Improved quality of life and medical cost offset. *Health and Quality of Life Outcomes, 1*(1), 1–9.

Centers for Disease Control and Prevention. (2013). *The state of aging and health in America 2013.* Retrieved from http://www.cdc.gov/features/agingandhealth/state_of_aging_and_health_in_america_2013.pdf

Crowther, M., Shurgot, G., Perkins, M., & Rodriguez, R. (2006). The social and cultural context of psychotherapy with older adults. In S. Qualls & B. Knight (Eds.), *Psychotherapy for depression in older adults* (pp. 179–199). Hoboken, NJ: John Wiley & Sons.

Dowrick, C., Gask, L., Perry, R., Dixon, C., & Usherwood, T. (2000). Do general practitioners' attitudes towards depression predict their clinical behaviour? *Psychological Medicine, 30*(2), 413–419.

Duncan, B.L. (1976). Differential social perception and attribution of intergroup violence: Testing the lower limits of stereotyping of Blacks. *Journal of Personality and Social Psychology, 34*(4), 590–598.

Fischtein, D., Herold, E., & Desmarais, S. (2007). How much does gender explain in sexual attitudes and behaviors? A survey of Canadian adults. *Archives of Sexual Behavior, 35*, 451–461.

Gosling, S.D., Vazire, S., Srivastava, S., & John, O.P. (2004). Should we trust web-based studies? A comparative analysis of six preconceptions about Internet questionnaires. *American Psychologist, 59*(2), 93–104.

Gott, M., Hinchliff, S., & Galena, E. (2004). General practitioner attitudes to discussing sexual health issues with older people. *Social science & medicine, 58*(11), 2093–2103.

Group, T.W. (1998). The World Health Organization quality of life assessment (WHOQOL): Development and general psychometric properties. *Social Science & Medicine, 46*(12), 1569–1585.

Harris, M., Greaves, F., Patterson, S., Jones, J., Pappas, Y., Majeed, A., & Car, J. (2012). The North West London integrated care pilot: Innovative strategies to improve care coordination for older adults and people with diabetes. *The Journal of Ambulatory Care Management, 35*(3), 216–225.

Hillman, J.L. (2000). *Clinical perspectives on elderly sexuality.* New York, NY: Kluwer/Plenum.

Hillman, J. (2012). *Sexuality and aging: Clinical perspectives.* Boston, MA: Springer.

Hillman, J.L., & Stricker, G. (1996). Predictors of college students' knowledge and attitudes toward elderly sexuality: The relevance of grandparental contact. *Educational Gerontology: An International Quarterly, 22*(6), 539–555.

Hinrichsen, G.A., & McMeniman, M. (2002). The impact of geropsychology training. *Professional Psychology: Research and Practice, 33*(3), 337–340.

Hinrichsen, G., Zeiss, A., Karel, M., & Molinari, V. (2010). Competency-based geropsychology training in doctoral internships and postdoctoral fellowships. *Training and Education in Professional Psychology, 4*(2), 91–98.

Huffstetler, B. (2006). Sexuality in older adults: A deconstructionist perspective. *Adultspan Journal, 5*(1), 4–14.

Kane, M.N. (2004). Ageism and intervention: What social work students believe about treating people differently because of age. *Educational Gerontology, 30*(9), 767–784.

Kane, M. (2008). How are sexual behaviors of older women and older men perceived by human service students? *Social Work Education, 27*(7), 723–743.

Karel, M.J., Knight, B.G., Duffy, M., Hinrichsen, G.A., & Zeiss, A.M. (2010). Attitude, knowledge, and skill competencies for practice in professional geropsychology: Implications for training and building a geropsychology workforce. *Training and Education in Professional Psychology, 4*(2), 75–84.

Koder, D.A., & Helmes, E. (2008). Predictors of working with older adults in an Australian psychologist sample: Revisiting the influence of contact. *Professional Psychology: Research and Practice, 39*(3), 276–282.

Lewis, S., & Bor, R. (1994). Nurses' knowledge of and attitudes towards sexuality and the relationship of these with nursing practice. *Journal of Advanced Nursing, 20*(2), 251–259.

Lindau, S.T., Schumm, L.P., Laumann, E.O., Levinson, W., O'Muircheartaigh, C.A., & Waite, L.J. (2007). A study of sexuality and health among older adults in the United States. *New England Journal of Medicine, 357*(8), 762–774.

Meeks, S. (1990). Age bias in the diagnostic decision-making behavior of clinicians. *Professional Psychology: Research and Practice, 21*(4), 279–284.

Miller, S.A., & Byers, E.S. (2008). An exploratory examination of the sexual intervention self-efficacy of clinical psychology graduate students. *Training and Education in Professional Psychology, 2*, 137–144.

Miller, A.S., & Byers, E.S. (2009). Psychologists' continuing education and training in sexuality. *Journal of Sex & Marital Therapy, 35*(1), 206–219.

Miller, A.S., & Byers, E.S. (2010). Psychologists' sexuality training and education in graduate school. *Canadian Journal of Behavioural Science, 42*(2), 93–100.

Ng, J.S.C. (2007). Sexuality and psychotherapy: An exploratory study of the subjectivities of psychotherapists with experience and expertise in working with sexuality. *Dissertation Abstracts International, 67*, 9B, 5416.

Padilla, M.A., & Veprinsky, A. (2012). Correlation attenuation due to measurement error: A new approach using the bootstrap procedure. *Educational and Psychological Measurement, 72*(5), 827–846. doi: 10.1177/0013164412443963

Pangman, V., & Seguire, M. (2000). Sexuality and the chronically ill older adult: A social justice issue. *Sexuality and Disability, 18*(1), 49–59.

Ports, K.A., Barnack-Tavlaris, J.L., Syme, M.L., Perera, R.A., & Lafata, J.E. (2014). Sexual health discussions with older adult patients during periodic health exams. *The Journal of Sexual Medicine, 11*, 901–908.

Preacher, K.J., & Hayes, A.F. (2004). SPSS and SAS procedures for estimating indirect effects in simple mediation models. *Behavior Research Methods, Instruments, & Computers, 36*(4), 717–731. doi:10.3758/BF03206553

Preacher, K.J., & Hayes, A.F. (2008). Asymptotic and resampling strategies for assessing and comparing indirect effects in multiple mediator models. *Behavior Research Methods, 40*(3), 879–891. doi:10.3758/BRM.40.3.879

Qualls, S., Segal, D., Norman, S., Niederehe, G., & Gallagher-Thompson, D. (2002). Psychologists in practice with older adults: Current patterns, sources of training, and need for continuing education. *Professional Psychology: Research and Practice, 33*(5), 435–442.

Reissing, E.D., & Di Giulio, G.D. (2010). Practicing clinical psychologists' provision of sexual health care services. *Professional Psychology: Research and Practice, 41*(1), 57–63.

Robinson, J.G., & Molzahn, A.E. (2007). Sexuality and quality of life. *Journal of Gerontological Nursing, 33*(3), 19–27.

Schick, V., Herbenick, D., Reece, M., Sanders, S.A., Dodge, B., Middlestadt, S.E., & Fortenberry, J.D. (2010). Sexual behaviors, condom use, and sexual health of Americans over 50: Implications for sexual health promotion for older adults. *The Journal of Sexual Medicine, 7*(s5), 315–329.

Schover, L. (1981). Male and female therapists' responses to male and female client sexual material: An analogue study. *Archives of Sexual Behavior, 10*(6), 477–492.

Steinke, E. (1994). Knowledge and attitudes of older adults about sexuality in ageing: A comparison of two studies. *Journal of Advanced Nursing, 19*, 477–485.

Snyder, R.J., & Zweig, R.A. (2010). Medical and psychology students' knowledge and attitudes regarding aging and sexuality. *Gerontology and Geriatrics Education, 31*, 235–255.

Træen, B., & Schaller, S. (2013). Talking to patients about sexual issues: Experiences of Norwegian psychologists. *Sexual and Relationship Therapy, 28*(3), 281–291.

United Nations, Department of Economic and Social Affairs, Population Division. (2013). World population prospects: The 2012 revision, DVD edition. Retrieved from http://esa.un.org/unpd/wpp/Excel-Data/population.htm

United States Census Bureau. (2012). *Older Americans month.* Washington, DC: Government Printing Office. Retrieved from http://www.census.gov/newsroom/releases/archives/facts_for_features_special_editions/cb12-ff07.html

Van Ryn, M. (2002). Research on the provider contribution to race/ethnicity disparities in medical care. *Medical Care, 40*(1), I–140.

Visalakshi, J., & Jeyaseelan, L. (2013). Confidence interval for skewed distribution in outcome of change or difference between methods. *Clinical Epidemiology and Global Health.* doi:10.1016/j.cegh.2013.07.006

White, C. (1982). A scale for the assessment of attitudes and knowledge regarding sexuality in the aged. *Archives of Sexual Behavior, 11*(6), 491–502.

Wiederman, M.W., & Sansone, R.A. (1999). Sexuality training for professional psychologists: A national survey of training directors of doctoral programs and predoctoral internships. *Professional Psychology: Research and Practice, 30*(3), 312–317.

Wittenbrink, B., Judd, C.M., & Park, B. (1997). Evidence for racial prejudice at the implicit level and its relationship with questionnaire measures. *Journal of Personality and Social Psychology, 72*(2), 262–274.

Zivin, K., Pfeiffer, P.N., Szymanski, B.R., Valenstein, M., Post, E.P., Miller, E.M., & McCarthy, J.F. (2010). Initiation of primary care-mental health integration programs in the VA health system: Associations with psychiatric diagnoses in primary care. *Medical Care, 48*(9), 843–851.

Sexuality of the ageing female – the underlying physiology

R.J. Levin

Sexual Physiology Laboratory, Porterbrook Clinic, Sheffield, UK

While the ageing process occurs both in males and females, the latter have the added effects of the changes brought about by the menopause. The review characterises the many menopausal changes that the decrease in oestrogens produces in neural, skeletal, circulatory and genital systems. Many of these changes can adversely affect the sexual functioning of women. The increase in female lifespan means that women can spend 30–40 years in the postmenopausal condition. Treatments need to be developed to ensure that their healthspan (those years spent without chronic-age related dysfunctions) is also increased.

Introduction

Normal somatic ageing progresses gradually and it causes a reduced function in most of the major systems of the body (neural, respiratory, cardiovascular, endocrinological, urinary, skeletal, muscle and motor). Why does this ageing take place? Two ageing processes have been identified. While cells are continuously being replaced, the terminally differentiated ones, like those in the brain, undergo "chronological ageing" and are rarely replaced but others, like skin and the gastrointestinal tract, undergo "replicative ageing" and are continually renewed (by the time you have read this sentence, 50 million of your cells have died and been replaced!). Each cell, however, can only multiply a certain number of times before it dies. Every time a cell divides to make two cells, special zones at the end of each chromosome (telomeres) shorten. When they reach a critical length, the cell stops dividing and dies. Pines (2013) in reviewing the literature could not find, however, any relationship between telomere length and the menopause or the use of hormone therapy (HT). As more cells are lost, the signs of the damage from ageing (from glucose cross-linking, free radicals, ultraviolet radiation, activation of oncogenes and agents that modify DNA or chromatin) become obvious.

While ageing is a common feature of both male and female lives, women have two other crucial experiences in relation to their changing life status. The first is "menarche", the initiation of menstruation and the subsequent continued regularity of her normally ovulatory menstrual cycles, and then, much later, the "menopause", defined as the permanent cessation of these cycles. The former has the connotation of becoming a female able to create and sustain a new life while the latter indicates that this function has ended. In the Western world, menopause occurs at around 45–50 years of age. There is no single time or event that one can say, "this is the menopause". The convention is that it is usually diagnosed retrospectively after 12 months of cessation of the menses (amenorrhea). However, it is common practice to use the term to indicate the time when the spontaneous menstruation ceases. The transition period before the last period is called the "perimenopause" (also known as the "climacteric") and can last for just a few months or can be as long as several years. Human life expectancy is increasing without any genetic intervention by an average of five hours per day (Walker, 2014). Because the life expectancy of women in the Western world is now approximately 80 years, they can expect to experience ageing in the postmenopausal condition for some 30–40 years. Menopause is now not an end-of-life event but a mid-life event (Parish et al., 2013).

What causes the menopause?

The physiology of the cause of menopause is reasonably well understood but its origin and evolution less well so. In brief, during embryogenesis of the female, some 2000 primordial germ cells migrate to the gonadal ridges where they quickly multiply forming 5–7 million follicles. Around the fifth month of embryonic development, the multiplication stops and the loss of primordial follicles by atresia begins so that by the time of birth, each ovary now contains only 1 million follicles and the loss by atresia continues. During the female life, while just a few hundreds ova are lost through ovulation, the vast decrement from atresia is maintained until a low critical number is reached. This brings about a dramatic reduction in the amount of oestrogen secreted (particularly oestradiol) and the menopause occurs with its many subsequent postmenopausal body changes due to the decrease in oestrogen (Burger, 1999; Margolskee & Selgrade, 2013; Rashidi & Shanley, 2009).

In relation to the origin and evolution of the menopause, the lack of a definitive explanation is shown by the number of competing hypotheses: all of which have their specific weakness. Morton, Stone, and Singh (2013) summarised the various evolutionary hypotheses in a table and characterised them briefly as follows:

(1) follicle depletion hypothesis (a limited number of eggs when depleted brings about the menopause),
(2) lifespan-artefact hypothesis (menopause is the consequence of increased longevity),
(3) senescence hypothesis (natural effect of ageing),
(4) reproduction-cost hypothesis (reproduction has a heavier cost on women leading to physical deterioration),
(5) mother hypothesis (survival of children increased by inability to procreate in mothers),
(6) grandmother hypothesis (improves the survival and reproduction of her grandchildren ensuing the continuation of her genes),
(7) patriarch hypothesis (allows men to mate with younger women),
(8) absent father hypothesis (consequence of decrease in paternal investment and extended maternal age),
(9) reproductive conflict hypothesis (competition between grandmothers, daughters and daughters-in-law and grandchildren),
(10) evolutionary trade-off hypothesis (balance between survival of children and female fertility).

For full references and discussion, the original reference of Morton et al. (2013) should be accessed.

Female sexual functioning during ageing and the menopause transition

Bancroft (2009) examined the conceptual difficulties as to whether the decrease during ageing in female sexual interest/responsiveness noted in many investigations was due to the ageing process per se or a consequence of the hormonal decreases associated with the menopause. The former process is complex because it involves social factors such as lack of sexual relationships (women tend to outlive their male sexual partners), partner sexual function (older men often have erectile and ejaculatory dysfunctions, Wylie & Kenney, 2010) and loss of privacy (communal residency). Despite many studies on the decrease in sexual activity of ageing women (for overviews, see DeLamater, 2012; DeLamater & Koepsel, 2014; Dennerstein, Alexander, & Kotz, 2003), no definitive conclusions have been produced. In a recent study, Mitchell et al. (2013), using a probability sample and a psychometrical valid questionnaire (Natsal-3),[1] surveyed 6777 women in Britain (Scotland, England and Wales) aged 16–74 years. Low sexual function (defined as the lowest quintile of the scores from the distribution of their Natsal-3 measure of sexual function) was associated with increasing age but levelled off at 55 years. The cause of this levelling off is as yet undetermined. Problems with sexual response were present with one or more problems for 51.2%. The most common were lack of interest in sex (34.2%), difficulty in reaching a climax (16.3%), an uncomfortably dry vagina (13.0%) and lack of enjoyment (12.1%). Over the age range of 16–24 years compared to that of 65–74 years, the problems with vaginal dryness increased from 9.4% to 20%. Unsurprisingly, in women who did not have sex within the previous year, their dissatisfaction with their sex life was substantially higher than those that did have such activity, 22.4% against 11.7%, respectively. However, distress or worry about their sex life was not different between those who were sexually active (10.9%) and those who were not (9.5%).

Changes in sexual functioning of women as they transitioned through the menopause were studied by Avis et al. (2009). It was a large community-based study of middle-aged women who reported a decrease in sexual desire and an increase in painful coitus starting in the late perimenopause. Those women reporting 1–5 days of vaginal dryness were at greater risk of having pain at coitus, had less arousal and more frequent masturbation compared to those who did not report vaginal dryness. It was suggested that the transient increase in masturbation during early perimenopause was possibly related to the concurrent pain at coitus and the subsequent decline at postmenopause was related to their decline in sexual desire.

Labial changes

The atrophic changes in the genitalia of postmenopausal women were observed in an magnetic resonance imaging (MRI) study of healthy premenopausal and postmenopausal subjects as the latter were found to have smaller labia minora width, vestibular bulb width, vaginal width and wall thickness and cervical diameter (Suh, Yang, Cao, Garland, & Maravilla, 2003). Basaran, Kosif, Bayar, and Covelek (2008) confirmed the thinner minora in postmenopausal women (15.4 mm ± 4.7 mm, $n = 50$) compared to those in premenopausal women (17.9 mm ± 4.1 mm, $n = 50$). The colour of the labia becomes a paler shade of red after the menopause (Stika, 2010) presumably because there is less blood in their reduced microcirculation.

Vaginal changes

The adult human vagina is a somewhat tubular organ with a W or H cross-section and an elongated, flattened S-shaped longitudinal section. It is a potential space and there is no single word for describing such a structure. Its walls are composed of three layers. The innermost wall consists of a stratified squamous epithelium, an ideal surface for coping with friction, which undergoes cell shedding and replacement from basal cells dividing under the influence of oestrogens secreted by the ovaries. Underneath this epithelium is the stratum consisting of connective tissue containing nerves and blood vessels while the final layer is composed of autonomically innervated smooth muscle (longitudinal and circular).

The degree of vaginal innervation appears to be strongly influenced by oestrogens. Griebling, Liao, and Smith (2012) found that postmenopausal women not receiving any HT had relatively high levels of innervation, the majority of axons expressing tyrosine hydroxylase (indicating nor-adrenergic sympathetic fibres associated mainly with smooth muscle of the vasculature and muscles) or VIP (vasoactive intestinal peptide expressed by cholinergic parasympathetic innervation associated predominantly with vascular and non-vascular smooth muscle). Some 20% of axons were non-cholinergic, non-adrenergic (NANC) presumed to be the unmyelinated sensory innervation which also showed decreases with the hormonal treatments but their small number did not allow quantitative analysis. The participants receiving systemic HT showed a reduction in their overall innervation while those treated with vaginal topical HT had the greatest reduction in their innervation. The conclusion was that HT reduces autonomic and sensory innervation density. Their findings may explain why perimenopausal and postmenopausal women who suffer from vaginal itching, burning, dryness and pain find that these symptoms are relieved by systemic or topical hormone treatment (Simon, 2011; Simon, Kojkot-Kierepa, & Goldstein, 2013)

The lack of oestrogen support, by reducing the stimulus for cell division in the basal vaginal epithelial layer, causes the loss of the rugae (the vaginal folds or the "the wrinkles of youth") and the wall can become paper thin. While the vagina decreases in length, this does not bring about penile contact with the cervix during coitus. First, because vaginal tenting (the lifting of the utero-cervix away from the thrusting penis) occurs during sexual arousal (Levin, 2011, 2012). Second, because the cervix itself decreases in length and can become flush with the vaginal wall instead of protruding into its lumen. The lack of oestrogen is also typically considered to be the cause of the reduced vaginal lubrication. VIP when injected into postmenopausal subjects does not cause an increase in vaginal vasocongestion as it does in premenopausal women (Palle, Bredkær, Fahrenkrug, & Ottesen, 1991). This reduction in vaginal lubrication is possibly the most important postmenopausal change that occurs in vaginal function influencing coital behaviour. In seven key studies examined by Parish et al. (2013), there was a prevalence of vulvo-vaginal atrophy (VVA) of about 50% but not all women with VVA have discomfort or pain. Moreover, not all assessments of the dyspareunia in postmenopausal women have correlated highly with the menopausal status, oestrogen levels or vaginal atrophy as a significant percentage experience pain not caused by lack of oestrogens (Kao, Binik, Kapuscinski, & Khalifé, 2008). The authors could not find any studies elaborating on this lack of correlation but suggested an explanation may be changes in tone of the pelvic musculature, especially hypotonus. This could lead to dyspareunia. Further studies are clearly needed to clarify the problem.

The increased lubrication is normally activated by sexual arousal to facilitate painless penile penetration. The vagina, in its basal condition, is maintained in a "just moist" condition, the epithelium being kept moist to prevent opposite wall adhesions developing if they touch. The mechanisms involved in the basal lubrication include the continuous formation of interstitial fluid by transudation of plasma from the vaginal capillaries leaking through and between the vaginal epithelial cells onto the vaginal wall surface. The fluid is recycled back into the blood by osmotic co-transfer with the lumen-to-blood Na^+ ion transfer operating in the basal layers of the vaginal epithelium (Levin, 1997). Sexual arousal causes an increase in the vaginal blood supply through its neural innervation by the release of the vasodilator neurotransmitter VIP and in the reduction of its sympathetic adrenergic constrictor tone. The basal vaginal microcirculation is regulated locally like many other tissues by vasomotion (Levin & Wylie, 2008), the mechanism by which most of the tissue's capillaries are closed and only open when the local build-up of metabolites and hypoxia relax their normally contracted pre-capillary sphincters. The enhanced blood flow induced opens many capillaries gradually reducing vasomotion until all the capillaries are maintained open. The increase in capillary surface area plus the enhanced blood flow creates a volumetric vasocongestion and a large increase in the transudation of interstitial fluid. This percolates through the vaginal epithelium and swamps the limited Na^+ reabsorption. The extra fluid appears on the vaginal surface as an increase in vaginal lubrication (Levin, 2003a; Levin & Wylie, 2008; Masters & Johnson, 1966). After the cessation of the sexual arousal, the vaginal fluid is reabsorbed by the Na^+ lumen-to-blood transfer. Notice that the process while lubricating the vagina on demand is still able to conserve the Na^+ and the fluid, a possible necessity in our prehistoric past. The vasomotion mechanism is preserved even in the absence of oestrogens in the menopausal woman (Levin & Wylie, 2008) thus highlighting its basic importance.

A further feature of vaginal function affected by the reduction in oestrogens is the control of its luminal fluid pH. During the premenopausal inter-menstrual periods, this ranges from pH 3.5 to 4 (Masters & Johnson, 1966) and is a factor in the prevention of harmful bacteria colonising the vagina. In the menopause, however, the pH rises to between 6.5 and 7.0 (Panda, Das, Singh, & Pala, 2014) but the acidity can be returned by oestrogen treatment (Roy, Caillouette, Roy, & Faden, 2004). One explanation for the generation of this acidity is that Döderlein's bacteria present in the vagina create the acidity from carbohydrate substrates in the lumen (Boskey, Cone, Whaley, & Moench, 2001). More recent studies, however, have shown that the vaginal and cervical epithelial cells can secrete H^+ ions per se, and oestrogens upgrade the secretion (Gorodeski, Hopfer, Liu, & Margles, 2005). Gorodeski (2001) also found, however, that while the vaginal cells of the postmenopausal women secreted H^+ ions, the secretion was reduced compared to the premenopausal cells and that oestrogen failed to increase the secretion as it did in the premenopausal participants. The interpretation was that other (not described) factors of the ageing process affected the function of the acid secretory mechanisms of the vaginal and ectocervical cells.

Clitoral changes

The clitoris has clearly both external and internal structures. The former are the obvious clitoral glans, shaft and prepuce while the latter consist of the two crus and the paired vestibular bulbs on either side of the urethra. It is claimed that the clitoris is the most highly innervated structure of the female body whose only function is the generation of sexual arousal/pleasure. It is the organ that needs the least amount of energy to induce an orgasm even in the postmenopausal woman. The clitoral tissues are hormone sensitive, the glans and shaft have androgen receptors that remain throughout the life of the female making the structures androgen sensitive while the prepuce (overlying hood of skin) is sensitive to oestrogens. During the menopause, the glans has better hormonal support (androgens) than the prepuce (oestrogens) which shrinks, thereby often exposing the glans. In some women, this allows friction through underwear rubbing and can become irritative and cause discomfort.

Age-related changes occur in the clitoral corpora cavernosae content of smooth muscle and connective tissue. Over the age range of 15−90 years, the former decreased from 65% to 37% (Tarcan et al., 1999). How or whether this decrease affects the functionality/ sensitivity of the clitoris has not been investigated.

Both the innervation and the function(s) of the vestibular bulbs and the internal clitoral "roots" are poorly described and it is not clear whether their functions are as structural support for the vaginal walls or erotic or both. It has been claimed that they are not innervated as part of the erogenous sexual arousal system (Puppo, 2011), but no evidence was presented for this conclusion.

It should be noted that those postmenopausal women who have regular coitus appear to have better vaginal functionality, as assessed by a vaginal atrophy index (gynaecological examination of six genital dimensions), than those who do not (Leiblum, Bachman, Kenman, Colburn, & Swartzman, 1983). The mechanical stimulation by the penile thrusting, the activated vaginal reflexes and the activity of the seminal prostaglandins on the vaginal mucosal blood flow may all play a part in this coital maintenance action (Levin, 2003b).

Uterine changes

The role of the uterus during orgasm is another poorly studied aspect of female sexual arousal. It is an organ consisting mainly of smooth muscle (myometrium) which is sensitive to oestrogen levels and thus becomes reduced in size after the menopause. At orgasm, it is induced to contract. These contractions were thought to be induced by the oxytocin released systemically from the posterior pituitary, but studies have shown that this is now thought unlikely and it is local oxytocin released from the endometrial lining of the uterus that is the cause (see Levin, 2011 for full references). The uterus also has sympathetic adrenergic innervation that also causes contraction of the smooth muscle while its VIP innervation inhibits such contractions. It is highly likely that this adrenergic innervation is also involved in the orgasmic contractions. Basson (1995) reported from her clinical patients that in some menopausal women, pain occurs during and after the uterine contractions of orgasm. A possible explanation for this induced pain is that in premenopausal women contractions of the uterus are reduced by the VIPergic innervation, but in postmenopausal women this does not exist so that the contractions are more severe and can become spasmodic causing uterine anoxia and creating the pain. According to Masters and Johnson (1966), the pain is relieved by oestrogen and progesterone treatment which would agree with the hypothesised mechanism of its induction.

Cervical changes

The cervix is the structure at the neck of the uterus connecting its lumen to that of the vagina through the agency of the endocervical canal with its internal os inside the uterus and its external os in the vagina. The endocervix inside the uterus is lined with columnar epithelial cells that secrete mucus under the influence of oestrogen (clear watery mucus type E_s) that allows sperm penetration and progesterone (thick, opaque mucus type G) which blocks their entry. The former is secreted in the follicular phase of the menstrual cycle up to ovulation while the latter is manufactured during the luteal phase. The ectocervix in the vagina is covered by squamous epithelial cells. The organ is a densely fibrous structure with a little smooth muscles and elastic fibres. There are no glands in the cervical epithelium but its infoldings form crypts (up to 10,000) giving the mistaken appearance of glandular structures often reported in inaccurate descriptive accounts in textbooks (Levin, 2005).

The decrease in oestrogens at menopause directly reduces the production of the watery mucus (type E_s) while ageing decreases the permeability of its epithelium due to tightening of the junctions between cells. These changes promote cervical dryness (Gorodeski, 2001). The cervix can become friable (easily damaged) and flush with the vaginal vault.

Cardiovascular changes

While there is an increasing risk of cardiovascular diseases with age in both males and females, in women the postmenopausal condition appears to increase this risk possibly due to the reduction in oestrogens. Randomised clinical trials of hormone replacement therapy (HRT), however, have not shown protective benefits of oestrogen treatments (Reslan & Khalil, 2012). This lack of effect may be due to using women in the late stage of their menopause. Evidence supports a "timing hypothesis" for using menopausal HT (oestrogen, with or without progestogen), benefits will be shown if it is applied in younger women during their perimenopausal period or within five years of amenorrhoea (Hodis & Mack, 2013; Lobo, 2014; Nastri et al., 2013; Reslan & Khalil, 2012).

One of the most characteristic and for many women a very distressing symptom of the menopause is the "hot flush" often concomitant with sudden sweating. While it is clear that the flushing occurs because of a disturbance in the hypothalamic temperature regulating mechanism, despite many studies over a considerable period the mechanism(s) is still enigmatic. According to Sturdee (2008), the physiological changes associated with the hot flushes are different from any other flushing condition as it occurs with an increase in peripheral blood flow, increased heart rate and a decrease in galvanic skin response unique to the condition. There is little doubt that the flushes involve the lack of oestrogens but the detailed mechanism of their involvement is not established. Rossouw, Manson, Kaunitz, and Anderson (2013) reported that menopausal HT was effective for relief of vasomotor symptoms but that the HT should be used for fewer than five years. Interestingly, the incidence of flushing varies in different female populations. Flushing is far less prevalent in the far east than in the Western world. The reason(s) for this is/are not understood clearly.

Skeletal changes

There are two types of bone, trabecular (spongy or cancellous) found in the ends of long bones and vertebrae and cortical (compact bone). The latter is the densest and is found primarily in the shaft of the long bones creating an outer shell around the former type. Bone is remodelled by osteoclasts that cause the resorption mainly of trabecular bone while osteoblasts rebuild the bone. Cytokine activity is involved in the system. While oestrogen's action on bone is complex, its major effect is to inhibit the osteoclasts. Bone loss of up to 1% per year begins at the age of 35–40 years, but during the menopause it increases by as much as 10-fold and then falls back to 1%–3% a year. There is loss with increasing age due to the decrease in the numbers of osteoblasts (Clarke & Khosia, 2010). The condition characterised by a decrease in bone mass and density is called osteoporosis and is most common in women after menopause. It can lead to bone fractures, disability and early death, especially from hip fractures. Osteoporosis leads to spine curvature (kyphosis) and a stooped posture ("dowager's hump") while falls are associated with fractures of wrist, spine, shoulder and hip and are one of the main causes of disability in postmenopausal women. This highlights the importance of the prevention of osteoporosis (National Institute for Health and Clinical Excellence [NICE], 2011; Peto & Allaby, 2011).

Skin changes

After the menopause, ageing of the skin accelerates. It becomes thinner with a decrease in its collagen and it becomes less elastic more wrinkled and crepy (Thornton, 2013).

Mental changes

The most common reported mental changes occurring in the perimenopause and meno-pause are mood changes, depression (more often in the former period), insomnia (from night sweats) leading to irritability during the day, cognitive and memory problems (short-term memory loss and concentration difficulties). The menopausal transition has been suggested as the "period of vulnerability" for the development of depression. How-ever, Judd, Hickey, and Bryant (2012) review of the available literature on depression and the menopause could find no clear evidence that depressive disorders occurred more frequently with the menopause. The prevalence of the disorder appeared to be no more frequent than other phases of female life. Marjoribanks, Farquhar, Roberts, and Lethaby (2012) examined the use of menopausal HT (oestrogens with or without progestogens) and concluded that it is not indicated for the primary or secondary prevention of dementia or for preventing deterioration of cognitive functions.

Orgasm and female ageing

There is significant variability in the sexual and mental satisfaction obtained from orgasms during the female life cycle. The early orgasms of youth are usually less pleasur-able and satisfying than those of later adulthood. There is an obvious suggestion of "sexual pleasure learning" during maturation (Levin, 1981). This is consistent with other pleasures obtained from food, music and art which also have a "learning" component often involving education and experiences (Levin, 2014). The factors that influence the pleasure and satisfaction created by orgasms are generally poorly understood. There are a few obvious physiological ones such as the hormonal background with androgens being of importance (Levin, 2014), the "tone" (degree of contraction) of the pelvic musculature (both hypo-tonus and hyper-tonus can cause orgasmic dysfunctions (Wylie & Levin, 2013), some drugs are pro-orgasmic (dopaminergic) but others are inhibitory (serotoner-gic) (Levin, 2014). The skill of the sexual partner's stimulation techniques and the emo-tional connection with him/her can also be highly influential.

Orgasms obtained after menopause are said to be harder to achieve needing a longer duration of stimulation and are of decreased intensity (Basson, 1995; Masters & Johnson, 1966). This latter conclusion from clinical assessments agrees with the experimental study that gave healthy premenopausal subjects injections of depot leuprolide, a down-regulator of the secretion of gonadotrophins, inducing hypogonadism that caused signifi-cant decreases in the intensity of their orgasms (Schmidt et al., 2009).

The fact that orgasm still exists in the postmenopausal woman despite the fact that she cannot reproduce has an important bearing on a presumed reproductive role. Brody (2010) has argued that because orgasm from penile vaginal intercourse is the only sexual behaviour that allows the propagation of genes, it has been rewarded by evolution with better health for females than orgasm attained by clitoral or other means. A number of authors have voiced their criticisms of these conclusions (Laan & Rellini, 2011; Levin, 2011, 2012; Prause, 2011, 2012). Clearly, orgasm in the postmenopausal woman cannot have any reproductive purpose but yet it is still retained despite its obvious energy demands (costs of maintenance of its neural, circulatory and metabolic needs). Orgasm maintenance in the postmenopause indicates that loading a specific procreative role onto orgasm does not create a robust argument or conclusion (see Levin, 2011, 2012 for a critical discussion).

The healthspan increase concept

The litany of changes that occur during ageing and the menopause can appear depressing in the extreme and suggest that postmenopausal life is beset with possible health problems. The lifting of the burden of menstruation, the freedom from possible pregnancy during coitus and of childbearing and rearing are obvious compensations allowing some benefit to postmenopausal sexual life. Often, especially in the Western world, an extensive holiday travel itinerary can be undertaken. However, it is said that few over 80 have perfect health. What is essential is that with the prevalent increase in lifespan, treatments are developed to ensure that there is also an increase in "healthspan", defined as those years spent without chronic age-related dysfunctions. Although simple changes like better diet and regular exercise can increase healthspan, new treatments for its facilitation need to be prioritised (see Fontana, Kennedy, Longo, Seals, & Melov, 2014). Finally, it should be noted that the use of HRT (also known as MHT – menopausal hormonal therapy) in randomised trials for treating the various effects of oestrogen deficiency of the menopause so prevalent in the 1980s became heavily criticised in the 2000s because of possible serious side effects, especially in relation to breast cancer and cardiovascular risks. These potential increased risks led to the abandonment of such treatments after 2002 by millions of women. More recent analysis of the trials has re-evaluated the initial reports (see section on Cardiovascular changes) and has not confirmed increased cardiovascular risks (apart from venous thrombosis) or of breast cancer using oestrogens alone (Lobo, 2014). In fact, recent data have shown a coronary benefit and a decrease in all-cause mortality (Lobo, 2014). Lobo (2014) provocatively suggests treatment at the onset of menopause to prevent the pathological changes which can occur some years later.

Note

1. Natsal-3, British National Survey of Sexual Attitudes & Lifestyles of 15,000 adults aged 16–74 between September 2010 and August 2012 who participated in interviews and questionnaires. The latter can be found at www.natsal.ac.ukmedia82473/bl.capi and casi questionnaire.pdf. Publications based on Natsal-3 can be found at www.natsal.ac.uk/natsal-3/publications.

References

Avis, N.E., Brockwell, S., Randolph, J.F., Jr., Shen, S., Cain, V.B.S., Ory, M., & Greendale, G.A. (2009). Longitudinal changes in sexual functioning as women transition through menopause: Results from the Study of Women's Health Across the Nation (SWAN). *Menopause, 16*, 442–452.

Bancroft, J. (2009). *Human sexuality and its problems*. (3rd ed.). Edinburgh: Churchill Livingstone and Elsevier.

Basaran, M., Kosif, R., Bayar, U., & Covelek, B. (2008). Characteristics of external genitalia in pre- and postmenopausal women. *Climacteric, 11*, 416–421.

Basson, R. (1995). Sexuality and the menopause. *Journal of the Society of Obstetricians and Gynecologists of Canada, 10–15* (Suppl, May).

Boskey, E.R., Cone, R.A., Whaley, K.J., & Moench, T.R. (2001). Origins of vaginal acidity: High D/L lactate ratio is consistent with bacteria being the primary source. *Human Reproduction, 16*, 1809–1813.

Brody, S. (2010). The relative health benefits of different sexual activities. *Journal of Sexual Medicine, 9*, 962–963.

Burger, H.G. (1999). The endocrinology of the menopause. *Journal of Steroid Biochemistry and Molecular Biology, 69*, 31–35.

Clarke, B.L., & Khosia, S. (2010). Female reproductive system and bone. *Archives of Biochemistry and Biophysics, 503*, 118–128.

DeLamater, J. (2012). Sexual expression in later life: A review and synthesis. *Journal of Sex Research, 49*, 125–141.

DeLamater, J., & Koepsel, E. (2014). Relationship and sexual expression in later life: A biopsychosocial perspective. *Sexual and Relationship Therapy*. doi:10.1080/14681994.2014.939506.

Dennerstein, L., Alexander, J.L., & Kotz, K. (2003). The menopause and sexual functioning: A review of population-based studies. *Annual Review of Sex Research, 14*, 64–82.

Fontana, L., Kennedy, B.K., Longo, V.D., Seals, D., & Melov, S. (2014). Medical research: Treat ageing. *Nature, 511*, 405–407.

Gorodeski, G. (2001). Vaginal-cervical epithelial permeability decreases after menopause. *Fertility and Sterility, 76*, 753–761.

Gorodeski, G.I., Hopfer, U., Liu, C.C., & Margles, E. (2005). Estrogen acidifies vaginal pH by up-regulation of proton secretion via the apical membrane of vaginal-ectocervical epithelial cells. *Endocrinology, 146*, 816–825.

Griebling, T.L., Liao, Z., & Smith, P.G. (2012). Systemic and topical hormone therapies reduce vaginal innervation density in post-menopausal women. *Menopause, 19*, 630–635.

Hodis, H.N., & Mack, W.J. (2013). The timing hypothesis and hormone replacement therapy: A paradigm shift in primary prevention of coronary heart disease in women. Part 1: comparison of therapeutic efficacy. *Journal of American Geriatric Society, 61*, 1005–1010.

Judd, H.C., Hickey, M., & Bryant, C. (2012). Depression and midlife: Are we over-pathologising the menopause? *Journal of Affective Disorders, 136*, 199–211.

Kao, A., Binik, Y.M., Kapuscinski, A., & Khalifé, S. (2008). Dyspareunia in postmenopausal women: A critical review. *Pain Research Management, 13*, 243–254.

Laan, E., & Rellini, A.H. (2011). Can we treat anorgasmia in women? The challenge to experiencing pleasure. *Sexual and Relationship Therapy, 26*, 329–341.

Leiblum, S., Bachmann, G., Kenmann, E., Colburn, D., & Swartzman, L. (1983). Vaginal atrophy in the postmenopausal woman. The importance of sexual activity and hormones. *JAMA, 249*, 2195–2198.

Levin, R.J. (1981). The female orgasm – a current appraisal. *Journal of Psychosomatic Research, 25*, 119–133.

Levin, R.J. (1997). Actions of spermicidal and virucidal agents on electrogenic ion transfer across human vaginal epithelium in vitro. *Pharmacology and Toxicology, 81*, 219–225.

Levin, R.J. (2003a). The ins and outs of vaginal lubrication. *Sexual and Relationship Therapy, 18*, 509–513.

Levin, R.J. (2003b). Do women gain anything from coitus apart from pregnancy? Changes in the human genital tract activated by coitus. *Journal of Sex and Marital Therapy, 29*, 59–69.

Levin, R.J. (2005). The involvement of the human cervix in reproduction and sex. *Sexual and Relationship Therapy, 20*, 251–260.

Levin, R.J. (2011). The human female orgasm: A critical evaluation of its proposed reproductive functions. *Sexual and Relationship Therapy, 26*, 301—314.

Levin, R.J. (2012). The deadly pleasures of the clitoris and the condom — a rebuttal of Brody, Costa and Hess. *Sexual and Relationship Therapy, 27*, 272—295.

Levin, R.J. (2014). The pharmacology of the human female orgasm — its biological and physiological backgrounds. *Pharmacology, Biochemistry and Behaviour, 121*, 63—70.

Levin, R.J., & Wylie, K. (2008). Vaginal vasomotion — its appearance, measurement and usefulness in assessing the mechanism of vasodilatation. *Journal of Sexual Medicine, 10*, 83—96.

Lobo, R.A. (2014). What the future holds for women after menopause: Where we have been, where we are, and where we want go. *Climacteric, 17*, 1—21.

Margolskee, A., & Selgrade, J.F. (2013). A lifelong model for the female reproductive cycle with an antimüllerian hormone treatment to delay menopause. *Journal of Theoretical Biology, 326*, 21—35.

Marjoribanks, J., Farquhar, C., Roberts, H., & Lethaby, A. (2012). Long term hormone therapy for perimenopausal and postmenopausal women. *Cochrane Database Systematic Review, 11*(7), CD004143. doi:10.1002/14651858.CD004143.pub4

Masters, W.H., & Johnson, V. (1966). *Human sexual response*. Boston, MA: Little Brown.

Mitchell, K.R., Mercer, C.H., Ploubidis, G.B., Jones, K.G., Datta, J., Field, N., ... Wellings, K. (2013). Sexual function in Britain: Findings from the third National Survey of Sexual Attitudes and Lifestyles (Natsal-3). *Lancet, 382*, 1817—1829.

Morton, R.A., Stone, R.J., & Singh, R.S. (2013). Mate choice and the origin of the menopause. *PLOS Computational Biology, 9*(6), e1003092. doi: 1371/journal.pcbi.1003092.

Nastri, C.O., Lara, L.A., Ferriani, R.A., Rosa-E-Siva, A.C., Figuerido, J.B., & Martina, W.P. (2013). Hormone therapy for sexual function in perimenopausal and postmenopausal women. *Cochrane Database Systematic Review,* (6). CD009672. doi:10.1002/14651858.CD00967.pub2

National Institute for Health and Clinical Excellence. (2011). *Alendronate, etidronate, risedronate, raloxifene, strontium ranelate, and teriparetide for the secondary prevention of osteoporotic fragility fractures in postmenopausal women*. Technology appraisal TAS 161.

Palle, C., Bredkær, H.E., Fahrenkrug, I., & Ottesen, B. (1991). Vasoactive intestinal peptide loses its ability to increase vaginal blood flow after menopause. *American Journal of Obstetrics & Gynecology, 164*, 556—558.

Panda, S., Das, A., Singh, A.S., & Pala, S. (2014). Vaginal pH: A marker for menopause. *Journal of Mid-life Health, 5*, 34—37.

Parish, S.J., Nappi, R.E., Krychman, M. Kellog-Spadt, S., Simon, J.A., & Goldstein, J.A. (2013). Impact of vulvovaginal health on postmenopausal women: A review of surveys on symptoms of vulvovaginal atrophy. *International Journal of Women's Health, 5*, 437—447.

Peto, L., & Allaby, M. (2012). *Screening for osteoporosis in postmenopausal women. A draft report for the UK National Screening Committee*. Oxford: Solutions for Public Health.

Pines, A. (2013). Telomere length and telomerase activity in the context of menopause. *Climacteric, 16*, 629—631.

Prause, N. (2011). The human female orgasm: Critical evaluations of proposed psychological sequelae. *Sexual and Relationship Therapy, 26*, 313—328.

Prause, N. (2012). A response to Brody, Costa and Hess (2012): Theoretical, statistical and construct problems perpetuated in the study of the female orgasm. *Sexual and Relationship Therapy, 27*, 260—271.

Puppo, V. (2011). Anatomy of the clitoris: Revision and clarifications about the anatomical terms for the clitoris proposed (without scientific basis) by Helen O'Connell, Emmanuelle Jannini, and Odile Buisson. *International Scholarly Research Network ISRN Obstetrics and Gynecology, 2011*, 261464. doi:10.5402/2011/261464

Rashidi, A., & Shanley, D. (2009). Evolution of the menopause: Life histories and mechanisms. *Menopause International, 15*, 26—30.

Reslan, O.M., & Khalil, R.A. (2012). Vascular effects of estrogenic menopausal hormone therapy. *Reviews on Recent Clinical Trials, 7*, 47—70.

Rossouw, J.E., Manson, J.E., Kaunitz, A.M. & Anderson, G.L. (2013). Lessons learned from the Women's Health Initiative trials of menopausal hormone therapy. *Obstetrics & Gynecology, 121*, 172—176.

Roy, S., Caillouette, J.C., Roy, T., & Faden, J.S. (2004). Vaginal pH is similar to follicle stimulating hormone for menopause diagnosis. *American Journal of Obstetrics and Gynecology, 190*, 1272–1277.

Schmidt, P.J., Steinberg, E.M., Negro, P.P., Haq, N., Gibson, C., & Rubinow, D.R. (2009). Pharmacologically induced hypogonadism and sexual function in healthy young women. *Neuropsychopharmacology, 34*, 565–576.

Simon, J.A. (2011). Identifying and treating sexual dysfunction in postmenopausal women: The role of estrogen. *Journal of Women's Health, 20*, 1453–1465.

Simon, J.A., Kojkot-Kierepa, M., & Goldstein, J. (2013). Vaginal health in the United States: Results from the Vaginal-Health: Insights, views and attitudes. *Menopause. The Journal of the North American Menopause Society, 20*, 1043–1048.

Stika, C.S. (2010). Atrophic vaginitis. *Dermatology Therapy, 23*, 514–522.

Sturdee, D.W. (2008). The menopausal hot flush – anything new? *Maturitas, 60*, 42–49.

Suh, D.D., Yang, C.C., Cao, Y., Garland, P.A., & Maravilla, K.R. (2003). Magnetic resonance imaging anatomy of the female genitalia in premenopausal and postmenopausal women. *Journal of Urology, 170*, 138–144.

Tarcan, T., Park, K., Goldstein, I., Maio, G. Fassina, A., Krane, R.I., & Azadzoi, K.M. (1999). Histomorphometric analysis of age-related structural changes in human clitoral cavernosal tissue. *Journal of Urology, 161*, 940–944.

Thornton, M.J. (2013). Estrogens and aging skin. *Dermatoendocrinology, 5*, 264–270.

Walker, A. (2014, July 10). Letter. *The Guardian*.

Wylie, K., & Kenney, G. (2010). Sexual dysfunction and the ageing male. *Maturitas, 65*, 23–27.

Wylie, K., & Levin, R.J. (2013). A self-treated case of female pleasure dissociative orgasmic disorder (PDOD). *Sexual and Relationship Therapy, 28*, 204–208.

Relationships and sexual expression in later life: a biopsychosocial perspective

John DeLamater[a] and Erica Koepsel[b]

[a]Department of Sociology, University of Wisconsin-Madison, Madison, WI, USA; [b]Department of Gender and Women's Studies, University of Wisconsin-Madison, Madison, WI, USA

The literature on sexual activity and ageing has grown substantially in the past 20 years. Until recently, a medicalized perspective dominated. In the past decade research based on a social-relational perspective has emerged. We summarize recent work from both perspectives. In addition to the effects of disease on sexual functioning of men and women over the age of 50, this review emphasizes sexual expression among older couples, newly emerging topics such as human immunodeficiency virus (HIV) in the older adult, and older lesbian and gay sexuality. Sexual functioning in both males and females continues in later life, while sexual satisfaction within their relationships is dependent upon individual responses to age-related changes. As the life course continues, some older married couples begin to desire emotional intimacy, stability, and continuity in addition to or instead of penetrative sex. This also appears to be characteristic of relationships involving two (older) women. As the world's population over 50 continues to grow there is an increasing interest in older adult's sexuality. This signals progress toward understanding healthy sexual relationships.

Introduction

Until recently, the research literature on later life sexual activity has been dominated by studies identifying physical and mental health barriers. The sexual expression of typical, healthy older persons is a relatively neglected topic of research, which makes it difficult to develop generalizable models of sexual relationships in later life. We cannot provide accurate information and support for older persons who wish to remain sexually active, or provide evidence-based advice to individuals and couples seeking counseling. There are little data on the potential benefits of sexual activity for quality of life. Data on which to base policy decisions regarding housing, sexual health care, and related programs for this age group are also limited.

We begin this review with a brief discussion of measures of sexuality. Next we summarize the data consistent with the medical model, focusing on ageing, physical health, mental health and medications as influences on sexual activity. In this context, we review the literature on sexual dysfunctions. Then we turn to research based on the alternative biopsychosocial model, focusing on attitudes, relationship status, and quality of relationship as important influences. We will review the limited literature on two new topics of research, the impact of human immunodeficiency virus (HIV) on sexual functioning and later life, and sexual expression of lesbian, gay, and bisexual (LGB) individuals and couples as they age.

An understanding of the realities and potential of sexual function at older ages is important for many reasons. First, there are a large number of older adults in the USA. In 2012, there were 41.5 million persons 65 and older, comprising 13.4% of the population (U.S. Census Bureau, 2012b). This group will double in size to 83.7 million in 2050, when one in five Americans will be 65 or older (U.S. Census Bureau, 2012c). Second, men and women in the United States are living longer. Life expectancy at birth increased from 70.8 in 1970 to 77.7 in 2006, and is expected to increase to 79.5 by 2020 (U.S. Census Bureau, 2012a). Even more significantly, *active life expectancy* at age 65 (years with no health-related difficulty performing instrumental activities of daily living) is estimated to increase by 2.5 years by 2022 (Manton, Gu, & Lamb, 2006). The number of years of potential sexual activity in later life will increase significantly as a result of these changes. Third, as families are smaller, and men and women are living longer, they no longer spend most of their adult years bearing and raising children. New stages of the later life course are emerging, including "empty nest" and "retirement" phases (Burgess, 2004). Individuals and couples may experience greater solitude and privacy during these years with more opportunity to engage in sexual activity. All of these changes have been observed globally.

Most importantly, regular (consensual) sexual expression contributes to physical and psychological well-being, and may reduce physical and mental health problems associated with ageing (Burgess, 2004; Edwards & Booth, 1994). Brody (2010), reviewing the literature, reports that engaging in penile–vaginal intercourse is correlated with higher quality of intimate relationships, lower rates of depressive symptoms, and improved cardiovascular health in both men and women. A study in South Korea also noted, "those who were maintaining a sexual life had significantly higher self-esteem than those who were not" (Choi, Jang, & Kim, 2011).

There are two fundamental perspectives in the research literature on sexuality beyond age 60. One is a medical perspective, which focuses on physical and mental health concomitants of ageing and their effect on sexual behavior. These studies generally consider the effects of various illnesses and treatments on sexual behavior, leading to a focus on *dysfunctions*.

In the past 15 years, research based on an alternative perspective has appeared with increasing frequency. In their analysis of sexuality across the life course, Carpenter and DeLamater (2012) develop and illustrate a *biopsychosocial* perspective, in which biology (health and illness) is only one of three influences on sexual functioning. Psychological influences (knowledge, attitudes) and relationship characteristics (quality, satisfaction) are also important. Increasingly, research on community samples of older adults has been published which reflects this more inclusive perspective.

Sexuality in later life

Sexual functioning

Until recently, the published literature on sexuality and ageing has concentrated on sexual interest or desire, capacity for sexual intercourse, and erectile dysfunction, particularly among older men. This reflects the medicalization of sexual functioning (Tiefer, 1996). However, in order to appreciate the role of sexuality in later life, we need to consider a range of sexual activities, including solo and partnered masturbation and oral sex. Moreover, the definition should include both objective and subjective components (Araujo, Mohr, & McKinlay, 2004). "Subjective sexual well-being" refers to the perceived quality of or satisfaction with the person's sexual life and relationships (Laumann et al., 2006).

Sexual behavior

Data on frequency of sexual behavior among older persons in the USA are available from three recent surveys: the American Association of Retired Persons survey conducted in 2009 (AARP, 2010), the National Social Life, Health and Aging Project (NSHAP) survey conducted in 2005–2006 (Waite, Laumann, Das, & Schumm, 2009), and the National Survey of Sexual Health and Behavior (2010), or NSSHB, conducted in 2009. The latter is a cross sectional survey of persons aged 14–94 years, and therefore covers the broadest age range. The sampling frame was constructed via a complex process, described by Herbenick et al. (2010). Persons in the frame were invited to complete an Internet survey, yielding 950 male and 958 female participants over the age of 50.

Table 1 presents data on the sexual activity reported by persons over 50 years of age in the year prior to the survey. The data include all respondents, whether partnered or not.

Solo masturbation is common among older American men and women; 46% of the oldest men (over 70) and 33% of the oldest women report engaging in the behavior. The data clearly indicate the extent of continuing sexual expression in this population. Men are somewhat more likely to report giving and receiving oral sex with a female partner (48% and 44%, respectively, for men aged 50–59), than women are to report these behaviors with a male partner (34% and 36% among those aged 50–59), and annual incidence declines with age among both. Vaginal intercourse is reported by 58% of men and 51% of women aged 50–59. The incidence declines to 43% among men aged over 70, and to 22% among women aged between 70 and older. Analyses of these data indicate that the decline among women is primarily related to relationship status, i.e., loss of a male partner (Schick et al., 2010).

Table 1. Sexual behaviors in the past year by gender and age.

	Male			Female		
	50–59	60–69	70+	50–59	60–69	70+
	$n = 454$	$n = 317$	$n = 179$	$n = 435$	$n = 331$	$n = 192$
	Percent					
Masturbated alone	72.1%	61.2%	46.4%	54.1%	46.5%	32.8%
Masturbated with partner	27.9%	17.0%	12.9%	17.7%	13.1%	5.3%
Received oral from female	48.5%	37.5%	19.2%	0.9%	0.6%	1.5%
Received oral from male	8.4%	2.6%	2.4%	34.2%	24.8%	7.8%
Gave oral to female	44.1%	34.3%	24.3%	0.9%	0.9%	1.5%
Gave oral to male	8.0%	2.6%	3.0%	36.2%	23.4%	6.8%
Vaginal intercourse	57.9%	53.5%	42.9%	51.4%	42.2%	21.6%
Inserted penis into anus	11.3%	5.8%	1.7%	0	0	0
Received penis in anus	4.6%	6.0%	1.7%	5.6%	4.0%	1.0%

Note: Data taken from National Survey of Sexual Health and Behavior (NSSHB).

These results are consistent with those reported by the NSHAP (Waite et al., 2009). A survey of 2341 German men and women aged 18–93 also found that engaging in sexual activity was primarily related to having a partner (Beutel, Stobel-Richter, & Brahler, 2007). Research on large samples of adults conducted in Great Britain (Mercer et al., 2013), Finland (Kontula, 2009), and Australia (Hyde et al., 2010) reports similar frequencies of and declines in sexual behavior in later life.

Thus, sexual activity remains a significant component of life and relationships well into the 70s. Having a sexual partner and being in good health are the primary influences or mechanisms for continued sexual activity (Karraker, DeLamater, & Schwartz, 2011). As noted earlier, maintaining sexual activity will likely increase in importance as more people live longer, and live more years in good health.

The medical perspective

Recently, the advent of Viagra and other forms of treatment have stimulated a substantial literature on the prevalence and pharmaceutical treatment of various sexual dysfunctions in later life. As noted by Tiefer (2007), much of this research is based on a biomedical perspective and assumes declining individual sexual functioning in later life, though there are exceptions (e.g., Laumann, Das, & Waite, 2008).

Research from a medical, rather than social scientific perspective, suffers from reliance on limited samples. Most of these studies involve small samples of older persons who have been diagnosed or treated for accident or illness, or who were taking a specific medication. Although informative, such research provides a little indication of typical patterns of sexual expression among healthy older adults who form the majority of people aged 50 and over.

In this section, we summarize the data consistent with the medical model, focusing on ageing, physical health, mental health, and medications as influences on sexual activity. We will review the limited medical literature on a new topic of research, the impact of HIV on sexual functioning, and later life. Then we turn to research based on the biopsychosocial model, focusing on attitudes, relationship status, and quality of relationship as important influences. We introduce recent research on sexual expression of LGB individuals and couples as they age.

Health and sexual activity

Physical changes associated with ageing

Ageing is associated with physical changes in women and men that may affect sexual functioning. The most noticeable changes in women are related to a decline of function of the ovaries during the climacteric. Due to the gradual decline in levels of estrogen in the body, women may experience vaginal dryness and atrophy. As many as 60% of postmenopausal women experience these conditions (Krychman, 2007), but there is little consistent evidence of the effect of such conditions/symptoms on the sexual activity. Some women report a less frequent sexual activity, possibly associated with negative feelings, others report no change, and some may experience greater excitement and desire after the menopause (Dillaway, 2012; Hinchcliff & Gott, 2008; Koch, Mansfield, Thurau, & Carey, 2005). Consequences associated with changes in estrogen levels vary considerably. Serious symptoms include aches and itching in the vulva and vagina, burning and dyspareunia. Obviously, these may lead to a reduced frequency or cessation of sexual activity. The experience of serious symptoms does not appear to be common. A study of a random sample of urban women aged 40–79 in Australia found that vaginal dryness was reported as always present by only 11.5% and never present by 35.8% (Howard, O'Neill, & Travers, 2006). Dyspareunia was experienced half of the time or more by only 14.6% of the women. The incidence of vaginal dryness and of dyspareunia did not differ significantly by age.

The analogous change in men is a slow decline in testosterone production. This is much more gradual than the decline in estrogen production in women, and so its consequences may take much longer to appear and may be subtle. Consequences for sexual functioning may include slower erections, less firm erections, decreased likelihood of orgasm, and a longer refractory period (Aubin & Heiman, 2004).

In short, there is little evidence that the normal physical changes that accompany ageing necessarily or irreversibly affect sexual functioning.

Cognitive perspectives suggest that it is the meaning of these changes, not the changes themselves that may determine their impact on sexual functioning. These meanings are derived from social values. Many people experience age-related changes in physical appearance, including changes in skin tone and firmness, and amount and coloring of hair. Physical vitality may also be affected. These changes are reminders of biological ageing and may be stressful for those who live in an ageist society (Slevin & Mowery, 2012). In a Western society surrounded by youthful media images, ageing means movement away from that youthful status, and may have negative effects on self-esteem and body image. Ageing men and women may feel that they are no longer physically or sexually attractive, undermining their sexual desire even though their physical capacity has not declined. Koch et al. (2005) found that women aged 39–56 who reported declining sexual desire and frequency of activity also reported that they felt less physically attractive than 10 years earlier, regardless of age.

Another influence on women's interest in and desire for sexual activity is pronatalism (Baker, 2005). Some men and women define womanhood in terms of motherhood. An inability to reproduce following menopause may result in the belief that there is no longer any reason to engage in sexual activity. Thus, social values may result in cessation of sexual activity by some (older) people.

Physical health

Lindau and Gavrilova (2010) calculated sexually active life expectancy "defined as the average number of years remaining spent as sexually active" (p. 3). Their estimates take into account the likelihood of having a partner and of being institutionalized at specific ages. At age 55, they estimate sexually active life expectancy for men at 15 years and for women at 10.6 years. Men in excellent or good health are estimated to gain 5–7 additional years of sexual activity compared to men in fair or poor health. Women in excellent or good health are estimated to gain 3–6 years.

Research on health often relies on a measure of self-reported health. Older men and women who report their health as excellent or good are more likely to be sexually active than those who report their health as fair or poor (Lindau & Gavrilova, 2010). In the AARP (2010) results, there is a strong positive association between the rating of one's health and reports of engaging in sexual intercourse at least once per week. Similar results were found in two nationally representative surveys in Finland in the 1990s (Kontula & Haavio-Mannila, 2009). Hence, good health is related to continuing sexual activity, and self-reported health does not inevitably decline with age.

Table 2. Conditions that respondents think restrict sexual activity.

	Men			Women		
	45−59	60−74	75+	45−59	60−74	75+
(Base)	(341)	(205)	(90)	(368)	(253)	(119)
Have conditions that restricts sexual activity	18.2%	39.0%	44.6%	15.8%	10.4%	13.3%
High blood pressure	8.2%	15.6%	11.1%	2.7%	4.0%	3.4%
Arthritis or Rheumatism	4.4%	4.9%	4.4%	5.7%	5.9%	4.2%
Diabetes	3.5%	10.7%	6.7%	1.1%	2.0%	2.5%
Depression	4.1%	0.5%	1.1%	4.1%	2.0%	1.7%
Enlarged or swollen prostate	2.1%	9.3%	7.8%	0	0	0
Prostate cancer	0.3%	4.4%	11.1%	0	0	0

Source: AARP (1999) survey.

We noted earlier the substantial literature on the impact of chronic conditions and illness on sexual functioning. AARP (1999) conducted a questionnaire survey of 1384 respondents aged 45 and older. The results indicated that less than 16% of the men and 6% of the women reported restrictions in their sexual activity due to serious medical conditions. At the same time, one-third of men and women had been diagnosed with high-blood pressure, 19% of men and 31% of women with arthritis, 15.6% of men with enlarged prostate, and 14% of men and 12% of women with diabetes mellitus (Table 2).

Lindau et al. (2007) reported results from NSHAP, based on face-to-face interviews with a national probability sample of 3005 adults aged 57−85. Respondents who reported that their health was fair or poor were less likely to be sexually active and reported a higher incidence of sexual problems. The results indicate that diabetes mellitus and hypertension are associated with sexual dysfunction among older men and women (Lindau et al., 2010). The AARP results indicate that the incidence of these diseases is less than 12%.

Howard et al. (2006) studied sexual functioning in a sample of 474 Australian women aged 40−79. These women reported a variety of medical conditions including breast cancer, diabetes mellitus, hypertension, and osteoarthritis. Howard and his colleagues conclude, "Overall, women with medical conditions showed no increase in sexual distress compared with women without medical conditions" (p. 363). Similarly, Kontula and Haavio-Manilla (2009), basing their conclusion on an analysis of the Finnish survey data, claimed that illness seldom causes sexual problems.

The evidence does not support the argument that medical illness is a major influence on declining sexual desire or behavior in later life. The literature does suggest that improvements in the health of a population will increase rates of sexual activity in later life.

Mental health

Mental health also influences sexual functioning in later life. Laumann et al. (2008), analyzing data from NSHAP, reported that scores on an anxiety scale were related to sexual difficulties among both men and women. Increased anxiety was associated with a lack of sexual interest in both women and men, with increased anorgasmia and lack of pleasure from sex among women (e.g., Moreira, Glasser, King, Duarte, & Gingell, 2008). Symptoms of depression were associated with anorgasmia and erectile problems among men. There was a correlation between self-rating of mental health as fair or poor and reports of problems in sexual functioning amongst women (e.g., Brody, 2010). Laumann and colleagues concluded that stress, a major contributor to anxiety and depression, may be a primary cause of reduced sexual functioning in later life.

There is a positive relationship between mental health and sexual functioning in later life.

Medications

Significant numbers of older adults take various medications, some of which are known to affect sexual functioning. The impression is created that increasing use of multiple medications, with the exception of drugs for erectile dysfunction, is a major reason why older people stop engaging in sexual activity. Therefore, it is important to assess this relationship in large samples of typical adults.

The AARP (2010) survey asked respondents aged 50 and above to identify the prescription drugs they took. Overall, 47% of men and women reported taking blood pressure medication, and 41% of men and 36% of women reported taking medication to lower cholesterol. Medication to relieve pain was being taken by 39% of men and by 43% of women. The frequency of use of all three prescribed drugs increased with age in both men and women. Three medications were reportedly taken by more than one-third of the respondents (Table 3).

Table 3. Prescription drug use.

	Males				Females			
	45−49	50−59	60−69	70+	40−49	50−59	60−69	70+
(Base)	82	198	151	92	77	205	188	113
Blood pressure pills	30%	36%	48%	69%	16%	40%	50%	54%
Medications for cholesterol	23%	28%	53%	56%	16%	23%	40%	51%
Pain killers	29%	32%	47%	43%	26%	39%	47%	46%
Pills or other med. to thin blood	11%	11%	37%	39%	5%	9%	11%	18%
Pills/paste patches or anything for heart or heart beat	4%	7%	25%	27%	5%	7%	8%	9%
Medications for depression	12%	8%	14%	7%	16%	18%	18%	10%
Sleeping pills of other meds to help you sleep	13%	13%	18%	11%	16%	20%	14%	22%
Medications for a nervous condition, such as tranquilizers	3%	5%	11%	2%	8%	11%	7%	9%
Medications to improve sexual functioning	6%	10%	13%	9%	1%	1%	0%	0%
Any androgens, testoderm, or bromocriptine	1%	2%	1%	4%	0%	0%	0%	0%

Source: AARP (2009) survey.

DeLamater and Sill (2005) conducted extensive analyses of the AARP (1999) data related to influences on sexual desire. A two-item index of desire was related negatively to regular use of anticoagulants, cardiovascular medications, medications to control cholesterol, and drugs to reduce hypertension among women. It was related negatively to taking anticoagulants and medications for hypertension among men. These correlations were significant and uniformly small; the largest was −.19. In multivariate analyses, the total number of drugs being taken regularly was significantly related to desire, but the coefficients were small. DeLamater and Moorman (2007) conducted regression analyses of the 1999 AARP data focused on influences on frequency of sexual behavior. Diagnosed illnesses and medication use were generally unrelated to frequency of sexual activity.

Sexual functioning

Sexual desire

Much of the literature on sexual functioning presumes, implicitly or explicitly, that sexual desire is important. Desire is thought to index motivation for sexual activity and gratification.

Reported sexual desire declines sharply with age, although there is some variation across studies. In the AARP (1999) data, 76.5% of men aged 45−59 reported desire a few times per week, declining to 43% among men aged 60−74, and 17% among men aged over 75. Among women, the comparable percentages were 36%, 11%, and 4%, respectively. Ergo, women were much less likely to report frequent sexual desire than men. Kontula and Haavio-Mannila (2009) reported data from two surveys in Finland with data from 705 men aged 45−74. They asked whether lack of sexual desire had caused problems very often or quite often in the past year. Thirteen percent of respondents aged 45−54, 12% aged 55−64, and 30% aged 65−74 replied affirmatively. In contrast, Moreira et al. (2008) found that 18% of 750 Australian men aged 40−80 reported lack of sexual interest with no variation by age. Similarly, lack of sexual interest was reported by 33% of 750 Australian women aged 40−80 with no variation by age.

Huang et al. (2009) assessed sexual desire/interest among an ethnically diverse group of US women participating in the Kaiser Permanente Medical Program using items from the Female Sexual Function Index. Scores indicating at least moderate sexual desire were obtained by 56% of women aged 45−54, 35% of women aged 55−64, and 29% of women aged over 65, indicating a less substantial decline than other studies. Of the female respondents 50% Black, 46% Latina, 41% White, and 39% Asian women reported at least moderate desire.

Lindau and Gavrilova (2010) analyzed data from two surveys, MIDUS (the national survey of Midlife Development in the USA) with 3032 respondents aged 25−74 and NSHAP. Both surveys assessed sexual interest. The results indicated that among men sexual interest was stable across age groups and did not vary by partner status. For women interest declined significantly after the age of 60 and was much lower among women without a partner.

The relationship between age and reported sexual desire varies across studies. Clearly, desire does not always decline as men and women age, suggesting that other variables such as partner status and health/stress are influential.

While reported desire varies, several studies indicate a link between sexual desire and sexual activity. In a study of healthy older women there was a positive association between sexual desire and frequency of arousal, lubrication, and orgasm (Trompeter,

Bettencourt, & Barrett-Conner, 2012). Two surveys of adults in Finland reported that frequency of desire predicted frequency of sexual intercourse (Kontula & Haavio-Manilla, 2009). The AARP data indicate, along with more frequent sexual activity, that there is an association between desire and increased masturbation (DeLamater & Moorman, 2007). It appears that desire is significantly associated with frequency of sexual activity in later life.

Sexual dysfunctions

As noted earlier, much of the recent literature on sexuality among older adults is focused on sexual dysfunctions, contributing to the stereotype that later life is a time of diminished or no sexual activity. The following discussion considers issues related to desire, arousal, orgasm, and sexual pain/use of lubricants.

Hypoactive sexual desire.   Hypoactive sexual desire disorder (HSDD) is defined as "the persistent or recurrent deficiency (or absence) of sexual fantasies/thoughts, and/or desires for, or receptivity to, sexual activity, which causes personal distress" (Aubin & Heiman, 2004, p. 481). This is considered a serious disorder. Hayes et al. (2007) measured HSDD by combining their measure of desire from the Profile of Female Sexual Function with a validated measure of sexual distress. They found that while lack of desire increased with age, especially in the European sample, the percentage of women distressed by their lack of desire declined from two-thirds of woman aged 20–29 to 37% of women aged 60–70 in the USA and 22% of women of the same age in Europe. They conclude that HSDD among women is not associated with age.

Problems of sexual arousal.   The occurrence of vaginal lubrication is an indicator of physiological arousal. The percentage of women reporting that lubrication was difficult, very difficult, or impossible increased from 17% among women aged 45–54 to 28% among women aged 55–64 and 27% among women over the age of 65 (Huang et al., 2009). While this age trend was not significant, Kontula and Haavio-Manilla (2009) reported a significant age trend among Finnish women, 13% of those aged 45–54, 36% of women aged 55–64, and 31% of women aged 65–74 reported lubrication difficulties quite often in the past year. Similar results were found in a survey of 750 Australian women (Moreira et al., 2008).

The most common disorder among men aged from 57 to 85 years is erectile dysfunction (Laumann et al. 2008, Table 2). Laumann, Paik, and Rosen (1999), analyzing National Health and Social Life Survey data, found that men aged 50–59 were three times more likely (17%) than those aged 18–29 to experience erectile difficulties in the past year. Results from NSHAP (Laumann et al., 2008) and the study of Australian men (Moreira et al., 2008) indicate that the incidence of erectile problems was significantly related to age. The AARP (1999) questioned men about impotence, defining the condition as "being unable to get and keep an erection that is rigid enough for sexual activity." Among men aged 45–59, only 2.5% rated themselves "completely impotent," increasing to 16% among men aged 60–74, and 38% among men aged over 75. Frequencies reported in the 2010 online survey are similar. However, in response to an open question about what conditions restricted their sexual activity, only 2%–4% of the men wrote "impotence." It appears as though many men with difficulties maintaining erections may be engaging in sexual activities other than those involving penile penetration. This issue should be investigated in future research.

Problems associated with orgasm.   Among men, in the NHSLS, with respondents aged 18–59, only 7%–9% of men reported "inability to climax or achieve orgasm" in the past year (Laumann, Paik, & Rosen, 1999). In the NSHAP data, inability to climax was reported by 16%, 23%, and 33% of men aged 57–64, 65–75, and 75–85, respectively. The age trend is highly significant (Waite et al., 2009).

Among women aged between 18 and 59, inability to climax or achieve orgasm was reported in the past year by 22%–26% of the respondents (Laumann et al., 1999). Among the older women in NSHAP, there is no significant age trend (Waite et al., 2009). In response to the AARP question regarding frequency of orgasm, the percentage saying "never" was 4% among women aged 45–49, 13% among women aged 50–59, 5% of women aged 60–69, and 7% among women aged 70 and over. In a survey of almost 2000 women aged 45–80, Huang et al. (2009) reported the percentage of women stating that achieving orgasm was difficult, very difficult, or impossible did not increase significantly with age from 45 to over 65. Thus, in all four of these studies, there is little evidence that orgasmic disorder increases with age among women, although the precise measure varies across studies.

Pain during intercourse.   Among male respondents in NSHAP, reports of experiencing pain during intercourse in the past year were very infrequent, less than 4%, and did not vary with age (Laumann et al., 2008). Similar results were found in the AARP (1999) questionnaire, indicating pain associated with sex appears to be a very uncommon experience among older men.

Among women, the NSHAP data indicates that 12%–19% experienced pain during intercourse in the preceding year. The incidence did not vary with age. Hispanic women were significantly more likely to report this experience (31%) than Black (9%) or White (17%) women. In three other studies, there are no differences with age in the frequency of reports of pain during intercourse (AARP, 1999; Huang et al., 2009; Leiblum, Hayes, Wanser, & Nelson, 2009). The experience of pain during intercourse appears to be unrelated to age among women.

Treatment.   With regard to treatment, the Associated Press-LifeGoesStrong (Knowledge Networks, 2010) poll asked respondents whether they have ever sought treatment from a medical professional for problems related to sexual functioning. Forty-six percent of people aged 45–65 said they had. Twelve percent of people aged 45–65 and 14% aged 66 and older reported taking medication or receiving treatment for such a problem.

Moreira et al. (2008) found that only 22% of Australian men and women who had reported at least one sexual difficulty had sought help from a medical professional, typically a medical doctor. Men experiencing erectile difficulties, women experiencing problems with lubrication, and those who believed sex is a very or extremely important part of life were more likely to have sought medical help.

The AARP (1999) survey indicates that 28% of the men and 13% of women had sought treatment for problems related to sexual functioning. About half of these participants consulted their primary care physician and half consulted a specialist physician. This clearly indicates the need for medical personnel to be trained in the assessment and management of sexual function in older people. About 6% of the men and 4% of the women reported using medication, hormone replacement therapy, or other treatments to improve sexual functioning at the time of the survey. Five percent of the men and 3% of the women reported using these in the past. Of the men who had ever received a treatment, one-half used Viagra. Among women, one-half reported using hormone replacement therapy. Those who received/accepted treatments did not report a significant increase in frequency of intercourse following treatment, but 60% of the men and women who were treated reported an increase in their satisfaction with sex.

HIV in the older adult

While HIV has been identified in populations of adults aged 55 years and older for the past decade, the literature has only recently recognized that this population is at risk of HIV infection. The *National HIV/AIDS Strategy for the United States* indicates a continual rise in the number of individuals aged 50 and over who contract HIV each year (White House Office of National AIDS Policy, 2010). The Centers for Disease Control and Prevention (CDC) estimates that by 2015 over half of HIV cases in the United States will be adults in this age range, with the majority being new cases (CDC, 2008). Of the older adults currently infected with HIV approximately 60% of males were infected due to sex with other males. In contrast, 80% of infected females contracted HIV from heterosexual contact (CDC, 2013).

The rise in HIV infection among older populations has been attributed to four main factors (Emanuel, 2014). First, as stated earlier, older adults are living longer and staying healthier. As a result older people are able to remain sexually active for longer than in the past. Second, even individuals who experience problems in sexual functioning have the assistance of Viagra or other drugs that enable enjoyment of penetrative sex for longer than was possible in previous generations. Third, retirement communities, where large numbers of people of similar aged live together and interact daily, provide a greater opportunity for older people to engage in sexual partnership. Finally, it appears that older, sexually active people may not have received safer sex information earlier in life. They also may have minimal information on condom use.

Not surprisingly, older individuals with HIV have similar reactions to the virus and medication as younger adults. It is common for HIV drugs to affect sexual functioning, by preventing arousal and erection, in ways similar to anti-depressant medication (Gay Men's Health Crises Inc., 2010). Other studies have identified HIV as a hindrance to sexual activity. HIV may also lead to loss of libido due to the emotional stress related to contracting a serious and stigmatizing illness (Sadeghi-Nejad, Wasserman, Weidner, Richardson, & Goldmeier, 2010). As HIV progresses it can be responsible for low testosterone levels and nerve damage, which in turn may cause erectile problems in men (Mayr & Bredeek, 2007; State of New York Department of Health, 2012). Women who may already have low postmenopausal estrogen levels are at a higher risk of contracting HIV due to the thinning of the vaginal walls (Brennan, Emlet, & Eady, 2011; Rural Center for AIDS/STI Prevention, 2013). A woman who is HIV positive may also experience altered production of progesterone and estrogen which may affect female sexual enjoyment by causing vaginal dryness, thrush, and pain (Carter, 2011). Unfortunately, these symptoms can be more intense or can escalate more quickly in older bodies due to the typical decline of the immune system.

Another factor affecting HIV rates in the older population is the social stigma surrounding the sexuality of older people (Brennan et al., 2011; CDC, 2013; Miller, 1996). Because it is typically assumed that older adults are sexually inactive, health care providers are less likely to inquire about older patients sexual habits, so rarely consider their risk of HIV and other STIs (CDC, 2013). Older patients may be embarrassed or uncomfortable and avoid discussing sexual activity with their health care providers. This may result in late diagnosis, which is often accompanied by a quicker progression of HIV/AIDS disease and more rapid bodily deterioration (Brennan et al., 2011). Because older individuals are expected to have bodily ailments in later life, many who experience symptoms of HIV fail to identify them as HIV related. They may also be misdiagnosed by doctors who attribute symptoms to ageing (CDC, 2008, 2013). In addition, the ability for more individuals to perform sexually into later life can lead to more sexual activity, which includes more risky sexual behaviors (Carter, 2011; Maes & Louis, 2003). This misunderstanding of older sexuality and failure of both older adults and care providers to discuss sexual health behaviors with one another results in an increased incidence of HIV infection in the older community.

Many older adults do not perceive themselves at risk for HIV. As a result single, older individuals are less likely to take necessary precautions to protect themselves from HIV and other STIs. Moreover, many women have already gone through the menopause and therefore are unconcerned about using contraception (Maes & Louis, 2003). The NSSHB indicated that older men are more likely to use condoms than older women, but rates of condom use decline significantly in older age (Reece et al., 2010; Schick et al., 2010). It appears that Black and Hispanic adults aged over 50 are more likely to use condoms and get tested for STIs than other adults (Dodge et al., 2010). Even if older adults are aware of the risks, they are often under-educated on the modes of transmission as well as proper condom use (Scudder, 2012). Organizations are trying to combat this knowledge gap with educational series in New York City, and books featuring lesson plans for sex education with older adults, e.g., *Older, Wiser, Sexually Smarter* are being published. However, it is unclear how these resources are being used (Brick, Lunquist, Sandak, & Taverner, 2009; Kilgannon, 2007). Research indicates that loneliness among single, older adults can lead to riskier sexual behavior, such as unprotected vaginal or anal sex and multiple or anonymous partners, especially when combined with drug and alcohol use (Golub et al., 2010). As part of a vicious cycle, lack of a support system and loneliness often have detrimental effects on the mental health of older individuals who have already contracted HIV.

Clearly current research on HIV in older individuals illustrates an interaction between biological and social influences that affect the sexual functioning and sexual health of older adults.

A biopsychosocial perspective

The variables employed in the medical perspective – ageing, health, medications, and sexual functioning – explain relatively little of the variation in reported sexual expression in older couples. Carpenter and DeLamater (2012) develop and illustrate a *biopsychosocial* perspective, in which biology is only one of three types of influence on sexual functioning.

Research based on the biopsychosocial perspective has been facilitated by the publication of articles and the release of data from several large studies of older populations. The samples include larger numbers of "well persons" and measure a broad range of variables. The vast majority of participants in research using community-based or representative samples are heterosexual, due to their predominance in populations. The data reviewed in this section are about partnered heterosexual activity and masturbation. A short review on the limited published research on typical patterns of sexual expression among older LGB persons follows.

Psychological factors

Attitudes about sex

Attitudes about sexuality are an important influence on frequency of partnered sexual behavior. The AARP (1999) survey included three measures of the *importance of sex to a relationship*, e.g., "Sexual activity is a critical part of a good relationship." One-third to one-half of men and women agreed with each item. Three additional items measured the *importance of sex to the person*, e.g., "Sexual activity is important to my overall quality of life," and "I would be quite happy never having sex again." Fifty-nine percent of the men agreed or strongly agreed with the first item, compared to 35% of the women. Conversely, 3% of the men agreed with the second item, compared to 20% of the women (DeLamater & Moorman, 2007). Therefore, men were more likely to rate sex as important than women. Results from the AARP (2010) online survey conducted 10 years later found similar results.

The AP-LifeGoesStrong (Knowledge Networks, 2010) surveyed 945 adults 45–75 years of age. Asked to choose between "Sexual activity is a critical part of a strong relationship," and "Couples can have a strong relationship without sexual activity," 45% of people aged 45–65 chose the former, compared to 29% of the people aged 65 and older. With regard to attitudes about sex as people age, 51% of respondents aged 45–65 endorsed the statement "Sex becomes less important to most people as they get older," as did 76% of those aged over 65.

The NSHAP survey included the attitude statement "sexual ability decreases with age." Among men, 68% of those aged 57–64 agreed, as did 72% of those aged 65–74 and 78.5% of men aged 75–85. Among women, the comparable percentages were 71%, 83%, and 89%, respectively (Waite et al., 2009).

Substantial percentages of older people believe that sex declines in importance as they age. The results of two surveys in Finland indicate that men and women (of all ages) who rated sex as important reported more frequent sexual activity (Kontula, 2009). DeLamater and Sill (2005), analyzing the 1999 AARP data, constructed three-item indices of attitudes about the importance of sex for the self, and of sex for relationships. Men and women who agreed that sex was important to them reported significantly greater desire ($r = .31$ and $.19$, respectively). Men and women who agreed they would be happy never having sex again reported significantly lower sexual desire ($r = -.47$ and $-.57$, respectively). In regression analyses with desire as the outcome variable, attitudes were associated with the largest beta coefficients after age.

This research demonstrates the importance of positive attitudes to continuing sexual activity.

Information about sexuality

It is plausible that information about sexuality and especially sexuality in later life influences sexual activity. There is almost no systematic empirical research on this issue. One exception is a survey of 844 adults over 65 years of age living in Melbourne (Minichiello, Plummer, & Loxton, 2004). Higher scores on a six-item sexual knowledge scale were associated with being in a sexual relationship, for both men and women. There are many anecdotal reports of older persons ceasing to engage in partnered sexual activity because they mistakenly believe that one should not do so following major health events, e.g., a heart attack, or fears about negative health consequences for self or partner. "Older adults are misinformed about normative patterns of ageing and often rely on stereotypes in order to understand sexuality and older adults" (Burgess, 2004, p. 439). This misinformation demonstrates the need for accurate sex education for older adults.

Relationships/social well-being

Most sexual activity is coupled (Gagnon, Giami, Michaels, & de Colomby, 2001). The foundation of couple relationships or partnering is a desire for sexual and emotional intimacy (Sassler, 2010). The research summarized above indicates that couple relationships are typically beneficial for physical and mental health. Couple relationships provide instrumental and emotional support, social support, and meaningful activity (Blieszner, 2006). As people age, their partner(s) may become more important as one, or perhaps the only, source of these rewards.

Relationship status

Table 4 describes the marital status of men and women aged over 45 years in the United States (U.S. Census Bureau, 2010). Among men, 67%–72% are married. Among women aged 45–64, about 63% are married. The percentage declines sharply to 40% among women aged over 65. This reflects two demographic characteristics. Women in the USA marry men who are on average 2.6 years older (England & McClintock, 2009). Typically women live 5–6 years longer than men. Therefore, many older women are widowed.

Married men and women report more frequent partnered sexual activity (once a week or more) than single individuals, including those who were formerly married and are divorced or widowed, particularly at older ages (Lindau & Gavrilova, 2010). This reflects cultural norms limiting intimate sexual activity to persons in committed relationships. The incidence of sexual activity (sexually active in the past six months) declines with age, in the age range 57–85 years of age, especially among women (Lindau et al., 2007) (see Table 1). The most significant contributor to the decline in frequency among women is the increase in percentage of widowed women (DeLamater & Moorman, 2007), as reflected in Table 4.

Across the range of statuses, frequency of sexual activity is highest among the currently married, intermediate among never married and divorced persons, and lowest

Table 4. Marital status, United States, 2009.

Age and sex	Total	Married (except separated)	Widowed	Divorced	Separated	Never married
Males						
45–54	21,493,896	66.80%	1.00%	15.60%	2.60%	14.00%
55–64	15,712,993	72.40%	2.50%	15.20%	2.00%	7.90%
65 and older	16,027,330	71.40%	13.80%	8.90%	1.30%	4.60%
Females						
45–54	22,152,876	64.10%	3.20%	18.40%	3.60%	10.80%
55–64	16,888,360	62.30%	9.10%	19.20%	2.40%	7.00%
65 and older	21,973,540	43.40%	43.40%	10.60%	1.00%	4.60%

Source: 2005–2009 American Community Survey, Table S1201.

among widowed persons (Smith, 2006). Smith attributes this variation primarily to availability of partners, recognizing that health becomes a factor as people age.

Population level changes in types or frequency of relationships may affect rates of sexual activity (Karraker et al., 2011). New relationship forms have emerged in the United States in the past two decades. Manning and Brown (2009) estimate that in 2009, 2% of older Americans were cohabiting. They suggest that one reason these couples do not marry is a desire to maintain financial autonomy. Part of this may be related to the disincentives of remarriage for older adults in the USA. Remarriage may result in higher American taxes due to combined income or loss of survivor benefits from social security, thus encouraging cohabitation and autonomy (Kahler, 2014). Research on sexual activity in a national representative sample indicates that cohabiters report more frequent partnered sexual activity than married couples (Yabiku & Gager, 2009), 12 times per month and 6 times per month, respectively. In contrast, when older adults live in separate residences, known as living apart together, there may be an associated decline in the frequency of sexual activity (Blieszner, 2006; Manning & Brown, 2009).

Between 9% and 19% of men and women aged over 45 in the USA are divorced (Table 4). As noted, frequency of sexual activity in this group is intermediate between married and widowed individuals. Research using the NHSLS data on people aged 18–59 found that resuming sexual activity following divorce or dissolution of a cohabiting relationship was related to how recently the event had taken place. There was a significant positive relationship between having left a relationship within the past year and more frequent sexual activity (Wade & DeLamater, 2002). Stack and Gundlach (1992), analyzing older General Social Survey data, reported that men were more likely to be sexually active following divorce than women, and that likelihood of being sexually active declined with age. Qualitative research (Lichtenstein, 2012) suggests that whether divorced women re-enter the dating scene and become sexually active depends partly on whether they are financially independent. Data from the AP-LifeGoesStrong (Knowledge Networks, 2010) poll indicate that one in three divorced women aged between 45 and 65 is dating, compared to only one in ten aged over 65. Poor adjustment to the stresses of divorce or the breakdown of a long-term relationship reduces the chance of forming a new romantic relationship (Coleman, Ganong, & Leon, 2006). As they age, women face the challenge of an increasingly lopsided sex ratio when attempting to form new relationships (England & McClintock, 2009). These data indicate that relationship or marital status is perhaps the major influence on the frequency of heterosexual sexual activity in later life.

Relationship satisfaction

The quality of, or satisfaction with, committed relationships is a major influence on sexual activity. Spousal support and relationship happiness were associated with more frequent and satisfying sexual episodes (McFarland, Uecker, & Regnerus, 2011). Smith (2006) also reported that rating one's marriage as happier is associated with more frequent sexual intercourse. In the AARP (1999) survey, 60% of the men and women aged between 45 and 59 were satisfied with their sex lives. By the age of 75 this had fallen to 35%. Satisfaction was associated significantly with frequency of partnered sexual activity. Greater satisfaction was associated with more frequent hugging and kissing, oral sex, and vaginal intercourse (DeLamater & Moorman, 2007). Satisfaction was also associated with less frequent reports of reduced sexual interest, lack of pleasure, and anorgasmia in women (Laumann et al., 2008).

Yabiku and Gager (2009) used the National Survey of Families and Households data to examine the relationship between frequency of sexual activity and separation. Using reported sexual frequency in 1987–1988, they looked at whether unions were intact in 1992–1994. The data include 5440 marriages and 462 cohabiting unions. Forty-seven percent of the cohabiting unions compared with 10% of the marriages dissolved in the interim. The results indicate that there is a significant association between low sexual frequency and dissolution, and the relationship was stronger among cohabiters. Infrequent sexual activity will create dissatisfaction which may lead to the breakdown of some relationships.

Huang et al. (2009) report data on an ethnically diverse sample of 1971 women aged 45–80. Overall, there was an age-related decline of just 7% in women who claimed to be moderately or very sexually satisfied (61% of those aged 45–50 and 54% for those aged over 65). The same trend was observed among sexually active women. In multivariate analyses, sexually active Latina women were more likely to report being sexually satisfied than sexually active White women. It should be noted that 29%45% of woman who were not sexually active still reported being satisfied. A similar trend was noted by Trompeter et al. (2012). The evidence suggests an overall increase in sexual satisfaction, independent of sexual activity, among community dwelling women.

Research has recently expanded to include the sexual satisfaction of married couples. For a variety of reasons most couples report less sexual activity as they age. Many indicate that this "loss" of sexual activity, while mourned by a few, is replaced with emotional attachment and alternative expressions of affection such as holding hands, hugging, and cuddling (Lodge & Umberson, 2012). Some older, sexually active women feel this emotional closeness results in more frequent arousal, lubrication, and orgasm (Trompeter et al., 2012). Similarly, some married couples experience the decrease in sexual activity as an increase in quality of sex. However, in heterosexual married couples where reports of quality were inconsistent between the two parties, women expressed satisfaction while men did not (Lodge & Umberson, 2012). None of the research focuses on the sexual satisfaction of single individuals outside a committed relationship.

However, to say individuals enjoy the sex they do have in older age does not mean it comes without occasional distress. It is common for older men to express distress at the inability to get or maintain an erection, while women often fault themselves, rather than their partners, for this obstacle. Many also seem to hold to societal notions about who should initiate sex, so many women feel uncomfortable with this new role of pursuer (Lodge & Umberson, 2012; Mitchell et al., 2013). Often, couples who have ceased all forms of sexual activity have done so due to erectile dysfunction, and show no interest in replacing penile–vaginal intercourse with other types of sex (Lodge & Umberson, 2012). This indicates a rather strict definition of sex, which may be limiting possible healthy expressions of sexuality.

Lesbian and gay older adults

As research on the sexuality of older adults expands to include topics within a psychosocial perspective, a new focus has developed on the sexual and emotional relationships of older lesbian and gay (LG) individuals. Little to no research has been done in other sexual minority groups. Similarities in sexuality between the general population of ageing adults and LG older people include more frequent sex with a life partner as opposed to a new partner, concerns of isolation, and a shifting focus from sex to intimate acts such as hand holding, hugging, and sleeping together. While there are many similar narratives in the experiences of ageing heterosexual adults and older LG individuals, researchers have indicated a major difference in the ability of older LG adults to express their sexuality throughout old age.

Older LG adults may have experienced a lifetime of victimization specifically related to their sexual identity. Although there is little research to indicate a compounded stigma of ageism and homophobia during later life, it is likely that experiences of violence and discrimination earlier in life may impede disclosure of information about sexuality to new friends, caretakers, or medical professionals. However, some researchers believe that the lifelong victimization experienced by these older adults may mean that they cope better with the transition to old age in an ageist society (D'Augelli & Grossman, 2001). Nevertheless, LG individuals are still confronted with societal standards of beauty. They react quite differently from one another and from their heterosexual counterparts. Lesbians may be more accepting of the changes to their ageing bodies than straight women due to a lack of interest in and pressure from the "male gaze." In contrast, older gay males may fare less well due to the continued emphasis on youth in the gay community. However, there are indications that LG individuals try to reject the ageing process as much as the general population does by controlling their ageing bodies through dieting, exercise, and cosmetic surgery (Slevin & Mowery, 2012).

For independent LG older adults, there seem to be distinct but varying changes in sexual behavior. Some consider themselves to be "sexually smarter" after a lifetime of sexual activity and so are able to enjoy stress-free sexual encounters (Slevin & Mowery, 2012). Those in primary relationships seem to benefit from this more relaxed attitude towards sexual behavior, as this is the population most likely to engage in frequent sexual activity (Averett, Yoon & Jenkins, 2012). On the other hand, lesbian older adults, like many ageing persons, notice a greater emphasis on affection rather than sex (Averett et al., 2012; Slevin & Mowery, 2012). However, the opportunity for LG adults to engage with a community of similarly identified individuals is limited when compared to those of heterosexual older adults. This may result in isolation and less sexual activity than is desired or in high-risk sexual behavior (Gay and Grey in Dorset, 2006; Kuyper & Fokkema, 2010).

Often, the isolation and loneliness experienced by LG individuals are the result of being confined to home care or long-term care (LTC) facilities. Furthermore, a move to LTC facilities may affect more LG older people, as many of these individuals have no children to help care for them (Bloomberg & Quinn, 2009). A recent study of staff perceptions and acceptance of sexual activity in LTC facilities discovered that staff members of one LTC facility were much more accepting of heterosexual pairings than same-sex pairings. They were least tolerant of male-to-male sexual contact (Hinrichs & Vacha-Haase, 2010). Another study emphasized that housebound LG individuals may feel alienated from their former queer communities (Cronin, Ward, Pugh, King, & Price, 2011). It is reasonable to believe that residents in LTC facilities without many other LG individuals may feel the same. Interviews with older LG persons in care facilities indicated disappointment with their inability to disclose information about long-term partners when other residents can freely talk about their spouses (Cronin et al., 2011). There is no question that these individuals experience stigma due to their sexual orientation. There is a fear that resistance, from unaccepting caregivers, to older LG sexual expression may cause a retreat back into the "closet" and a suppression of sexual desire and identity (Bloomberg & Quinn, 2009; Cronin et al., 2011; Gay and Grey cited in Dorset, 2006; Hinrichs & Vacha-Hasse, 2010). While this stigma may certainly change based on the location of the older adult and their dependence on caretakers, there is certainly a question to be asked about how these facilities can become gay friendly places.

It appears that regardless of sexual identity, older adults are in need of an accepting community that allows them to express their sexuality, and engage in healthy sexual activity.

Summary: sexual expression in later life

Research indicates that men and women remain sexually active into their 80s. Men report greater incidence and frequency of sexual activity, including sexual intercourse than women. The differences increase with age due to differential loss of partners, and variations in health (Karraker et al., 2011).

We reviewed research based on a medical perspective. There is little evidence that physical changes associated with ageing necessarily lead to reduced sexual activity. Hormonal changes may affect sexual functioning negatively in some men and women, but these effects are often treatable. Men are more likely to report difficulties with sexual arousal and erection as they age; women are more likely to report at least occasional orgasmic difficulty as they age.

There is a positive relationship between good physical and mental health and frequency of sexual activity in both men and women. Diabetes mellitus and depression are associated with reduced sexual activity for both sexes, but are reported by relatively small percentages of the participants in recent large-scale surveys. These associations between physical and mental health and sexual activity are found across several Western societies.

Turning to the research based on a biopsychosocial model, positive attitudes about the importance of sexual expression for oneself and in one's relationships are associated with more frequent sexual activity. Men, particularly older men, are more likely to rate sex as important to themselves. Loss of a sexual partner may explain why older women do not rate sexual activity as highly as younger women. It may also reflect the impact of ageist and pronatalist attitudes.

Relationship status is a major influence on whether a person engages in partnered sexual activity. Differences in relationship status – married, cohabiting, single, divorced, and widowed – are related to differences in frequency of sexual activity among persons over 50 years of age. For persons within relationships, satisfaction is an important correlate of frequent sexual activity.

Newer studies on the sexuality of LG older adults indicate some unique challenges the older LG individual may face. Standards of appearance seem to differ between the LG communities and result in more potential for acceptance of ageing among older lesbians and more pressure to appear young for older gay men. Older LG individuals may also experience LTC facilities much differently than their heterosexual peers and may find it more difficult to develop new sexual relationships in old age due to social stigma and silence surrounding homosexuality.

Limitations

The scope of this review is constrained by the limits of the literature.

First, the research is overwhelmingly descriptive. There has been little effort to develop a theoretical model that encompasses all of the major influences and outcomes studied. Clearly, an interdisciplinary or biopsychosocial framework would be beneficial. Although HIV risks among older people are being studied, there is little clear information suggesting how medical experts and community leaders are dealing with the issue.

Further research should work to identify successful interventions and educational programs for older adults at risk of contracting HIV.

It is also important that future research further explores the sexual satisfaction of individuals who are not in committed relationships. Those who are sexually active and those who only engage in masturbation must also be the focus of future studies.

The nature of samples studied is a continuing problem, and much of the available data reflects white, heterosexual, and primarily middle-class patterns of behavior. Most of the research involving sexual and racial/ethnic minorities in the United States is focused around HIV risk behavior. We need research on all aspects of older adult sexuality that is inclusive of racial/ethnic minority groups, and facilitates the study of intersectionality that undoubtedly influences sexual expression. While the research includes more information on LG individuals, it is necessary to expand this information beyond HIV prevention behaviors to include information about sexual desire and sexual satisfaction. It is also vital to continue expanding this research to emerging sexualities.

In the last 20 years we have learned much about sexuality beyond the age of 50 but there is more to do. This review provides a map indicating some of the routes we need to take.

References

American Association of Retired Persons. (1999). *AARP/modern maturity sexuality study*. Washington, DC: AARP.

American Association of Retired Persons. (2010). *Sex, romance, and relationships: AARP survey of midlife and older adults*. Washington, DC: AARP.

Araujo, A.B., Mohr, B.A., & McKinlay, J.B. (2004). Changes in sexual function in middle-aged and older men: Longitudinal data from the Massachusetts male aging study. *Journal of the American Geriatrics Society, 52*, 1502−09.

Aubin, S., & Heiman, J. (2004). Sexual dysfunction from a relationship perspective. In J. Harvey, A. Wenzel, & S. Sprecher (Eds.), *The handbook of sexuality in close relationships* (pp. 477−519). Mahwah, NJ: Lawrence Erlbaum.

Averett, P., Yoon, I., & Jenkins, Carol L. (2012). Older lesbian sexuality: Identity, sexual behavior, and the impact of aging. *Journal of Sex Research, 49*(5), 495−507.

Baker, M. (2005). Medically assisted conception: Revolutionizing family or perpetuating a nuclear and gendered model? *Journal of Comparative Family Studies, 36*, 521−543.

Beutel, M.E., Stobel-Richter, Y., & Brahler, E. (2007). Sexual desire and sexual activity of men and women across their lifespans: Results from a representative German community sample. *BJU International, 101*, 76−82.

Blieszner, R. (2006). Close relationships in middle and later adulthood. In A. Vangelisti & D. Perlman (Eds.), *The Cambridge handbook of personal relationships* (pp. 211−227). Cambridge, UK: Cambridge University Press.

Bloomberg, M.R., & Quinn, C.C. (2009). Age friendly NYC: Enhancing out city's livability for older New Yorkers. Retrieved from http://www.nyc.gov/html/dfta/downloads/pdf/age_friendly/agefriendlynyc.pdf

Brennan, D.J., Emlet, C.A., & Eady, A. (2011). HIV, sexual health, and psychosocial issues among older adults living with HIV in North America. *Ageing International, 36*, 313–333.

Brick, P., Lunquist, J., Sandak, A., & Taverner, B. (2009). *Older, wiser, sexually smarter.* Morristown, NJ: Center for Family Life Education.

Brody, S. (2010). The relative health benefits of different sexual activities. *Journal of Sexual Medicine, 7*, 1336–1361.

Burgess, E.O. (2004). Sexuality in midlife and later life couples. In J. Harvey, A. Wenzel, & S. Sprecher (Eds.), *The handbook of sexuality in close relationships* (pp. 437–454). Mahwah, NJ: Lawrence Erlbaum.

Carpenter, L., & DeLamater, J. (2012). Studying gendered sexuality over the life course: A conceptual framework. In L. Carpenter & J. DeLamater (Eds.), *Sex for life: From virginity to Viagra, how sexuality changes throughout our lives.* New York, NY: NYU Press.

Carter, M. (2011, April 8). Sexual dysfunction. *Aidsmap.* Retrieved from http://www.aidsmap.com/Sexual-dysfunction/page/1044891/#item1044896

Centers for Disease Control and Prevention. (2008, October). HIV prevalence estimates – United States, 2006. *MMWR Morbidity and Mortality Weekly Report, 57*(39), 1073–1076.

Centers for Disease Control and Prevention. (2013, November). *HIV among older Americans.* Retrieved from http://www.cdc.gov/hiv/risk/age/olderamericans/

Choi, K.B., Jang, S.H., & Kim, K.H. (2011). Sexual life and self-esteem in married elderly. *Archives of Gerontology and Geriatrics, 53*, e17–e20.

Coleman, M., Ganong, L., & Leon, K. (2006). Divorce and postdivorce relationships. In A. Vangelisti & D. Perlman (Eds.), *The Cambridge handbook of personal relationships* (pp. 157–173). Cambridge, UK: Cambridge University Press.

Cronin, A., Ward, R., Pugh, S., King, A., & Price, E. (2011). Categories and their consequences: Understanding and supporting the caring relationships of older lesbian, gay and bisexual people. *International Social Work, 54*(3), 421–435.

D'Augelli, A.R., & Grossman, A.H. (2001). Disclosure of sexual orientation, victimization, and mental health among lesbian, say, and bisexual older adults. *Journal of Interpersonal Violence, 16*(10), 1008–1027.

DeLamater, J., & Moorman, S. (2007). Sexual behavior in later life. *Journal of Aging and Health, 19*, 921–945.

DeLamater, J., & Sill, M. (2005). Sexual desire in later life. *Journal of Sex Research, 42*, 138–149.

Dillaway, H.E. (2012). Reproductive history as social context: Exploring how women talk about menopause and sexuality at midlife. In L. Carpenter & J. DeLamater (Eds.), *Sex for life: From virginity to Viagra, how sexuality changes throughout our lives.* New York, NY: NYU Press.

Dodge, B., Reece, M., Herbenick, D., Schick, V., Sanders, S.A., & Fortenberry, J.D. (2010). Sexual health among U.S. black and hispanic men and women: A nationally representative study. *Journal of Sexual Medicine, 7*, 330–345.

Edwards, J.N., & Booth, A. (1994). Sexuality, marriage, and well-being: The middle years. In A.S. Rossi (Ed.), *Sexuality across the life-course* (pp. 233–259). Chicago, IL: University of Chicago Press.

Emanuel, E.J. (2014, January 18). Sex and the single senior. *New York Times.* Retrieved from http://www.nytimes.com/2014/01/19/opinion/sunday/emanuel-sex-and-the-single-senior.html?_r = 0

England, P., & McClintock, E. (2009). The gendered double standard of aging in US marriage markets. *Population and Development Review, 35*, 797–816.

Gagnon, J., Giami, A., Michaels, S., & de Colomby, P. (2001). A comparative study of the couple in the social organization of sexuality in France and the United States. *Journal of Sex Research, 38*, 24–34.

Gay and Grey in Dorset. (2006). *Lifting the lid: on sexuality and ageing.* Bournemouth: Help and Care Development Ltd.

Gay Men's Health Crisis, Inc. (2010). *Growing older with the epidemic: HIV and aging.* Retrieved from http://www.gmhc.org/files/editor/file/a_pa_aging10_emb2.pdf

Golub, S., Tomassilli, J.C., Pantalone, D.W., Brennan, M., Karpiak, S.E., & Parsons, J. (2010). Prevalence and correlates of sexual behavior and risk management among HIV-positive adults over 50. *Sexually Transmitted Diseases, 37*(10), 615–620.

Hayes, R., Dennerstein, L., Bennett, C., Koochaki, P.E., Leiblum, S.R., & Graziottin, A. (2007). Relation between hypoactive sexual desire disorder and aging. *Fertility and Sterility, 87*, 107–112.

Herbenick, D., Reece, M., Schick, V., Sanders, S.A., Dodge, B., & Fortenberr, J.D. (2010). Sexual behavior in the United States: Results from a national probability sample of men and women ages 14 to 94. *Journal of Sexual Medicine, 7*(suppl 5), 255−265.

Hinchcliff, S., & Gott, M. (2008). Challenging social myths and stereotypes of women and aging: Heterosexual women talk about sex. *Journal of Women and Aging, 20*, 65−81.

Hinrichs, K.L.M., & Vacha-Haase, T. (2010). Staff perceptions of same-gender sexual contacts in long-term care facilities. *Journal of Homosexuality, 57*, 776−789.

Howard, J.R., O'Neill, S., & Travers, C. (2006). Factors affecting sexuality in older Australian women: Sexual interest, sexual arousal, relationships, and sexual distress in older Australian women, *Climacteric, 9*, 355−367.

Huang, A., Subak, L., Thom, D.H., Van Den Eeden S.K., Ragins, A.I., Kuppermann, M., . . . Brown, J.S. (2009). Sexual function and aging in racially and ethnically diverse women. *Journal of the American Geriatrics Society, 57*, 1362−1368.

Hyde, Z., Flicker, L., Hankey, G.J., Almeida, O.P., McCaul, K.A., Chubb, S.A., . . . Yeap, B.B. (2010). Prevalence of sexual activity and associated factors in men aged 75 to 95 years. *Annals of Internal Medicine, 153*, 693−702.

Karraker, A., DeLamater, J., & Schwartz, C. (2011). Sexual frequency decline from midlife to later life. *Journals of Gerontology Series B: Psychological Sciences and Social Sciences, 66*B(4), 502−512.

Khaler, R. (2014, April 13). Reasons not to marry or remarry. *USA Today*. Retrieved from http://www.usatoday.com/story/money/personalfinance/2014/04/13/reasons-not-to-marry-or-remarry/7648231/

Kilgannon, C. (2007, February 14). Greatest generation learns about great safe sex. *The New York Times*. Retrieved from http://www.nytimes.com/2007/02/14/nyregion/14sex.html?_r=1&

Knowledge Networks. (2010). Associated Press-LifeGoesStrong.com relationships survey. Retrieved from http://www.lifegoesstrong.com/sex-poll

Koch, P.B., Mansfield, P.K., Thurau, D., & Carey, M. (2005). "Feeling frumpy": The relationship between body image and sexual response changes in midlife women. *Journal of Sex Research, 42*, 215−223.

Kontula, O. (2009). *Between sexual desire and reality: The evolution of sex in Finland*. Helsinki: Vaestoliitto: The Family Federation of Finland.

Kontula, O., & Haavio-Mannila, E. (2009). The impact of aging on human sexual activity and sexual desire. *Journal of Sex Research, 46*, 46−56.

Krychman, M. (2007). Vaginal atrophy: The 21st Century health issue affecting quality of life. *Medscape Ob/Gyn & Women's Health*. Retrieved from http://www.medscape.com/viewarticle/561934

Kuyper, L., & Fokkema, T. (2010). Loneliness among older lesbian, gay and bisexual adults: The role of minority stress. *Archives of Sexual Behavior, 39*, 1171−1180.

Laumann, E.O., Das, A., & Waite, L.J. (2008). Sexual dysfunction among older adults: Prevalence and risk factors from a nationally representative U.S. probability sample of men and women 57−85 years of age. *Journal of Sexual Medicine, 5*, 2300−2311.

Laumann, E.O., Paik, A., Glasser, D.B., Kang J., Wang, T., Levinson, B., . . . Gingell, C. (2006). A cross-national study of subjective sexual well-being among older women and men: Findings from the global study of sexual attitudes and behaviors. *Archives of Sexual Behavior, 35*, 145−161.

Laumann, E.O., Paik, A., & Rosen, R.C. (1999). Sexual dysfunctions in the United States: Prevalence and predictors. *Journal of the American Medical Association, 281*, 537−544.

Leiblum, S.R., Hayes, R.D., Wanser, R.A., & Nelson, J.S. (2009). Vaginal dryness: A comparison of prevalence and interventions in 11 countries. *Journal of Sexual Medicine, 6*, 2425−2433.

Lichtenstein, B. (2012). Starting over: Dating risks and sexual health among midlife women after relationship dissolution. In L. Carpenter & J. DeLamater (Eds.), *Sex for life: From virginity to Viagra, how sexuality changes throughout our lives*. New York, NY: NYU Press.

Lindau, S.T., & Gavrilova, N. (2010). Sex, health, and years of sexually active life gained due to good health: Evidence from two US population based cross sectional surveys of ageing. *British Medical Journal, 340*. doi:10.1136/bmj.c810

Lindau, S.T., Schumm, L.P., Laumann, E.O., Levinson, W., O'Muircheartaigh, C.A., & Waite, L.J. (2007). A study of sexuality and health among older adults in the United States. *New England Journal of Medicine, 357*, 762−774.

Lindau, S.T., Tang, H., Gomero, A., Vable, A., Huange E.S., Drum, M.L., . . . Chin, M.H. (2010). Sexuality among middle-aged and older adults with diagnosed and undiagnosed diabetes. *Diabetes Care, 33*(10), 2202–2210.

Lodge, A.C., & Umberson, D. (2012). All shook up: sexuality of mid- to later life married couples. *Journal of Marriage and Family, 74*, 428–443.

Maes, C.A., & Louis, M. (2003). Knowledge of AIDS, perceived risk of AIDS, and at-risk sexual behaviors among older adults. *Journal of the American Academy of Nurse Practitioners, 15*(11), 509–516.

Manning, W., & Brown, S. (2009). The demography of unions among older Americans: 1980-present.*Working Paper* 09-14. National Center for Family and Marriage Research, Bowling Green State University.

Manton, K.G., Gu, X., & lamb, V.L. (2006). Long-term trends in life expectancy and active life expectancy in the United States. *Population and Development Review, 32*, 81–105.

Mayr, C., & Bredeek, U.F. (2007). Sexual dysfunction in HIV/AIDS. In *HIV Medicine 15th Edition* (pp. 679–686). Paris: Flying Publisher.

McFarland, M.J., Uecker, J.E., & Regnerus, M.D. (2011). The role of religion in shaping sexual frequency and satisfaction: Evidence from married and unmarried older adults. *Journal of Sex Research, 48*(2–3), 297–308.

Mercer, C.H., Tanton, C., Prah, P., Erens, B., Sonnenberg, P., Clifton, S., . . . Johnson, A.M. (2013). Changes in sexual attitudes and lifestyles in Britain through the life course and over time: Findings from the National Surveys of Sexual Attitudes and Lifestyles (Natsal). *The Lancet, 328*, 1781–1794.

Miller, R. (1996). The aging immune system: Primer and prospectus. *Science, 273*(5271), 70–74.

Minichiello, V., Plummer, D., & Loxton, D. (2004). Factors predicting sexual relationships in older people: An Australian study. *Australasian Journal on Ageing, 28*(3), 125–130.

Mitchell, K.R., Mercer, C.H., Ploubidis, G.B., Jones, K.G., Datta, J., Field, N., . . . Wellings, K. (2013). Sexual function in Britain: findings from the third National Survey of Sexual Attitudes and Lifestyles (Natsal-3). *The Lancet, 328*, 1817–1829.

Moreira, E.D., Jr., Glasser, D.B., King, R., Duarte, F.G., & Gingell, C. (2008). Sexual difficulties and help-seeking among mature adults in Australia: Results from the global study of sexual attitudes and behaviours. *Sexual Health, 5*, 227–234.

Reece, M., Herbenick, D., Schick, V., Sanders, S.A., Dodge, B., & Fortenberry, J.D. (2010). Condom use rates in a national probability sample of males and females ages 14 to 94 in the United States. *Journal of Sexual Medicine, 7*, 266–275.

Rural Center for AIDS/STD Prevention. (2013). With proper treatment, life expectancy of HIV +persons is approaching those negative. *R A P Time, 17*(9), 1.

Sadeghi-Nejad, H., Wasserman, M., Weidner, W., Richardson, D., & Goldmeier, D. (2010). Sexually transmitted diseases and sexual function. *Journal of Sexual Medicine, 7*, 389–413.

Sassler, S. (2010). Partnering across the life course: Sex, relationships, and mate selection. *Journal of Marriage and Family, 72*, 557–575.

Schick, V., Herbenick, D., Reece, M., Sanders, S.A., Dodge, B., Middlestadt, S.E., & Fortenberry, J.D. (2010). Sexual behaviors, condom use, and sexual health of Americans over 50: Implications for sexual health promotion for older adults. *Journal of Sexual Medicine, 7*(suppl 5), 315–329.

Scudder, L. (2012). Talking to older adults about HIV risk. *Journal of the Association of Nurses in AIDS Care, 23*, 487–499.

Slevin, K.F., & Mowery, C.E. (2012). Exploring embodied aging and ageism among old lesbians and gay men. In L. Carpenter & J. DeLamater (Eds.), *Sex for Life: From Virginity to Viagra, How Sexuality Changes throughout Our Lives*. New York, NY: NYU Press.

Smith, T. (2006). *American sexual behavior: Trends, socio-demographic differences, and risk behavior* (GSS Topical Report No. 25, Version 6.0). National Opinion Research Center, University of Chicago.

Stack, S., & Gundlach, J. (1992). Divorce and sex. *Archives of Sexual Behavior, 21*, 359–367.

State of New York Department of Health. (2012, May). Sex never gets old. Retrieved from http://www.health.ny.gov/publications/9102.pdf

Tiefer, L. (1996). The medicalization of sexuality: Conceptual, normative, and professional issues. *Annual Review of Sex Research, 7*, 252–282.

Tiefer, L. (2007). Beneath the veneer: The troubled past and future of sexual medicine. *Journal of Sex & Marital Therapy, 33*, 473–477.

Trompeter, S.E., Bettencourt, R., & Barrett-Conner, E. (2012). Sexual activity and satisfaction in healthy community-dwelling older women. *The American Journal of Medicine, 125*(1), 37–43.

U.S. Census Bureau. (2010). Marital status. S1201. American community survey. Retrieved December 17, 2010, from http://factfinder.census.gov

U.S. Census Bureau. (2012a). Expectation of life at birth, 1970 to 2008, and projections, 2010 to 2020. *Statistical Abstract of the United States, 20*(No. 2), Table 104.

U.S. Census Bureau. (2012b). Population by age and sex, 2012 current population survey, annual social and economic supplement, Table 1.

U.S. Census Bureau. (2012c). Projections of the population by selected age groups and sex for the United States: 2015 to 2060. Population Division, Table 2.

Wade, L., & DeLamater, J. (2002). Relationship dissolution as a life stage transition: Effects on sexual attitudes and behaviors. *Journal of Marriage and Family, 64*, 898–914.

Waite, L.J., Laumann, E.O., Das, A., & Schumm, L.P. (2009). Sexuality: Measures of partnerships, practices, attitudes, and problems in the National Social Life, Health, and Aging Project. *Journals of Gerontology: Social Sciences, 64B*(Suppl. 1), i56–i66.

The White House Office of National AIDS Policy. (2010, July). *National HIV/AIDS Strategy for the United States*, Retrieved from http://www.whitehouse.gov/sites/default/files/uploads/NHAS.pdf

Yabiku, S., & Gager, C. (2009). Sexual frequency and the stability of marital and cohabiting unions. *Journal of Marriage and Family, 71*, 983–1000.

The influence of health over time on psychological distress among older couples: the moderating role of marital functioning

Laurence Villeneuve[a,b], Gilles Trudel[a,b], Luc Dargis[a,b], Michel Préville[b,c,d], Richard Boyer[b,e] and Jean Bégin[a]

[a]Department of Psychology, Université du Québec à Montréal, Montreal, Canada; [b]Axe Santé Mentale, Réseau Québécois de Recherche en Vieillissement, Montreal, Canada; [c]Department of Community Health Sciences, Université de Sherbrooke, Sherbrooke, Canada; [d]Research Center of Charles Lemoyne Hospital, Longueuil, Canada; [e]Department of Psychiatry, Université de Montreal, Montreal, Canada

This study examines the longitudinal links between self-rated health, chronic diseases, marital functioning and psychological distress over an 18-month period among a representative sample of 384 community-dwelling couples. The moderator role of marital functioning on the longitudinal association between physical health measurements and psychological distress will also be explored. Dyadic data analyses with structural equation modelling were performed. The results indicate that the number of chronic diseases and the level of marital functioning predict a significantly higher level of psychological distress for both men and women. Self-rated health significantly predicts psychological distress over time, but only among older women. No partner effects were found in the present study. Results show a significant moderator role for marital functioning on the longitudinal association between self-rated health and psychological distress among older women. This study underlines the importance of marital functioning and health status as predictors of further psychological distress among older couples.

Introduction

Many changes occur in aging, such as the emergence of health problems, a decrease in functional status, retirement and the loss of financial resources (Shields & Martel, 2006; Turcotte & Schellenberg, 2007). Studies reveal that many older people present psychological distress, depression symptoms or mental health disorders. In the United States, the U.S. Federal Interagency Forum on Aging-Related Statistics (2010) reported that almost 18% of older women and 10% of older men presented clinical symptoms of depression in 2006. In Canada, Préville et al. (2008) found similar results among a representative sample of 2798 older adults living at home in Quebec, 12.7% of which meet the diagnostic criteria for depression, mania, anxiety disorders and benzodiazepine dependency. Considering that the majority of older people live as couples (Statistics Canada, 2007; U.S. Census Bureau, 2011), more studies should be conducted among this population in order to better understand the emergence of psychological distress in aging.

After retirement, many changes occur in the marital life of older couples, some of which can have negative effects on the couple's functioning, such as a redefining of the roles within the couple, a reduction of the couple's social network, children leaving home and more time spent together (e.g., Kim & Moen, 2001; Trudel, Turgeon, & Piché, 2010). Many studies reveal that marriage can have a protective effect on mental health (e.g., Kim & McKenry, 2002; Weissman, 1987). However, some authors have pointed out that marriage itself is not a sufficient moderating factor against mental health problems. While a satisfactory marital relationship is a protective factor, an unsatisfactory marital relationship has the opposite effect (e.g., Levenson, Cartensen, & Gottman, 1993; Proulx, Helms, & Buelher, 2007; Sandberg & Harper, 2000; Sandberg, Miller, & Harper, 2002; Tower & Kasl, 1995, 1996a, 1996b).

Many authors have found a strong association between marital functioning and psychological distress (e.g., Beach, Katz, Kim, & Brody, 2003; Beach & O'Leary, 1992; Bookwala & Franks, 2005; Tower & Kasl, 1995, 1996a, 1996b). However, with regard to research on marital functioning and psychological distress, the majority of those studies used transversal data rather than longitudinal data. As underlined by Whisman and Uebelacker (2009), the majority of researchers who examined the longitudinal association between marital functioning and psychological distress conducted their studies with a sample of young couples. In addition, some authors argue that it is impossible to presuppose that results for younger couples will match those for older couples because, as reported by Levenson et al. (1993), older couples express greater pleasure and fewer conflicts than middle-aged couples.

Aging is generally marked by increasing health problems, such as a higher number of chronic diseases and disabilities (Shields & Martel, 2006). Many authors underline the detrimental impact of physical health on psychological distress (e.g., Joshi, Kumar, & Avasthi, 2003; Penninx et al., 1996; Pinquart, 2001; Schulz et al., 1994; Scott et al., 2007). However, very few studies have examined, in a longitudinal perspective, the effect of health and marital functioning on psychological distress among a sample of older couples living at home. In this context, it would appear important to examine whether or not marital functioning can play a moderator role against this effect. Five studies were found to address this topic among older people living together (Bookwala, 2011; Bookwala & Franks, 2005; Mancini & Bonanno, 2006; Tower, Kasl, & Moritz, 1997; Waldinger & Schulz, 2010). In summary, their results suggest that marital functioning can exacerbate the effects of health problems on psychological difficulties in dysfunctional relationships. On the other hand, a positive relationship can diminish these effects, thus playing a moderator role between those variables. For example, a study by Bookwala and Franks (2005), conducted among a representative sample of 1044 older people living together (555 men and 489 women) reveals that marital disagreements moderate the association between disabilities and the depressed affect. Similarly, a study by Mancini and Bonanno (2006), conducted with a sample of 1532 older participants with a high disability level, found that higher levels of marital closeness diminish the impact of functional disability on psychological distress. However, methodological gaps were identified within the studies surveyed, since many did not use a longitudinal design (Bookwala, 2011; Bookwala & Franks, 2005), while others used a very short period of time between the test and the retest – some retest periods were as short as eight days (Waldinger & Schulz, 2010). Also, certain studies did not include both spouses in the research (Bookwala, 2011; Bookwala & Franks, 2005; Mancini & Bonanno, 2006) and, for those that did, no dyadic data analysis was performed (Tower et al., 1997). This creates problems for the non-independence of data between spouses. Moreover, many of these studies used samples with specific health conditions (Bookwala, 2011; Tower et al., 1997) and high disability levels (Mancini & Bonnano, 2006), limiting the generalisation of results to a representative sample of older couples living at home and exhibiting a variety of diseases and disabilities. In addition to these methodological gaps, a large portion of the research examined only number of chronic diseases or functional status as health measurement. Nevertheless, with regard to physical health, Schulz et al. (1994) reported that the participants' perception of their own health is another useful and quick method for rating the health of a population. According to Pinquart (2001), objective and subjective health evaluated, for example, by the self-reported number of chronic health conditions and the subjective interpretation of one's health appear to make up two distinctive dimensions of the broader concept of health. Both dimensions should be considered in gerontological research. Moreover, self-rated health is reportedly linked to depressive symptoms (Schneider et al., 2004; Schulz et al., 1994), mortality (Benyamini & Idler, 1999; Idler & Benyamini, 1997) and objective health measurements (Lee & Shinkai, 2003; Leinonen, Heikkinen, & Jylhä, 2002). Furthermore, with regard to the moderator role of marital functioning, a study by Waldinger and Schulz (2010) found that higher levels of marital functioning diminish the impact of poorer self-rated health on daily happiness among a sample of octogenarian couples.

The main goal of this study was to examine the longitudinal role of marital functioning as a moderator effect on the longitudinal relationship between physical health (measured according to the self-reported number of chronic health conditions and self-rated health) and psychological distress among community-dwelling couples over an 18-month period.

In accordance with the data provided in the existing literature, the following hypotheses have been formulated:

(1) A lower level of marital functioning and a higher level of physical health status, as measured by both the number of chronic health conditions and the perception of health, at Time 1 ($T1$) will lead to a higher level of psychological distress at Time 2 ($T2$).

(2) Marital functioning at $T1$ will moderate the association between the physical health status ($T1$) and psychological distress ($T2$) among older couple. More specifically, a lower level of marital functioning at $T1$ will exacerbate the longitudinal association between the physical health status and psychological distress.

Considering that many authors underline the impact of gender differences on marital functioning, psychological distress and physical health, gender differences are also examined in the present study. Indeed, few studies have found that the longitudinal effect of marital functioning on psychological distress is stronger for women than men (e.g., Beach et al., 2003; Fincham, Beach, Harold, & Osborne, 1997). On the other hand, other studies have failed to identify any impact of gender differences on this longitudinal effect (e.g., Beach & O'Leary, 1992; Dehle & Weiss, 1998; Whisman & Ubelacker, 2009). With regard to physical health levels, a study by Levenson et al. (1993) reveals that, in unsatisfying relationships, women present more physical and mental health problems than men, while no such gender distinctions were found in satisfying relationships. In lines with the theory of symptom contamination between spouses suggested by Coyne et al. (1987), this study also examines partner effects between spouses. Examining partner effects helps to identify the effect of a person's score variable on their spouse's outcome variable.

Those research questions were also formulated on an exploration basis:

(1) Do gender differences impact the longitudinal effect of marital functioning and physical health on psychological distress?
(2) Do gender differences impact the moderator effect of marital functioning on the longitudinal association between physical health and psychological distress?
(3) Do partner effects impact the longitudinal association between marital functioning and psychological distress?
(4) Do partner effects impact the longitudinal association between physical health and psychological distress?

Methodology

The data were obtained from a longitudinal survey of community-dwelling older couples ($n = 508$) living in Quebec (ESA-Couple). This research project is part of a larger study conducted among Quebec's older people living at home (Enquête sur la santé des aînés (ESA); see Préville et al., 2008). From the 2798 participants involved in the ESA core data, 1358 were living as couples. Those living in relationships were contacted to participate in the ESA-Couple research project and were recruited from a stratified random sampling procedure conducted in three residential areas, namely, metropolitan (36%), urban (32%) and rural areas (32%). Inclusion criteria for this study involved the following: participants were required to read and understand French, to be in a relationship, to be living at home with their spouse for at least one year, and both spouses had to agree to participate. Moreover, at least one spouse had to be 65 years old or over, and both spouses were required to exhibit no moderate or severe cognitive impairments, as defined by the Mini Mental State Examination described in Folstein, Folstein, and McHugh (1975). The minimum score required for participation was 22. At the time of the first measurement ($T1$), the study included 508 older couples, and 390 couples at $T2$; approximately 18 months later (a range of 16–21 months). The response rate equalled 72% and the attrition rate equalled 23%. The dropout rate was primarily caused by the participants' refusals to participate, or to the fact that the couples failed to meet the selection criteria (e.g., they relocated or separated; one spouse dropped out due to illness or death). Ethical approval of the project (No. 061886) for both measurement periods was obtained from the Ethics Committee of the *Université du Québec à Montréal*.

Procedure

During both the measurement periods, the couples that were selected through the sampling procedure were contacted by phone, and those wishing to participate in the study received a letter containing a description of the research project, along with the interviewer's name and photograph. All participants were interviewed at their home (or in a place of their choice) by a nurse trained in research projects.

Each interview was conducted separately and each spouse answered marital and sexual questionnaires using a keypad to ensure confidentiality between the spouses and the nurse. An asterisk appeared on the interviewer's computer screen when a participant answered a question. As an incentive, each couple received $30 for participating in the study.

Instruments of measurement

Marital functioning was measured by the Dyadic Adjustment Scale (Spanier, 1976). This questionnaire was translated to French and validated by Baillargeon, Dubois, and Marineau (1986). It includes 32 questions representing four aspects of marital functioning: consensus, cohesion, satisfaction, and affective expression. A higher score indicates a higher level of marital functioning, and total scores range between 0 and 151 points. The validation study by Baillargeon et al. (1986) shows strong measurement reliability, with an internal alpha coefficient consistency of .91 for all items. Similar results were obtained by Spanier (1976). In this study, the internal coefficient consistency for all items at $T1$ equals .88 for older men, and .91 for older women. Similar results were obtained at $T2$. A confirmatory factor analysis supports the validity of the structure proposed by Spanier among a sample of older couples (Villeneuve, Préville, Trudel, & Boyer, 2010). In accordance with recommendations by Sabourin, Bouchard, Wright, Lussier, and Boucher (1988), only the total score was used in this study.

The participant's self-reported health status was assessed using a measurement based on an inventory of chronic health conditions contained in the International Classification of Diseases (ICD-10). This measurement assesses the health of a participant by using a list of 19 chronic conditions based on ICD-10, a commonly used procedure (e.g., Bennett, 2005; Chipperfield, 1993). Many authors have used this as an objective health measurement (e.g., Angner, Ray, Saag, & Allison, 2009; Cappeliez et al., 2004). All participants were asked to answer if the display showed one or more sets of chronic diseases. Another global measure of health was used to assess the perception of health as evaluated by the participant. Self-rated health was evaluated with a single question, asking participants to estimate their level of health by comparing it to others of the same age ("When comparing yourself to other people of your age, would you say that your physical health is generally: excellent, very good, good, average, or poor?"). This question has often been used in other studies (e.g., Chipperfield, 1993; Dening et al., 1998).

Psychological distress was measured using the Quebec Health Survey's Index of Psychological Distress (IDPESQ-14), developed by Préville, Boyer, Potvin, Perrault, and Légaré (1991). This questionnaire, adapted from the Psychiatric Symptom Index (Ilfeld, 1976), is designed to evaluate symptoms of depression, anxiety, irritability, as well as the cognitive problems experienced during the previous week. The version developed by Préville et al. (1991) is shorter by comparison. It contains 14 items that represent a more parsimonious concept of psychological distress when compared to the original version, which includes 29 items. Scores range between 0 and 100. A higher score indicates a higher level of psychological distress. A validation study shows a high level of reliability, with an internal alpha coefficient consistency of .89 for all items (Préville et al., 1991). In the present study, the internal alpha coefficient consistency at $T1$ equals .79, and .86 for both older men and older women, respectively. Similar results were obtained at $T2$.

Statistical analysis

Research on couples must take the non-independence of the data between spouses into consideration because they are reputed to share similar characteristics (Kenny, Kashy, & Cook, 2006). To counter the data's non-independence between spouses, dyadic data analyses were performed using structural equation modelling with AMOS 8.0 software. This type of analysis allows for the simultaneous testing of both actor and partner effects. As described by Kenny et al. (2006), actor effects provide information on the association between two variables of the same participants (e.g., the effects of the participant's marital functioning at $T1$ on psychological distress at $T2$), while partner effects provide information on the relationship between participant variables and spousal variables (e.g., the effects of the participant's marital functioning at $T1$ on the spouse's psychological distress at $T2$). Moreover, using structural equation modelling, gender differences can be examined in the same analysis, which increases the statistical power.

The hypotheses were tested using structural equation modelling strategies with nested models (Bentler & Bonnett, 1980). According to this analytical strategy, the first model (M_0) represents a complete independence model between dependant and independent variables. It was used as a reference model to evaluate the fit of the hypothetical model (M_1), which represents the hypotheses. Based on the results obtained at this stage, a second model (M_2) was tested, one that represents a more parsimonious model and a better fit. To evaluate the moderator effect, an interaction term was calculated by the product of the standardised marital functioning and each component of the health status (i.e., objective health and self-rated health).

To estimate the models' parameters, the maximum estimation likelihood method (ML) was used. To examine the fit of the model against the data, the chi-square test was used, in which a non-significant result indicates an acceptable fit. This means that the model can adequately replicate the sample covariance matrix. However, as underlined by Kline (2005), this kind of test is very sensitive to sample size. In order to compensate for the large sample size contained in this study, a normed chi-square test was used (Kline, 2005). The normed chi-square test represents the chi-square value divided by the number of degrees of freedom ($\chi^2/\underline{df}$). Ratios lower than 3 indicate a satisfactory fit (Carmines & McIver, 1981). To evaluate the goodness-of-fit of the models, the root-mean-square error of approximation (RMSEA) was used, along with the adjusted goodness-of-fit index (AGFI). A RMSEA value below .08 indicates a satisfying fit, and an AGFI value above .90 also indicates a good fit (Kline, 2005). In accordance with Bollen (1989), chi-square value difference tests ($\Delta\chi^2$) were used to compare the models. This test indicates the improvement percentage obtained between theoretical and baseline models. To examine gender differences between significant path coefficients on actor and partner effects, the critical difference ratios (C.R.s) provided by AMOS 8.0 were used between parameters. Considering the high degree of freedom in the intra-group variance, C.R. values can be interpreted as a Z score. All estimated parameters presented here have been standardised and a significance level of 5% was used for the study.

Regarding the hypotheses, two separate models were tested for each component of the health status: the first model tested the moderator role of marital functioning on the longitudinal association between objective health (number of chronic diseases) and psychological distress (M_2), while the second model tested the moderator role of marital functioning on the longitudinal association between subjective health (self-rated health) and psychological distress (M_2').

Results

Preliminary analysis

A review of the missing data indicates that one participant had not answered the question on self-rated health, which led to the elimination of both the participant and her spouse. Moreover, considering that a multivariate normal distribution was assumed with ML, univariate and multivariate normal distributions were examined. Results show a non-normal univariate distribution on the variables and, in accordance with Tabachnick and Fidell (2007), transformations were applied. After the normalisation of the variables, multivariate distribution was examined and five participants appeared to be multivariate outliers. These participants and their spouses were eliminated, reducing the final sample to 384 couples. Concerning the question of self-rated health, it was not possible to normalise this variable. The question was, therefore, subdivided into two groups: those who perceived their health as excellent or very good when compared to others of the same age (246 men and 216 women), and those who perceived their health as good, fair or poor (138 men and 168 women). This subdivision was based on the idea that a participant who claimed to have good, fair or poor health when compared to others of the same age perceived their health more negatively than the other group of participants who evaluated their own health as either excellent or very good.

Subsequent analyses were performed to examine the appropriateness of including age, family income and length of relationship as control variables, but none of these were statistically significant with regard to psychological distress among men and women. However, to maintain the comparison between models, and because chronic diseases and self-rated health are reportedly correlated (Lee & Shinkai, 2003; Leinonen et al., 2002), self-rated health and the number of chronic diseases were introduced in both models as control variables.

Demographic characteristics are presented in Table 1 and few significant gender differences have been found. Wives appear to be younger [paired t-test(383) = -12.03, $p < .001$] with lower levels of education [$\chi^2(2, 788) = 19.74$, $p < .001$] than their husbands. Descriptive data are shown in Table 2 and results indicate that women express more psychological distress [$T1$: paired t-test(383) = -4.81, $p < .001$; $T2$: paired t-test (383) = -4.81, $p < .001$] and lower levels of marital functioning [$T1$: paired t-test(383) = 4.27, $p < .001$; $T2$: paired t-test(383) = 4.46, $p < .001$] than their husbands. No gender differences appeared regarding the number of chronic diseases between both

Table 1. Demographic characteristics of participants at baseline ($N = 384$ older couples).

Demographic characteristics	Men	Women
Age (M, SD)	75.1 (5.2)	72.3 (6.0)
Education (%)		
Elementary (0–7 years)	18.2	14.1
Secondary (8–15 years)	53.9	69.5
Post-secondary (16–30 years)	27.9	16.4
Nationality (%)		
Canadian	96.9	96.6
Others	3.1	3.4
Marital status (%)[†]		
Married		94.9
Common law		5.1
Years of cohabitation (M, SD)		44.8 (12.1)
Family income (%)		
Less than $25,000		9.9
$25,000–$35,000		20.8
Higher than $35,000		59.1
Not available		10.2

[†]Results concerning marital status, years of cohabitation and family income were combined for men and women because they refer to conjugal unity.

Table 2. Descriptive data of men and women at both times of measure ($N = 384$ couples).

Variables	T1		T2	
	Men	Women	Men	Women
Marital functioning				
Mean (SD)	121.20 (14.49)	117.62 (16.14)	120.99 (15.63)	117.58 (15.40)
Minimum	70	55	61	67
Maximum	149	149	148	151
Number of chronic diseases				
Mean (SD)	3.18 (2.04)	3.43 (2.11)	3.10 (2.05)	3.34 (2.11)
Minimum	0	0	0	0
Maximum	10	10	10	11
Psychological distress				
Mean (SD)	9.77 (8.80)	13.70 (11.94)	10.95 (9.96)	14.71 (12.73)
Minimum	0	0	0	0
Maximum	61.90	73.81	59.52	73.81
Self-rated health (%)				
Excellent–very good	64.06	56.25	59.27	53.91
Good, fair, poor	35.94	43.75	40.73	46.09

measurement periods [$T1$: paired t-test(383) $= -1.87, p = .063$; $T2$: paired t-test(383) $= -1.71, p = .089$]. However, wives evaluated their own health more negatively at $T1$ than their husbands [$\chi^2(1, 768) = 4.89, p = .027$], but no such gender difference appears at $T2$ [$\chi^2(1, 767) = 2.24, p = .134$]. Over time, no gender differences were found regarding marital functioning between husbands [paired t-test(383) $= -0.09, p = .929$] and wives [paired t-test(383) $= .231, p = .817$]. Similar results were found regarding the number of chronic diseases in husbands [paired t-test(383) $= 1.06, p = .292$] and wives [paired t-test (383) $= 1.24, p = .217$]. For psychological distress, no differences appear for wives [paired t-test(383) $= -1.62, p = .105$], but husbands show a significant increase in psychological distress over time [paired t-test(383) $= -2.58, p = .01$]. For self-rated health, wives evaluated their health more negatively at $T2$ than at $T1$ [$\chi^2(1, 384) = 117.66, p < .001$]. The same result was found for husbands [$\chi^2(1, 383) = 70.61, p < .001$].

Moderator effect of marital functioning on the number of chronic disease

The first model tested included the moderator effect of marital functioning on the association between the number of chronic diseases at $T1$ and psychological distress at $T2$. Table 3 shows that the hypothetical model (M_1) presents a better fit than the complete independence model (M_0), which assumes no association between variables. However, the goodness-of-fit indexes of M_1 suggest that the model could be improved by eliminating non-significant parameter estimates. Thus, all parameter estimates were examined and eliminated one by one by forcing them to be equal to "0" when they were not significant for either gender. This procedure has been used to facilitate comparison between men and women.

Regarding non-significant parameters, all partner effects appeared to be non-significant between the exogenous and endogenous variables and were therefore eliminated. Moreover, the interaction terms between the number of chronic diseases and marital functioning were not significant for both genders and were therefore eliminated. The final

Table 3. Goodness-of-fit statistics for nested models of the first model tested (marital functioning × number of chronic diseases).

	χ^2	df	χ^2/df	AGFI	RMSEA	90% C.I. for RMESA	$\Delta\chi^2$
M_0	462.30	45	10.27	0.74	0.16	0.14–0.17	
M_1	51.33	15	3.42	0.90	0.08	0.06–0.10	410.97**
M_2	67.06	29	2.31	0.93	0.06	0.04–0.08	15.73

Note: C.I., confidence interval; ** $p < .01$.

model (M_2) is presented in Figure 1. Results suggest that, when the chi-square differences of the tests are examined, the elimination of the non-significant parameters does not deteriorate the model significantly, but it does improve the goodness-of-fit statistics (see Table 3). According to this final model, results show that the number of chronic diseases

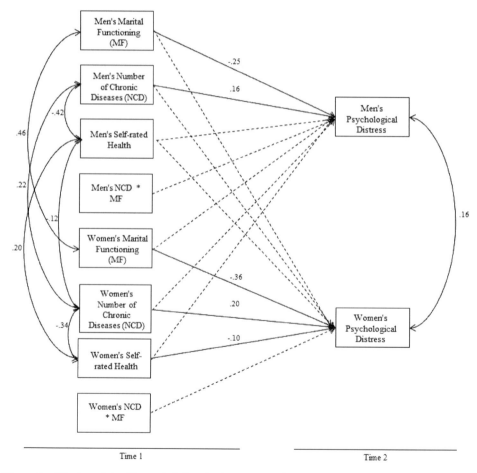

Figure 1. Final model with marital functioning as a moderator in the longitudinal link between number of chronic diseases and psychological distress ($N = 384$ older couples). Note: All parameter estimates presented are standardised and significant at $p < .05$. Dotted lines refer to a non-significant parameter estimate.

at $T1$ can significantly predict psychological distress for wives at $T2$ ($\beta = .20, p < .001$), as well for husbands ($\beta = .16, p = .003$). This explains the respective 4.03% and 2.56% variance values obtained. No gender difference was found ($Z = .80, p = .42$). After an 18-month period, marital functioning can significantly predict psychological distress for wives ($\beta = -.36, p < .001$), and for husbands ($\beta = -.25, p < .001$). This explains the respective 13.09% and 6.19% psychological distress variance values obtained. No gender difference was found ($Z = -1.96, p = .050$). Self-rated health can significantly predict psychological distress for older wives ($\beta = -.10, p = .036$), but not for older husbands ($\beta = .04, p = .466$). Significant gender differences were found ($Z = -2.01, p = .044$). The self-rated health of older wives explains 1.02% of the psychological distress value obtained over time. With regard to the main goal of this study, and contrary to what was expected, no significant interaction terms between the number of chronic diseases and marital functioning over an 18-month period were found for older husbands and wives. In short, this model can predict the respective 8.36% and 20.14% of their psychological distress at $T2$ for both husbands and wives.

Moderator effect of marital functioning on self-rated health

The second model tested included the moderator role of marital functioning on the longitudinal association between self-rated health status and psychological distress. Table 4 presents the goodness-of-fit statistics of the hypothetical model (M_1') as compared to the independent model (M_0'). M_1' appears to provide a better fit than M_0'. However, regarding the goodness-of-fit statistics of M_1', this model can be improved. All non-significant partner effects were eliminated one by one and this significantly improved the final model (M_2') when compared to M_1' (see Table 4). The final model is illustrated in Figure 2. Marital functioning can significantly predict psychological distress over time for older husbands ($\beta = -.26, p < .001$) and wives ($\beta = -.35, p < .001$). This variable explains the respective 6.69% and 12.31% of their psychological distress at $T2$. No significant gender difference was found ($Z = -1.62, p = .105$). Self-rated health at $T1$ can significantly predict psychological distress at $T2$ for older wives ($\beta = -.10, p = .032$). This explains the 1.06% of their psychological distress. However, among husbands, self-rated health at $T1$ does significantly predict psychological distress at $T2$ ($\beta = 0.04, p = .481$), and this gender difference appears to be significant ($Z = -2.02, p = .043$). Concerning the number of chronic diseases, this variable can significantly predict psychological distress at $T2$ for older husbands ($\beta = .16, p = .003$) and wives ($\beta = .21, p < .001$). This explains the respective 2.42% and 4.20% variance values obtained. No gender difference was found ($Z = 0.90, p = .368$). Regarding the interaction term between marital functioning and self-rated health, a significant interaction was found among older wives ($\beta = -.09, p =$

Table 4. Goodness-of-fit statistics for nested models of the second model tested (marital functioning × self-rated health).

	χ^2	df	χ^2/df	AGFI	RMSEA	90% C.I. for RMESA	$\Delta\chi^2$
M_0'	459.38	45	10.21	0.74	0.16	0.14–0.17	
M_1'	45.89	15	3.06	0.91	0.07	0.05–0.10	413.49**
M_2'	59.49	27	2.20	0.94	0.06	0.05–0.08	13.60

Note: C.I., confidence interval; **$p < .01$.

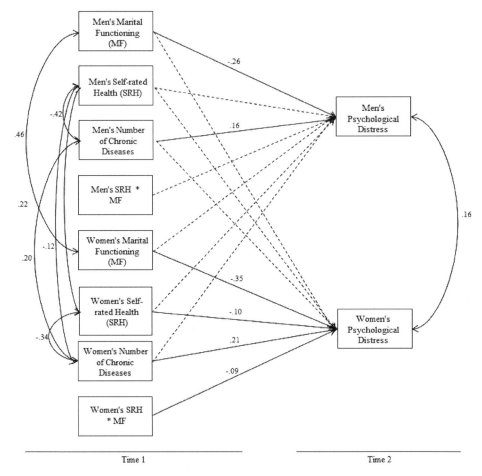

Figure 2. Final model with marital functioning as a moderator in the longitudinal link between self-rated health and psychological distress ($N = 384$ older couples). Note: All parameter estimates presented are standardised and significant at $p < .05$. Dotted lines refer to a non-significant parameter estimate.

.045). This explains 0.81% of the variance. Among husbands, this interaction was not significant ($\beta = .04$, $p = .400$) and gender differences were found ($Z = -2.02$, $p = .043$). This model can predict the respective 20.42% and 8.91% of their psychological distress at $T2$ for husbands and wives at $T2$.

For the interpretation of the interaction term, the marital functioning of older wives was subdivided into two groups on ± 1 standard deviation of the means (SD = 16.14). The strength of the correlation between self-rated health at $T1$ and psychological distress at $T2$ for older wives was studied for both subdivisions. Surprisingly, results show that, for older wives, self-rated health at $T1$ is unrelated to psychological distress at $T2$ when marital functioning is low ($r = -.195$, $p = .116$), but the same variables are significantly related when marital functioning is high ($r = -.489$, $p < .001$). Results show significant differences between those correlations [t-test(121) $= 7.26$, $p < .001$]. As illustrated by Figure 3, for older women with a high level of marital functioning, psychological distress is significantly higher when they have a less positive view of their health than when they

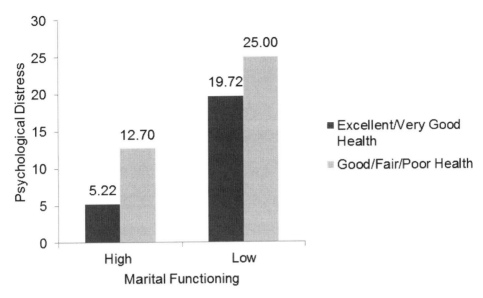

Figure 3. Average score of psychological distress at *T*2 depending on the level of self-rated health and marital functioning at *T*1 among older wives (*N* = 384).

have a high positive view of their health [t-test(55) = 4.15, $p < .001$]. Among wives with lower levels of marital functioning, no significant differences were found regarding psychological distress in relation to self-rated health [t-test(64) = 1.56, $p = .12$].

Discussion

As expected, variables surrounding marital functioning along with the self-reported number of chronic diseases and self-rated health can significantly predict psychological distress in women and men living in relationships over an 18-month period. Higher levels of marital functioning can predict lower level of psychological distress for both genders. This result supports the marital discord model of depression (Gotlib & Beach, 1995), which proposes that marital difficulties lead to less adaptive behaviour and an increase in negative behaviour which, in turn, increases psychological distress. These findings are consistent with other studies conducted with couples (e.g., Proulx et al., 2007; Villeneuve et al., in press; Whisman & Uebelacker, 2009). A recent study also found that negative marital support is related to further psychological distress for both older men and women living in relationships (Trudel, Dargis-Damphousse, Villeneuve, Boyer, & Préville, 2013). In this way, marital functioning appears to play a pivotal role in the well-being of older couples, as reported by Levenson et al. (1993). Gender differences were found and it appears that the longitudinal link between marital functioning and psychological distress is stronger for wives than for husbands. These findings are similar to those of other studies (e.g., Beach et al., 2003; Fincham et al., 1997). As reported by Fincham et al. (1997), this result may be explained by the fact that, compared to husbands, wives tend to be more relationship-oriented and feel more responsible for making their marriage work. Consistent with other studies (e.g., Joshi et al., 2003; Penninx et al., 1996; Scott et al., 2007), this study also found that a higher number of chronic diseases are significantly related to psychological distress occurring later on for husbands and wives, at times as much as 18 months into the future. For this link, no gender differences were found, meaning that the number of chronic diseases seems to have the same impact on psychological distress for both genders over time. Concerning self-rated health, this variable can significantly predict psychological distress at $T2$ for wives only, underlying an important gender difference. It appears that the groups of wives who evaluated their health as excellent or very good when compared to others of the same age had less psychological distress 18 months later than those who evaluated their health less positively (i.e., good, fair or poor). These findings are consistent with other studies, which found a significant association between self-rated health and psychological well-being (Cappeliez et al., 2004; Schneider et al., 2004; Schulz et al., 1994). With regards to the disablement process model identified by Verbrugge and Jette (1994), it is possible that wives who perceive their health less positively than others are less confident in their capacity to respond to environmental demands which, in turn, exacerbates their psychological distress over time. Other studies will have to be undertaken to support this hypothesis.

One of the main strengths of this study is the examination of partner effects between variables. However, contrary to the theory of symptom contamination proposed by Coyne et al. (1987), no partner effects were found to impact measurements surrounding the number of chronic diseases and self-rated health, as with the impact of marital functioning on psychological distress in the longitudinal perspective. These results may seem surprising considering the fact that spouses tend to share similar characteristics (Kenny et al., 2006), but we must keep in mind that our sample was composed of representative older couples living at home with, on average, lower levels of psychological distress, higher levels of marital functioning, few chronic diseases and, globally, a positive view of their health. It may be possible that partner effects can only be revealed in samples with more psychological or conjugal distress, or those with more disabilities. Moreover, in our sample, it is possible that partner effects could be detected with another kind of measurement, since well-being better represents their global characteristics of functioning.

The second goal of this study is to examine the moderator role of marital functioning on the association between health measurements and psychological distress over an 18-month period. Contrary to our hypotheses, marital functioning does not moderate the impact of the self-reported number of chronic diseases on psychological distress over time for both wives and husbands. This finding may appear to be in contrast with other studies, which found that marital functioning can have a moderator effect between those variables. However, we must keep in mind that the majority of these studies were conducted with cross-sectional data (Bookwala, 2011; Bookwala & Franks, 2005; Mancini & Bonanno, 2006) and a sample exhibiting specific diseases and higher levels of disability (e.g., Mancini & Bonanno, 2006; Tower et al., 1997). Moreover, none of these studies examined the influence of the moderator effect of marital functioning on the longitudinal relation between physical health and psychological distress. On this point, we tested the hypothesis that the moderator effect of marital functioning between objective health measurements and psychological distress only exists transversely. However, results show no significant moderator effect for either gender. In line with these findings, it is possible that marital functioning may only have a moderator effect among older couples with more chronic diseases or disabilities. Considering our findings, further studies should be conducted with older couples to better understand the context in which marital functioning plays a moderator role between objective health and psychological distress. For example, it may be interesting to conduct studies that compare older couples exhibiting a lower functional status against older couples exhibiting a higher functional status.

Concerning the self-rated health measurements, a weaker interaction term was found with marital functioning for older women only. An examination of the interaction term led to surprising results because the longitudinal association between self-rated health and psychological distress is stronger for older women with higher levels of marital functioning than it is for those with lower levels of marital functioning. It seems that a less positively perceived health has more impact over time on psychological distress for women with higher levels of marital functioning, which leads us to think that older women have more room to react to lower stressors. Indeed, the present study shows that, overall, marital functioning has the biggest impact on psychological distress, suggesting that, among women with lower levels of marital functioning, it represents the main source of psychological distress, which decreases the impact of new stressors, such as poorer health perception. This result may suggest the existence of a ceiling effect and seems to support the stress reactivity model proposed by Steptoe (1991). This model states that the reactivity to stress will depend on many variables, such as the characteristics of the stressor (e.g., chronicity, intensity, complexity) and the availability of resources to deal with this stressor (e.g., coping skills, social support, personality). As reported earlier, another explanation of the interaction effect may involve the fact that women tend to be more relationship-oriented. It is possible that women with higher levels of marital functioning show more psychological distress when they have a lower perception of their health, as compared to those with higher levels of self-rated health, because they anticipate further difficulties when responding to environmental demands. As for the objective health measurements, we examined transversely the moderator effect of marital functioning on the link between self-rated health and psychological distress. However, no significant moderator effect was found for either gender, suggesting that the moderator effect of marital functioning found among older wives only existed longitudinally. Thus, negatively perceived health might constitute a prodromal symptom of further difficulties, like marital dissatisfaction or psychological distress. Further studies are needed to better understand this result. Among older men, the main effects of self-rated health, like their interaction term effect, are not related to their psychological distress. These findings can be explained by the fact that the older men in our study had lower levels of psychological distress and a very positive view of their health, which probably left fewer opportunities to find negative effects for self-rated health on psychological distress over time.

The strengths and limitations of this study must be underlined. First, it is impossible to generalise the results by applying them to older couples living in institutions, or to those suffering from specific chronic health conditions, because they are underrepresented in our sample. Second, objective health is assessed by a self-reported health measurement and may involve recall bias. Also, this kind of measurement does not assess disease severity, which may be more strongly related to psychological distress. Although this measurement has the potential to introduce recall bias, it is often used in the context of epidemiological studies, where cost and time are limited (e.g., Angner et al., 2009; Cappeliez et al., 2004). Some may also criticise the fact that self-rated health is assessed by means of a single question. However, as underlined by Cappeliez et al. (2004), using a single question to evaluate self-rated health allows for the assessment of health in a global manner. Considering the characteristics of the sample, results may only be generalised for older French-Canadians heterosexual couples living at home. Further studies have to be made among older couples from other countries or cultures, such as older Haitian-Canadian couples, because they are underrepresented in the present study. The same recommendation can be made for older homosexual couples. With regard to its strengths, this study includes a representative sample of older couples living together. It also includes dyadic analyses that consider data dependency between spouses, which represents a major strength when compared to other studies. Indeed, because both spouses were recruited, it was possible to examine partner effects, which was never done in previous studies examining the moderator role of marital functioning between health status and psychological distress. Moreover, this study examines the moderator effect of marital functioning on the association between physical health measurements and psychological distress from a longitudinal perspective. Finally, this study assesses health in a broad manner, using both objective and self-rated health measurements.

In summary, these findings underline the importance of marital functioning and health on further psychological distress for both genders. It can be expected that promoting chronic disease prevention and marital interventions to increase marital functioning would contribute to less psychological distress over time among older couples. For women, a less positive view of their health has a negative impact on their psychological distress, underlining the importance of taking women's perception of their own health into account. It may be of interest if health professionals were to ask older women the same, single question about their health perception to prevent further psychological distress. Moreover, it appears that the emergence of this stressor among older women with a less positive view of their health has a more profound impact on psychological distress for those with higher levels of marital functioning than it does for those with lower levels of marital functioning. These findings suggest how important it is to pay special attention to the evaluation of marital functioning among those women. It suggests the same for older men with lower levels of marital functioning, because they are more at risk of showing further psychological distress. To our knowledge, this study is the first to use a representative sample of older couples in order to examine the longitudinal association between marital functioning, health and psychological distress through dyadic analysis. However, we have to take into account the fact that the majority of participants in the study were in good health, had lower levels of psychological distress and higher levels of marital functioning, which limits our results to older couples with similar characteristics.

Funding

This work was supported by grants to Dr Gilles Trudel (trudel.gilles@uqam.ca) as the principal researcher from the Canadian Institute of Health Research (MOP – 81281), Mental Health Axis of Quebec Network for Research on Aging and by Faculty of Human Sciences of Université du Québec à Montréal (trudel.gilles@uqam.ca). Laurence Villeneuve received a doctoral fellowship from "Les Fonds de Recherche en Santé du Québec" [grant number 20389].

References

Angner, E., Ray, M.N., Saag, K.G., & Allison, J.J. (2009). Health and happiness among older adults: A community-based study. *Journal of Health Psychology, 14*, 503–512.

Baillargeon, J., Dubois, G, & Marineau, R. (1986). French translation of the Dyadic Adjustment Scale. *Canadian Journal of Behavioural Science, 18*(1), 25–34.

Beach, S.R.H., Katz, J., Kim, S., & Brody, G.H. (2003). Prospective effects of marital satisfaction on depressive symptoms in established marriages: A dyadic model. *Journal of Social and Personal Relationships, 20*, 355–371.

Beach, S.R.H., & O'Leary, K.D. (1992). Treating depression in the context of marital discord: Outcome and predictors of response for marital therapy vs. cognitive therapy. *Behavior Therapy, 23*(4), 507–528.

Bennett, K.M. (2005). Social engagement as a longitudinal predictor of objective and subjective health. *European Journal on Ageing, 2*, 48–55.

Bentler, P.M., & Bonnett, D.G. (1980). Significance tests and goodness of fit in the analysis of covariance structures. *Psychological Bulletin, 88*, 588–600.

Benyamini, Y., & Idler, E.L. (1999). Community studies reporting association between self-rated health and mortality. *Research on Aging, 21*(3), 392–401.

Bollen, K.A. (1989). *Structural equations with latent variables. Wiley series in probability and mathematical statistics.* New York, NY: Wiley. p. 514.

Bookwala, J. (2011). Marital quality as a moderator of the effects of poor vision on quality of life among older adults. *The Journal of Gerontology: Series B: Psychological Sciences and Social Sciences, 66*(5), 605–616.

Bookwala, J., & Franks, M.M. (2005). Moderating role of marital quality in older adults' depressed affect: The main effects model. *The Journal of Gerontology: Series B: Psychological Sciences and Social Sciences, 60B*, 338–341.

Cappeliez, P., Sèvre-Rousseau, S., Landreville, P., Préville, M., & Scientific Committee of ESA Study. (2004). Physical health, subjective health, and psychological distress in older adults: Reciprocal relationships concurrently and over time. *Ageing International, 29*(3), 247–266.

Carmines, E.G., & McIver, J.P. (1981). Analyzing models with unobserved variables: Analysis of covariances structures. In G.W. Bohmstedt & E.F. Borgatta (Eds), *Social measurement: Current issues* (pp. 65–115). Beverly Hills, CA: Sage Publications.

Chipperfield, J.G. (1993). Incongruence between health perceptions and health problems. *Journal of Aging and Health, 5*(4), 475–496.

Coyne, J.C., Kessler, R.C., Tal, M., Turnbull, J., Wortman, C.B., & Greden, J.F. (1987). Living with a depressed person. *Journal of Consulting and Clinical Psychology, 55*(3), 347–352.

Dehle, C., & Weiss, R. (1998). Sex differences in prospective associations between marital quality and depressed mood. *Journal of Marriage and the Family, 60*, 1002–1011.

Dening, T.R., Chi, L.Y., Brayne, C., Huppert, F.A., Paykel, E.S., & O'Connor, D.W. (1998). Changes in self-rated health, disability and contact with services in a very elderly cohort: A 6-year follow-up study. *Age and Aging, 27*, 23–33.

Fincham, F.D., Beach, S.R.H., Harold, G.T., & Osborne, L.N. (1997). Marital satisfaction and depression: Different causal relationship for men and women? *Psychological Science, 8*(5), 351–356.

Folstein, M.F., Fostein, S.E., & McHugh, P.R. (1975). Mini-mental state: A practical method for grading the cognitive state of patients for the clinician. *Journal of Psychiatric Research, 12*(3), 189–198.

Gotlib, I.H., & Beach, S.R.H. (1995). A marital/family discord model of depression: Implications for therapeutic intervention. In N.S. Jacobson & A.S. Gurman (Eds.), *Clinical handbook of couple therapy* (pp. 411–436). New York, NY: Guilford Press.

Idler, E.L., & Benyamini, Y. (1997). Self-rated health and mortality: A review of twenty-seven community studies. *Journal of Health and Social Behavior, 38*, 21–37.

Ilfeld, F.W. (1976). Further validation of a psychiatric symptom index in a normal population. *Psychological Reports, 39*(3), 1215–1228

Joshi, K., Kumar, R., & Avasthi, A. (2003). Morbidity profile and its relationship with disability and psychological distress among elderly people in Northern India. *International Journal of Epidemiology, 32*, 978–987.

Kenny, D.A., Kashy, D.A., & Cook, W.L. (2006). *Dyadic data analysis.* New York, NY: Guilford Press. p. 458.

Kim, H.K., & McKenry, P.C. (2002). The relationship between marriage and psychological well-being: A longitudinal analysis. *Journal of Family Issues, 23*, 885–911.

Kim, J.E., & Moen, P. (2001). Is retirement good or bad for subjective well-being? *Current Directions in Psychological Science, 10*(3), 83–86.

Kline, R.B. (2005). *Principles and practice of structural equation modeling* (2nd ed.). New York, NY: Guilford Press.

Lee, Y., & Shinkai, S. (2003). A comparison of correlates of self-rated health and functional disability of older persons in the Far East: Japan and Korea. *Archives of Gerontology and Geriatrics, 37*, 63–76.

Leinonen, R., Heikkinen, E., & Jylhä, M. (2002). Changes in health, functional performance and activity predict changes in self-rated health: A 10-year follow-up study in older people. *Archives of Gerontology and Geriatrics, 35*, 79–92.

Levenson, R.W., Cartensen, L.L., & Gottman, J.M. (1993). Long-term marriage: Age, gender, and satisfaction. *Psychology and Aging, 8*(2), 301–313.

Mancini, A.D., & Bonanno, G.A. (2006). Marital closeness, functional disability, and adjustment in late life. *Psychology and Aging, 21*(3), 600–610.

Penninx, B.W., Beekman, A.T., Ormel, J., Kriegsman, D., Boeke, A.J., van Eijk, J.T., & Deeg, D.J. (1996). Psychological status among elderly people with chronic diseases: Does type of disease play a part? *Journal of Psychosomatic Research, 40*(5), 521–534.

Pinquart, M. (2001). Correlates of subjective health in older adults: A meta-analysis. *Psychology and Aging, 16*(3), 414–426.

Préville, M., Boyer, R., Grenier, S., Dubé, M., Voyer, P., Punti, R., ... Brassard, J. (2008). The epidemiology of psychiatric disorders in Quebec's older adult population. *The Canadian Journal of Psychiatry, 53*(12), 822–832.

Préville, M., Boyer, R., Potvin, L. Perrault, C., & Légaré, G. (1991). *La détresse psychologique: Détermination de la fiabilité et de la validité de la mesure utilisée dans l'Enquête Santé Québec* [Psychological distress: Determining the reliability and validity of the measure used in the Quebec Health Survey]. Québec: Ministère de la Santé et des Services Sociaux, Gouvernement du Québec.

Proulx, C.M., Helms, H.M., & Buehler, C. (2007). Marital quality and personal well-being: A meta-analysis. *Journal of Marriage and Family, 69*(3), 576–593.

Sabourin, S., Bouchard, G., Wright, J., Lussier, Y., & Boucher, C. (1988). *L'influence du sexe sur l'analyse factorielle de l'Échelle d'Ajustement Dyadique* [The influence of sex on factor analysis of the Dyadic Adjustment Scale]. *Science et comportement, 18*, 187–201.

Sandberg, J.G., & Harper, J.M. (2000). In search of a marital distress model of depression in older marriages. *Aging and Mental Health, 4*(3), 210–222.

Sandberg, J.C., Miller, R.B., & Harper, J.M. (2002). A qualitative study of marital process and depression in older couples. *Family Relations, 51*(3), 256–264.

Schneider, G., Driesch, G., Kruse, A., Wachter, M., Nehen, H.-G., & Heuft, G. (2004). What influences self-perception of health in the elderly? The role of objective health condition, subjective well-being and sense of coherence. *Archives of Gerontology and Geriatrics, 39*, 227–237.

Schulz, R., Mittelmark, M., Kronmal, R., Polak, J.F., Hirsch, C.H., German, P., & Bookwala, J. (1994). Predictors of perceived health status in elderly men and women. *Journal of Aging and Health, 6*(4), 419–447.

Scott, K.M., Bruffaerts, R., Tsang, A., Ormel, J., Alonso, J., Angermeyer, M.C., ... Von Korff, M. (2007). Depression-anxiety relationships with chronic physical condition: Results from the World Mental Health surveys. *Journal of Affective Disorders, 103*(1–3), 113–120.

Shields, M., & Martel, L. (2006). *Des aînés en bonne santé* [Healthy Living among Seniors]. *Rapport sur la santé* [Health Report]. Vol. 16, Supplement. Retrieved from http://dsp-psd. tpsqc.qc.ca/Collection/Statcan/82-003-SIF2005000.pdf

Spanier, G.B. (1976). Measuring dyadic adjustment: News scales for assessing the quality of marriage and similar dyads. *Journal of Marriage and the Family, 38*, 15–28.

Statistics Canada. (2007). *Aînés* [Elderly], *Annuaire du Canada* (Statistics Canada Catalogue No. 11-402-XPF). Ottawa: Government of Canada. pp. 21–34.

Steptoe, A. (1991). The links between stress and illness. *Journal of Psychosomatic Research, 35*(6), 633–644.

Tabachnick, B.G., & Fidell, L. S. (2007). *Using multivariate statistic*. Boston, MA: Allyn and Bacon.

Tower, R.B., & Kasl, S.V. (1995). Depressive symptoms across older spouses and the moderating effect of marital closeness. *Psychology and Aging, 10*, 625–638.

Tower, R.B., & Kasl, S.V. (1996a). Depressive symptoms across older spouses: Longitudinal influences. *Psychology and Aging, 11*, 683–697.

Tower, R.B., & Kasl, S.V. (1996b). Gender, marital closeness, and depressive symptoms in elderly couples. *Journal of Gerontology: Psychological Sciences, 51B*(3), 115–129.

Tower, R.B., Kasl, S.V., & Moritz, D.J. (1997). The influence of spouse cognitive impairment on respondents' depressive symptoms: The moderating role of marital closeness. *Journal of Gerontology: Social Sciences, 52B*(5), S270–S278.

Trudel, G., Dargis-Damphousse, L., Villeneuve, L., Boyer, R., & Préville, M. (2013). Marital support, psychological distress, and disability among community-dwelling older couples: A longitudinal study. *Sexual and Relationship Therapy, 28*(4), 350–363.

Trudel, G., Turgeon, L., & Piché, L. (2010). Sexual and marital aspects of old age. *Sexual and Relationship Therapy, 25*, 316–341.

Turcotte, M., & Schellenberg, G. (2007). *Un portrait des aînés au Canada: 2006* [A portrait of seniors in Canada: 2006]. (Product no 89-519-XIF in index of Statistic Canada). Ottawa: Government of Canada.

U.S. Census Bureau. (2011). *Current population survey. Annual social and economic supplement.* Retrieved from http://www.census.gov.proxy.bibliotheques.uqam.ca:2048/

U.S. Federal Interagency Forum on Aging-Related Statistics. (2010). *Older Americans 2010: Key indicators of well-being*. Retrieved from http://www.agingstats.gov/agingstatsdotnet/Main_Site/Data/2010_Documents/Docs/OA_2010.pdf

Verbrugge, L.M., & Jette, A.M. (1994). The disablement process. *Social, Science, & Medicine, 38*(1), 1–14.

Villeneuve, L., Préville, M., Trudel, G., & Boyer, R. (2010). *Validation study of dyadic adjustment scale among community-dwelling French elderly couples*. Poster session presented at the congress of the Canadian Association on Gerontology, Montreal.

Villeneuve, L., Trudel, G., Dargis, L., Préville, M., Boyer, R., & Bégin, J. (in press). Marital functioning and psychological distress among older couples over an 18-month period. *Journal of Sex and Marital Therapy*.

Waldinger, R.J., & Schulz, M.S. (2010). What's love got to do with it? Social functioning, perceived health, and daily happiness in married octogenarians. *Psychology and Aging, 25*(2), 42–431.

Weissman, M.M. (1987). Advances in psychiatric epidemiology: Rates and risks for major depression. *American Journal of Public Health, 77*, 445–451.

Whisman, M.A., & Uebelacker, L.A. (2009). Prospective associations between marital discord and depressive symptoms in middle-aged and older adults. *Psychology and Aging, 24*(1), 184–189.

Individual and relational contributors to optimal sexual experiences in older men and women

A. Dana Ménard, Peggy J. Kleinplatz, Lianne Rosen, Shannon Lawless, Nicholas Paradis, Meghan Campbell and Jonathan D. Huber

Optimal Sexual Experience Research Team, University of Ottawa, Ottawa, Canada

Research on sexual development has tended to focus on those events and experiences (e.g., poor sex education, sexual violence, chronic illness, and disability) that lead to sexual dysfunctions rather than on those that might facilitate optimal sexual experiences. The sexual development of older individuals and couples has been pathologized and marginalized, with the assumption that sexual deterioration will be the inevitable accompaniment to ageing. As part of a larger study on the contributors to optimal sexual experiences, semi-structured interviews were conducted with 30 men and women, aged 60–82, who had been in relationships for 25–52 years and who reported having experienced "great sex." A phenomenologically oriented content analysis was conducted using interview transcripts to identify the factors that had contributed to optimal sexual experiences. The individual and relational contributors across the lifespan that led to optimal sexual experiences for older people are described (e.g., overcoming early learning, openness to experience, mutual empathy, structure and depth of the relationship). The ramifications of these findings for sex and relationship therapy are considered.

"What factors contribute to optimal sexual experiences among older men and women? Simply asking this question represents a stark departure from what we "know" about sexuality in older adults. Existing research findings paint a bleak picture of ageing as a slow loss of energy, desirability, and sexual interest. Many research questions are informed by ageist or medicalized stereotypes of sexuality and ageing, generating misleading findings. Some evidence suggests that older adulthood may instead be a time of sexual growth and heightened enjoyment; despite this, little empirical knowledge defines what heights we may strive for in our sexual lives or how these experiences are realized.

Sexual stereotypes of older adults

Older adults have often been depicted as largely asexual: physically unattractive, uninterested in sex, and/or physiologically unable to engage in sexual behaviours (Bouman, Arcelus, & Benbow, 2006; Gott & Hinchliff, 2003; Waltz, 2002). The media has reinforced this message. Explicit depictions of sexualized older adults remain taboo or marginalized as the subject of ridicule (i.e., "dirty old man"; Vares, 2009).

These traditional stereotypes are beginning to shift towards an emphasis on lifelong sexuality (Gott, 2006; Potts, Grace, Vares, & Gavey, 2006). Ironically, this view stems from and reflects the overall medicalization of sexuality; in other words, "normal" sexuality requires sufficient physiological functionality to permit vaginally penetrative, heterosexual intercourse and any performance challenges require medical intervention. This trend is exemplified by the prevalence of advertisements for sexual performance-enhancing medications (Moynihan & Mintzes, 2010); targeting these products at an older adult demographic normalizes the desire for sexual activity later in life yet implies that successful or normative sexual activity equates to vaginally penetrative intercourse (Hillman, 2008). Furthermore, these expectations surrounding sexual normalcy have specific implications for older adults; in particular, sexual activity has been deemed a key component of successful ageing. However, this approach is problematic as it creates a binary of functional versus dysfunctional, thereby restricting the meaning and range of sexual expression.

Sexual functioning of older adults

Recent survey data indicate that the majority of partnered older adults engage in sexual activities and regard sexuality as an important element of life, indeed the frequency of sexual activity in older adults is comparable to that of young adults identified in earlier population-based studies (Lindau et al., 2007). Findings suggest that sexuality remains a priority for partnered adults in mid to late life (Hyde et al., 2010; Woloski-Wruble, Oliel, Leefsma, & Hochner-Celnikier, 2010). However, the literature remains scarce in delineating normal or healthy expectations for sexuality in older adulthood.

In accordance with stereotypes for sexuality among older adults, research has focused on the incidence and prevalence of sexual dysfunctions. Many of these findings reinforce the notion that sexual activity and interest are difficult or challenging for this age group (DeLamater, 2012). Problems with desire, arousal, orgasm, and sexual pain have been documented among older adults in population-based samples; however, incidence rates rarely differ significantly from those of younger adults (e.g., Huang et al., 2009; Waite, Laumann, Das, & Schumm, 2009). When they were asked about conditions that affect their sexual expression, very few individuals in a sample of older adults from the United States cited erectile difficulties (AARP, 2010); similarly, when asking why older adults in a large population-based sample had not sought medical attention for their reported sexual difficulties, approximately one-quarter of respondents indicated that they were comfortable the way they were (Laumann, Glasser, Neves, & Moreira, 2009). DeLamater (2012) suggests that older men may engage in sexual activities other than intercourse, which maintains satisfaction in their sexual relationships.

Similarly, studies have examined the impact of physiological and health changes associated with ageing. Findings are somewhat contradictory regarding the impact of menopause on sexual functioning; some argue that changes in hormone levels greatly influence rates of sexual dysfunctions while others report mixed findings or no changes in sexual desire (e.g., Dennerstein, Guthrie, & Alford, 2004; Hinchliff & Gott, 2008). Accordingly, it has been argued that the impact of menopause on sexual functioning is dependent on the meaning ascribed by the individual (e.g., Koch, Mansfield, Thurau, & Carey, 2005). In sum, the social context or expectations surrounding menopause are tied to the loss of both reproductive capacity and youthfulness, both of which are equated with sexual desirability in Western culture. The elevated incidence of chronic medical conditions among middle and older adults is also a key area of research attention. Although a significant proportion of older adults report experiencing some type of chronic health condition, individuals rarely cite these as barriers to sexual functioning and enjoyment (Kontula & Haavio-Mannila, 2009).

Overall, research has long been focused on charting the decline in sexual functioning of older adults without accounting for subjective satisfaction or the possibility of further growth. Although older individuals often report decreases in sexual functioning or increases in health concerns, these do not seem to have a significant effect on their ratings of sexual satisfaction and enjoyment. Some findings suggest that older individuals may be more likely to move away from conventional sexual stereotypes or "scripts" (i.e., culturally defined, internalized norms for acceptable sexual activity; Simon & Gagnon, 2003) in adapting their sexual activity to suit their needs or capacities. Such a shift may also have benefits in altering the nature of their sexual experiences dramatically. Some authors suggest that peak or optimal sexuality may occur in the context of age and maturity (e.g., Shaw, 2012; Zilbergeld, 2004).

Optimal sexual experiences and older adults

The current medical model of sexuality equates sexual normalcy with physiological functioning and has little to offer individuals if they are deemed suitably functional. Despite this, popular conceptions of sexuality remain focused on the attainment of ultimate sexual satisfaction. It is clear that many individuals desire sex lives that go beyond mere adequacy, as demonstrated by the pervasive emphasis on better sex in popular culture. Magazines and self-help books promise greater, more passionate sexual experiences through novel techniques and the promotion of gendered sexual stereotypes (Gupta & Cacchioni, 2013; Ménard & Kleinplatz, 2008). Individuals comparing their sexual experiences to the unrealistic expectations found in much modern North American society often feel inferior or discouraged. Empirically based research on actual, optimal sexual experiences may help to advance understanding of what is actually feasible.

Research into the breadth of human sexuality has begun to explore the limits of wonderful sexual experiences. These have been termed "sexual ecstasy" (e.g., Ogden, 2006), "spectacular sex" (e.g., Sprinkle, 2005), and "profound sexual experiences" (e.g., Schnarch, 1991, 1997). Kleinplatz, Ménard, Paquet, et al. (2009) conducted semi-structured interviews with individuals who self-reported experiencing "great sex," with a particular emphasis on highlighting the experiences of those with the greatest breadth of knowledge and experience (i.e., older adults). Their analyses revealed eight components of optimal sexual experiencing that were consistent regardless of sex, sexual orientation, health status, age, or socioeconomic status. These components included being present in the moment, connection, intimacy, exceptional communication, authenticity, transcendence, risk-taking/exploration, and personal vulnerability. In sum, great sexual experiences are most likely to occur in the context of "...time, experience, and the commitment to making sex extraordinary" (Kleinplatz, 2010b, p. 60).

The consequent research question is thus to determine what helps to bring about optimal sexual experiences. Sexual interactions are uniquely and simultaneously informed by intrapersonal, interpersonal, and sociocultural elements; interviewing those who have lived such peak experiences will enable the documentation of this complexity. Furthermore, identifying factors that facilitate optimal sexuality for older adults can be contrasted with existing sexual stereotypes, providing empirical evidence of the potential experiences of these individuals. The aim of this study is to discover and document the particular elements that help to bring about and contribute to optimal sexual experiences among older adults.

Methods

Purpose

The developmental contributors to optimal sexual experiences were identified as part of a larger investigation on the factors that bring about or predispose someone towards optimal sexuality. Given the absence of previous research on optimal sexual experiences, descriptive phenomenology was selected to provide a qualitative framework for the investigation. Ultimately, the result of descriptive phenomenological analysis is a clear, accurate, and complete description of the experience as it appears to those who have experienced it, including the essential constituents and their variations (Moustakas, 1994; Polkinghorne, 1994). Within phenomenological investigations, understanding of an experience is pursued for its own sake (Langdridge, 2007; Moustakas, 1994) rather than to test hypotheses or identify "objective" truths. Instead, researchers try to get closer to the truth by investigating the richness of a phenomenon from different subjective realities (Camic et al., 2003). Because there is no desire within phenomenological investigations to generalize findings to other populations or settings (Polkinghorne, 1994; Thomas & Magilvy, 2011), the recruitment of a random sample of participants is neither desirable nor advisable. Rather, individuals who have expert knowledge regarding the phenomenon being studied, and who are able to describe their experiences thoroughly, are asked to participate (Moustakas, 1994; Polkinghorne, 1994). It is believed that the essential constituents and meaning of the experience remain constant despite variations in the subjective manifestations among participants (Polkinghorne, 1994).

The goal of phenomenological research is to represent accurately participants' experiences and actions (Polkinghorne, 1989). To that end, qualitative researchers attempt to set aside their own perspectives as much as possible through the process of epoché or "bracketing," where previous thoughts, biases, presuppositions, assumptions, judgments, and beliefs about a phenomenon are set aside in the hopes of approaching the subject from a fresh and naïve perspective (Giorgi & Giorgi, 2003; Holstein & Gubrium, 1995; Moustakas, 1994; Polkinghorne, 1994). Proper bracketing involves rigorous self-reflection (Hein & Austin, 2001); however, it is not assumed that researchers will be able to completely dispense with assumptions and presuppositions as new ones may be uncovered during the research process (Langdridge, 2007). Rather, bracketing is done in order to achieve a fresh perspective on the phenomenon being studied (Giorgi & Giorgi, 2003), and not necessarily because previous knowledge is incorrect or faulty (Wertz, 2005).

Participants

As part of the larger study on the contributors to optimal sexual experiences, 30 interviews were conducted with men and women who self-reported having "great sex." Participants were 60–82 years of age (mean age 65.6 years) and had been in partnered relationships for at least 25 years (mean length 28.3 years). In terms of sexual orientation, 22 described themselves as straight, six as bisexual and two as gay. When asked about physical disabilities, 19 self-identified as "able-bodied" and 11 reported disabilities of varying severity (e.g., cancer, cardiovascular problems, chronic obstructive pulmonary disease, multiple sclerosis, epilepsy, Human Immuno-deficiency Virus, and iatrogenic disorders). Half the participants reported that they were currently in polyamorous or open relationships ($n = 15$) and the rest described themselves as monogamous ($n = 15$).

Procedure

The following research protocol was approved by the ethics committee at Carleton University in 2005 and again by the University of Ottawa in 2007. Older individuals in long-term relationships were recruited from associations for the elderly as well as social and community groups using notices placed on bulletin boards, as well as online. Additional participants were identified based on snowball sampling (Neuman, 2004). Semi-structured interviews were conducted over the telephone and recorded with informed consent by two of the authors (a clinical psychologist and a graduate student in psychology). Prompts included: What are the elements or characteristics of "great sex"? At what point in your life did sex become great? What leads to great sex? What do you do to have great sex? The interviews, which lasted between 45 minutes and 120 minutes, were transcribed by members of the research team and verified for accuracy by one of the original interviewers. Identifying information was removed as was demographic information (e.g., sex, sexuality, sexual orientation, and age).

An analysis of the interview data was conducted within a research team ranging in size from five to seven members. Conducting phenomenological research within a larger research group may help members of the team become aware of their own personal biases and enhance their abilities to bracket pre-existing assumptions (Langdridge, 2007; Polkinghorne, 1994). Research team members read interview transcripts individually and attempted to identify contributors to optimal sexual experiences, that is, elements that might help to bring about or facilitate the occurrence of extraordinary sex.

Team members met to discuss potential categories and integrate ideas. Every meeting was then followed by a return to the data by each team member, an iterative process that is characteristic of qualitative investigations. The process for identifying themes was repeated for each broad contributor and it was repeated to identify specific themes within each contributor. Given the relatively large size of the research team, percentage agreement was calculated on a selection of statements and a threshold value of 70% was set before any classification system was considered final (Hunsley & Mash, 2008). In this study, percentage agreement among 5–7 raters ranged from 70% to 93% for the themes within each category.

Results

Participants described personal growth, that is, the broad contributor of individual development as well as the maturation of their relationships, as two major contributors to optimal sexual experiences. The themes arising in the major contributor of individual developmental factors will be described below and will be followed by the themes of relational contributors.

Individual developmental factors

Many of the older participants spontaneously and separately remarked that their sexual experiences had steadily improved in quality over their lifetimes. For many, the discovery that optimal sexual experiences continued into their 60s and beyond was a very pleasant and welcome surprise. An older man described the changes in his thinking:

> When I turned 40 I thought, 'Oh this is it, I'll never get laid again.' But that turned out not to be true and then when I turned 50, I thought the same thing and again it turned out not to be true and then it happened again when I was 60 and when I was 70. And I'm still having great sex and I think that's really quite wonderful.

Older participants reported that their capacity for having great sex was something that had developed over a lifetime; in other words, great lovers were made and not born. An older man said, "It takes a long time to learn it. And so, ideally sex is better for older people because they have more experiences and more learning." A female participant echoed this sentiment: "To me, great sex sort of implies a maturational kind of process ... there are just certain life experiences that you can only get through time, and different experiences and patience."

Within the larger category of developmental contributors to optimal sexual experiences, several distinct themes could be identified. These included letting go, overcoming, and unlearning; seeking, choosing, and practice; openness to experience, paying attention, and focusing.

Letting go, overcoming, and unlearning

For many participants in this investigation, optimal sexual experiences became possible when they learned to let go of and overcome certain destructive messages. For some, these negative messages centred on issues of gender identity, sexual orientation, and/or body image; others had received harmful messages focused on their specific sexual interests or about sex itself. For many, the negative beliefs that they developed about themselves and sex continued into adolescence and adulthood. An older male participant described the change in his beliefs over time:

> I think I underwent some very serious changes. You know, everything from the Catholic, monogamy, darkness, sex is for procreation and not for pleasure ... now I look for the opportunity for somebody to show me something or do something that I haven't done before and hopefully I'll like that too. So it's much more open and expressive now.

Working through shame and doubt with a view to transcending these negative messages was a crucial step on the path towards optimal sexual experiences. An older woman described this process as, "Really living our lives based on values that we embrace rather than those that have been imposed on us." For many participants, unlearning these destructive messages was the work of years rather than weeks or months. Participants explained that this process took time and could be difficult but emphasized that the reward for their labours had been better quality sex than they had ever dreamed possible. One older man described how he had overcome the negative messages he had received and why he believed this was important:

> It really is important for people to become liberated from that sex negativity in order to, um, to continue and to attain better and better what you might call 'great sex'. And that takes work, that takes psychological work and self-evaluation and understanding where your hang-ups are, what your fears are and dealing with them and however that might happen so that you become free of them to be totally human. And that's one of the reasons why, why sex for

older people is better than for younger people. Younger people are still socialized into a mold of expectations that, um, are sometimes very difficult to overcome. I certainly was.

For some participants, the overcoming and unlearning process continued well into old age, as they unlearned the messages they had received about sexuality and ageing. Other participants discovered the need to re-evaluate their understanding of sex and sexuality because of their experiences with disability and chronic illness. Again, many expressed surprise and delight at the discovery that optimal sexual experiences were still possible despite objective difficulties in sexual and/or physical functioning. A male participant described his journey as a result of neurodegenerative illness:

> I'm not even sure I had a definition of great sex until a few years ago ... after I was sort of forced to accept that, um, my previous definitions of sex weren't working, and I just wasn't, you know, and just kind of gave up on trying to do that. And was, became much more open to experimenting and, and communicating and, and, um, responding to what [my wife] wanted ... Sex was much more intense than it ever was before. And I like that, even though, I mean, even though I still wasn't, um, um, having erections or orgasms myself, but the whole experience as a whole was, I thought, was much greater than anything I had back then.

Seeking, choosing, and practice

Participants repeatedly emphasized that the occurrence of optimal sexual experiences in their lives was the result of very deliberate choices. Interviewees talked about purposefully cultivating their understanding and experience of sex and sexuality throughout their lives. They intentionally sought out experiences and practised skills that they believed might help to bring about optimal sexual experiences, speaking of "exploration" or "setting out on a journey." One older man described his experiences with his wife as, "A life of sexual exploration and adventure and excitement." One participant describes the process as: "I think it comes through experience ... Lots of practice [laughing] ... The more you do it, the better you enjoy it, the better you become at it."

Participants took a variety of different routes in their journeys towards optimal sexual experiences. Some said that they had honed their knowledge and skills on various subjects (e.g., communication, pleasure, and massage) through reading books, joining groups, and/or attending workshops. Others emphasized the opportunities to learn with and from sexual partners, whether these relationships were short- or long-term. Regardless of their individual choices, participants emphasized the need for continuous exploration, practice, repetition, and refinement. When asked how great sex became possible in her life, a female participant responded, "Um from doing it a lot! Uh, from having lots of partners, um, from putting myself out there and saying, 'Hey I'd like to have sex with you!' Um and then having lots of different kinds of sex." It is important to note that even though some participants made comparable choices (e.g., choosing to live more authentically with regards to their sexual orientation), most did not experience identical results. It seems likely that participants came to very different conclusions about themselves or about sex as a result of seemingly similar learning experiences. In other words, the journey towards optimal sexual experiences appeared to be unique for each separate traveller.

Many older participants emphasized the need for this learning process to continue indefinitely. In fact, many expressed eagerness at the idea of there being much more for them to learn about themselves, their partners or sex itself. During the interviews, some participants deliberately focused on insights that they had gained after mid-life:

My experience is not only that I experience something more fabulous, more uh, expansive and energetic and engaging a larger horizon, but that I become aware that there are other horizons that, that, you know, I'm, that I'm climbing a hill and every time I think I see a crest it's really just another one of these experiences where I come up over a crest which I thought was a crest and then it turns out the mountain is looming higher in front of me.

Openness to experience, paying attention, and focusing

Participants both sought out learning opportunities and took advantage of unexpected experiences that might not have been planned or anticipated. They described a state of openness where they deliberately paid attention to and focused on their experiences as they occurred so that they might learn more about themselves, their partners, and sex itself. An older man stated, "I think experience teaches a lot *for people who want to learn*" (italics added). One woman described this state of openness: "I feel you learn something from every sexual encounter that you have, from every person that you're with, uh, is a teachable moment if you choose to pay attention to it." An older woman described her experience of learning by being open to the possibilities:

> In seeking great sex, um, I think, yeah there was a certain amount of learning in that I certainly kept my eyes open, listened, heard other people and, and what made their sex feel wonderful to them, um, experimented with myself and my own body ... you know ... just more in an openness to it, not necessarily I'm going to sit down and learn how to have great sex.

Development of the relationship

For some of the participants in this investigation, their best sexual experiences occurred primarily within the context of their long-term relationships. They might have good or very good sex with others but optimal sexual experiences happened only with their partners of 30 or 40 years. For many, the quality of their experiences improved over time; some said that their best sex happened only after mid-life and after their children had left home.

In describing their long-term relationships, there appeared to be a core set of qualities related to the structure and development of the relationship over time that contributed to optimal sexual experiences. These important elements described below included having common values, "peerness" (a term used by our participants as indicated below) and good fit; growth, fluidity, and maturing of the relationship; emotional maturity of the partners and emotional independence in the relationship; and knowledge of one's partner, knowledge of a partner's body/desires/feelings/erotic wishes and depth.

In addition, empathy represented an essential and indispensable relational contributor to optimal sexual experiences, both in its own right and as a quality of every other relational contributor.

Structure and depth of the relationship

Common values, "peerness," agreement, and good fit

Many participants expressed the need to have common values, agreement, and a "good fit" with their partners in order for optimal sexual experiences to be possible. They defined "good fit" across the entire spectrum: sexually, physically, mentally, spiritually, emotionally, financially, philosophically, etc. An older man put it, "You got to be on level. You got to be on an emotional level with each other, you have to be, I'd go so far as to say you have to be intellectually level ... great sex is between equals." The word "peer" came up repeatedly when participants referred to their very best relationships. An older man described a relatively new relationship that involved fantastic sex: "Ultimately what goes on is there's a great peerness that, that sex between us becomes genderless. That's never happened to me. It's fantastic." Some interviewees alluded to the idea that over time, the relationship as a whole became greater than the sum of its parts.

Changing, evolution, growth, fluidity, maturing of relationship, and shared relationship history

Participants emphasized the importance of accepting and embracing change over time in themselves, in their partners, and in their relationships. They talked about actively seeking out and encouraging growth, maturation and development. When asked her definition of "great sex," one older woman replied, "...time coupled with a partnership that's a growing, that's a growthful partnership, where people are learning and it's so multifaceted ...."

In many cases, adaptation to change was necessary as many participants described the impact of illnesses, injuries, and/or treatment effects on themselves or on their partners. An older woman said:

> The fact is that people, especially in long-term relationships, change, for physical reasons or other reasons. And part of the secret of a good relationship is being able to adapt together to those changes and that includes in sex. Things may not work the way they always did so do you just shut it off and say 'I'm not going to do this anymore because it doesn't work the way it should' or do you say 'Okay, let's find another way to express our intimacy'?

Many participants said that their relationships had become stronger over time and emphasized the contribution of shared relationship history to the intimacy of the relationship. In turn, the quality of their sexual experiences, the connection that they experienced and the depth of the intimacy was enhanced by their shared history together. An older woman described her experiences in her marriage: "We have been through so much and through so many changes and have so much history makes a relationship that is just rich beyond measure ... We, we have become like the spiral helix. We have constructed our mutual DNA with each other's." Many other participants echoed the idea that shared relationship history could help couples get through stressful periods together. "You've gone through uh, so many ups and downs and ... the shit hitting the fan and, and so on, that you know that you're going to come out okay ... through the other side of it," said one participant. The knowledge that the relationship had already been tested and grown provided the foundation to take emotional and sexual risks, thereby enabling couples to attain extraordinary erotic intimacy.

Emotional maturity of the partners, ability to tolerate own anxiety in relationship, emotional independence in relationship, and self-soothing

Emotional maturity, involving the ability to self-soothe and tolerate anxiety, was an important relational contributor to optimal sexual experiences. Participants talked about learning to take risks with their partners "in a safe way" and being able to calm their anxieties as needed. One participant emphasized the need to avoid "no-growth" contracts in relationships so that both partners were free to develop and mature over time without these changes being seen as threatening to the relationship. An older woman described the contribution of emotional maturity to optimal sexual experiences:

> [Partners] can tolerate discomfort, even though they don't like it they can tolerate it — I'm not talking about physical discomfort here, I'm talking about emotional. Um, change is inherent in the relationship ... Each person can manage their own anxiety and share their growth with the other one. And great sex can happen ... It gets better as you get older if you're smart enough to grow into your capacity for being human.

Knowledge of partner, knowledge of partner's body/desires/feelings/erotic wishes and depth

Knowledge of one's partner was an important relational contributor to optimal sexual experiences and was especially relevant in long-term relationships. Participants talked about the sexual and non-sexual knowledge that they had accumulated about their beloveds throughout the course of the relationship. A male participant used a musical analogy to explain the development of optimal sexual experiences in a relationship over time:

> It takes practice. You know, a great symphony, um, a great concert ... has a conductor who knows what he's doing, has a score that's well-written, and has an orchestra that is professional and knows what they're doing ... and perhaps a great concert hall. But you put those four things together all at once and they don't know each other, it's going to take practice to produce that great symphonic concert.

Many participants said that it was important for this discovery process to be ongoing, that is, that they not take their partners for granted but strive to know more about them even after 25-plus years. This theme is conceptually related to the idea of personal change, growth and development over time: As both partners grow and mature, they need to constantly revisit their knowledge of one another and update it. An older man described his understanding of what made optimal sexual experiences possible with his wife:

> The kind of great sex that I have now, I learned by some academic study, I did. But mostly I learned in experiential learning with my partner. I betcha that if I tried to have the same great sex that I have now, the principles that I have figured out with my wife, I could still use with somebody else but it'd be learning. It, it, it's not just like once you learn a bicycle, you don't fall off. You learn different bicycles. But there's a lot of transfer. So I could have great sex with somebody besides my wife. But I couldn't, um, do it auto-matically. It wouldn't happen the first time or first five or six or ten times out of the box.

Other participants echoed this idea, saying that the great sex they experienced in their current relationship might not be possible in other relationships, or would take significant time to develop.

Depth

Participants emphasized the contribution of depth in the relationship to optimal sexual experiences. The word "depth" was used by participants to describe the connection, the intimacy, the love, the caring and the levels of trust, safety and communication that they felt with their partners. Some participants expressed the belief that the depth present in their longer relationships was what distinguished good from great sex. One participant stated:

Over time, it gets deeper, the connection gets, between the people, between the partners, gets deeper over time and they learn about themselves and each other more joyfully, physically, as they learn about each other in relationships and a lot of other ways.

One woman expressed the belief that optimal sexual experiences were not possible without this depth:

I have several friends who have been married for thirty, forty, fifty, one of them married sixty years and um, they have fabulous sex, they said that sex is better than it's ever been, because their connection with each other is so deep and so strong that there's no anxiety about rejection or inhibitions. They just can really let go and let loose and be intimately connected in a sweetness that they tell me they've not had before their seventies. And one of them's in their eighties.

Empathy

Participants emphasized and re-emphasized the importance of empathy as a contributor to optimal sexual experiences. Empathy was considered to be a separate contributor to optimal sexual experiences, as well as an element that coloured every other relational contributor. Perhaps the other relational contributors were only possible because of the degree of empathy that existed in the relationship.

Participants defined empathy in various ways. Some described it as the ability to be sensitive, perceptive, attentive, and responsive to another partner. A female participant described her best lovers as having, "An almost uncanny ability not only to hear what's said but what isn't said ... One time I told my current partner, 'You know, you're doing just what I wanted' and she said, 'Well, I'm watching your reactions.'" Some participants said that empathy involved tuning in to one's partner, reading the other person's body language, "feeling into another person's space" and trying to get on the same wavelength so as to create a connection with the other person's body and mind.

Flexibility and adaptation to change over time was crucial for the development of empathy. One woman explained, "Things change from time to time and circumstance to circumstance and what might have felt, worked great one time doesn't do it the next time." Whether the relationship was short- or long-term, generating deep empathy required openness, vulnerability, care, compassion, consideration, and respect between partners. Empathy also required that both partners be completely and fully present as well as willing to connect deeply with one another. A female participant stressed that empathy between partners was a far more important contributor to optimal sexual experiences than technical skills:

I think the skills are more mental skills and emotional skills than they are physical skills because if you the, if you have the empathy and you have the, um, desire to connect, you're going to be led in the right, you know, if you're, if you're paying attention to the feedback you're getting from your partner, nonverbal as well as verbal, that's, that'll give you the physical skills you need.

Discussion

The findings of this study suggest that contrary to popular belief, often reinforced and duplicated in the professional literature, some older adults are quite capable of having optimal sexual experiences. From a developmental perspective, one might question if these participants were able to attain extraordinary sexuality despite their age or because of it. These participants' own reflections suggest that personal maturity and relational growth were important contributors to the calibre of their sexual intimacy.

Rather than a simple and direct route between ageing and erotic enhancement, choices were required that would facilitate optimal sexual development. The first step on this pathway involved overcoming early negative sexual attitudes and experiences. Many participants had grown up in sex-negative environments and had been exposed to myths, taboos or silence surrounding sexuality, leading to shame and guilt. Some had been sexually abused. Almost without exception, participants reported having had to jettison early learning and its consequences to pave a more positive pathway for future sexual development. Participants noted "revisioning sexuality," that is, re-examining limiting concepts and values around sexuality to open up and imagine anew the possibility of what sex could become. The years required to *un*learn early messages meant that time, experience and choice were allies in enabling new directions.

Two kinds of important choices led to optimal sexuality: active pursuit and receptive openness to experience. For some, this involved seeking out partners, groups, books, or courses that might enhance sexual development and then practising. For others, their attitudes towards opportunities proved to be pivotal. Whether they encountered good or poor fortune, they set out to learn more about sexuality, about themselves as sexual beings and what would lead to greater fulfilment by cultivating attention to experience. In either case, these choices served them well and would prove advantageous in the face of losses associated with ageing, for example, chronic illness, disability and the loss of one's life partner.

The participants in this study were all in relationships of 25 years or longer. Contrary to the common assumption that sex peaks in the "honeymoon" (early) phase of a relationship, the participants in this study found that their best sexual experiences began in mid-life and beyond. The depth and maturing of the relationship seemed crucial in bringing about extraordinary sexual intimacy. Ironically, one of the constants seemed to be aware of the need for fluidity over the lifespan of the relationship. Changes in individuals and their partners were inevitable for those participants who had been pursuing optimal sexual experiences for years or decades. An ability to cope with the anxiety brought on by change (e.g., chronic illness and disability) and the flexibility to adapt were required. Instead of minimizing or avoiding anxiety, participants welcomed opportunities to discover themselves and their partners in the context of sexual intimacy, even though this involved taking interpersonal risks.

The need to maintain oneself within the relational context was balanced with mutual caring and respect. Trust was nurtured in an atmosphere of emotional accessibility and goodwill. Empathy was crucial for remaining in touch with one another and continually renewing the depth of mutual knowledge. These participants illustrated that like sexual passion itself, emotional connection does not happen naturally; it takes energy and effort to continue to know and value one's partners afresh.

Although, there has been some debate in the couples therapy literature about the relative importance of differentiation (cf., Schnarch, 1991, 1997) versus attachment (cf., Johnson, 2004), the participants here suggest that each has a crucial role in creating and maintaining sexual connection. Individual maturity and self-knowledge helped to create an atmosphere of trust and trustworthiness (Shaw, 2012). Correspondingly, mutual interest, knowledge and especially empathy created just enough safety to access and reveal deep vulnerabilities which in turn enabled intense, erotic exploration.

This study carries important implications for therapists working with clients/patients across the lifecycle and especially for sex therapists dealing with older couples. It is never too soon — or too late — to deconstruct the myths learned in one's youth, which prevent individuals and couples from discovering their own notions about sexuality. Letting go of these constricting beliefs can then allow clients to follow their own paths towards optimal sexual experience. Conspicuous among these notions are the assumptions surrounding ageing and the demise of sexuality. More subtly, this means enquiring as to patients' implicit beliefs about sexuality, including the notions that sex equals intercourse; sex should be "natural and spontaneous"; sex is for the young, firm, and able-bodied; do not start anything you cannot finish; and sex requires a hard penis and a lubricated vagina (cf., Zilbergeld, 1999, 2004). Questioning these imperatives may allow clients/patients at any age to determine which of these notions inhibits them from the full flowering of their erotic development as they grow.

Participants in this study indicated that emotional maturity was an important prerequisite for optimal sexual experience. Although "maturity" is often used euphemistically, it is hardly identical with ageing. Much depends on how one grows older. Sex therapists have stated the importance of personal differentiation, growth and openness to sexual and non-sexual changes (Broder & Goldman, 2004; Metz & McCarthy, 2012; Morin, 1995; Schnarch, 1997; Shaw, 2012). This sentiment was reflected in this study. Therapists are called upon here to support clients as they struggle with substantive personal growth and relational depth rather than merely helping them to attain normative sexual function (Kleinplatz, 2010a; Kleinplatz, Ménard, Paradis, et al., 2009; Ogden, 2006; Schnarch, 1997; Shaw, 2012).

Similarly, couples in long-term relationships often come to therapy with entrenched patterns, hoping that therapy can help with their sexual difficulties while mostly maintaining the status quo. (Therapists, too, may be afraid of de-stabilizing the relationship.) Whilst this may — or may not — allow couples to ameliorate the symptoms of sexual dysfunction, it will not help them to attain optimal sexual experiences. However, therapists may consider acknowledging the risks of emotional, interpersonal, and erotic stagnation alongside the risks of erotic exploration over the course of a lifetime.

This study does not suggest that couples *ought* to aim outside their comfort zones. That is a personal choice and the findings here are not intended to promote yet higher performance standards. On the contrary, if anything, these findings suggest that erotic development must be predicated on the individual's choices, searching within and with each paying attention to his/her own aspirations and path. The facilitating factors described here are not a checklist of requirements; they are intended to provide specific examples of the contributions of various factors to optimal sexual experiences in older adults.

Limitations

Given the nature of the phenomenological approach, generalizations of these findings to other populations are neither possible nor advisable. These results may provide useful information for those inclined towards the development of optimal erotic potential at any age but they are not intended to be universally prescriptive.

The results of this study showed that ageing, disability, and illness need not represent insurmountable obstacles to wonderful sexuality; however, the focus of this investigation was on individuals who had already identified as having optimal sexual experiences. It remains to be seen whether anyone can have these types of experiences if they wish to or whether fundamental barriers might exist that were not identified in this investigation.

Conclusions

Results of this study challenge the traditional belief that sexuality and sexual satisfaction necessarily deteriorate with age. Rather, sex can potentially improve with age, maturity, personal growth and relational depth. Furthermore, letting go of conventional sex scripts can open the door to this possibility, particularly if individuals and couples are open to charting their own sexual pathways. This is not merely a matter of discarding sex negativity but of re-defining sexuality per se beyond genital functionality and the imperative of penetration.

The findings here have notable implications not only for our perceptions of sexuality and ageing but for those seeking to enhance their sexuality throughout the life cycle. Rather than regarding older adults as pitiful, decrepit sexual relics, the alternative is to continue to learn from those who have optimal sexual experiences. For sex and relationship therapists, the lessons suggested here entail helping individuals develop comfort with self, openness to experience, and the courage to fulfil sexual potential. It will require that we promote clients' intimate knowledge of themselves and their partners as developing sexual beings. For couples, this will likely mean attaining impressively high levels of sexual and non-sexual empathy. For therapists and for lovers, spaces may need to be created in which trust and risk can be fostered, so that partners can connect authentically and lay themselves bare, daring to be seen and known as they truly are.

Funding

This study was funded by doctoral fellowship [grant number 752-2007-1803] to A. Dana Ménard from the Social Sciences and Humanities Research Council of Canada.

References

American Association of Retired Persons. (2010). *Sex, romance and relationships: AARP survey of midlife and older adults*. Washington, DC: Author.

Bouman, W.P., Arcelus, J., & Benbow, S.M. (2006). Nottingham study of sexuality & ageing (NoSSA I). Attitudes regarding sexuality and older people: A review of the literature. *Sexual and Relationship Therapy, 21*(02), 149–161.

Broder, M., & Goldman, A. (2004). *Secrets of sexual ecstasy*. New York, NY: Penguin.

Camic, P.M., Rhodes, J.E., & Yardley, L. (2003). Naming the stars: Integrating qualitative methods into psychological research. In P.M. Camic, J.E. Rhodes, & L. Yardley (Eds.), *Qualitative research in psychology: Expanding perspectives in methodology and design* (pp. 3–16). Washington, DC: American Psychological Association.

DeLamater, J. (2012). Sexual expression in later life: A review and synthesis. *Journal of Sex Research, 49*(2–3), 125–141.

Dennerstein, L., Guthrie, J.R., & Alford, S. (2004). Childhood abuse and its association with mid-aged women's sexual functioning. *Journal of Sex & Marital Therapy, 30*, 225–234.

Giorgi, A.P., & Giorgi, B.M. (2003). The descriptive phenomenological psychological method. In P.M. Camic, J.E. Rhodes, & L. Yardley (Eds.), *Qualitative research in psychology: Expanding perspectives in methodology and design* (pp. 243–273). Washington, DC: American Psychological Association.

Gott, M. (2006). Sexual health and the new ageing. *Age and Ageing, 35*(2), 106–107.

Gott, M., & Hinchliff, S. (2003). How important is sex in later life? The views of older people. *Social Science & Medicine, 56*(8), 1617–1628.

Gupta, K., & Cacchioni, T. (2013). Sexual improvement as if your health depends on it: An analysis of contemporary sex manuals. *Feminism & Psychology, 23*(4), 442–458.

Hein, S.F., & Austin, W.J. (2001). Empirical and hermeneutic approaches to phenomenological research in psychology: A comparison. *Psychological Methods, 6*(1), 3–17.

Hillman, J. (2008). Sexual issues and aging within the context of work with older adult patients. *Professional Psychology: Research and Practice, 39*(3), 290.

Hinchliff, S., & Gott, M. (2008). Challenging social myths and stereotypes of women and aging: Heterosexual women talk about sex. *Journal of Women and Aging, 20*, 65–81.

Holstein, J.A., & Gubrium, J.F. (1995). *The active interview*. Thousand Oaks, CA: Sage.

Huang, A.J., Subak, L.L., Thom, D.H., Van Den Eeden, S.K., Ragins, A.I., Kuppermann, M., ... & Brown, J.S. (2009). Sexual function and aging in racially and ethnically diverse women. *Journal of the American Geriatrics Society, 57*(8), 1362–1368.

Hunsley, J., & Mash, E.J. (Eds.). (2008). *A guide to assessments that work*. New York, NY: Oxford University Press.

Hyde, Z., Flicker, L., Hankey, G., Almeida, O., McCaul, K., Chubb, S., & Yeap, B. (2010). Prevalence of sexual activity and associated factors in men aged 75 to 95 years: A cohort study. *Annals of Internal Medicine, 153*(11), 693–702.

Johnson, S.M. (2004). *The practice of emotionally focused marital therapy: Creating connection*. New York, NY: Bruner/Routledge.

Kleinplatz, P.J. (2010a). "Desire disorders" or opportunities for optimal erotic intimacy. In S.R. Leiblum (Ed.), *Treating sexual desire disorders: A clinical casebook* (pp. 92–113). New York, NY: Guilford.

Kleinplatz, P.J. (2010b). Lessons from great lovers. In S. Levine, S. Althof, & C. Risen (Eds.), *Handbook of clinical sexuality for mental health professionals* (2nd ed.; pp. 57–72). New York, NY: Brunner-Routledge.

Kleinplatz, P.J., Ménard, A.D., Paquet, M.-P., Paradis, N., Campbell, M., Zuccarini, D., & Mehak, L. (2009). The components of optimal sexuality: A portrait of "great sex". *Canadian Journal of Human Sexuality, 18*(1–2), 1–13.

Kleinplatz, P.J., Ménard, A.D., Paradis, N., Campbell, M., Dalgleish, T., Segovia, A., & Davis, K. (2009). From closet to reality: Optimal sexuality among the elderly. *The Irish Psychiatrist, 10*(1), 15–18.

Koch, P.B., Mansfield, P.K., Thurau, D., & Carey, M. (2005). "Feeling frumpy": The relationship between body image and sexual response changes in midlife women. *Journal of Sex Research, 42*, 215–223.

Kontula, O., & Haavio-Mannila, E. (2009). The impact of aging on human sexual activity and sexual desire. *Journal of Sex Research, 46*, 46–56.

Langdridge, D. (2007). *Phenomenological psychology: Theory, research and method*. Harlow: Pearson Education.

Laumann, E.O., Glasser, D.B., Neves, R.C.S., & Moreira, E.D. (2009). A population-based survey of sexual activity, sexual problems and associated help-seeking behavior patterns in mature adults in the United States of America. *International Journal of Impotence Research, 21*(3), 171–178.

Lindau, S.T., Schumm, L.P., Laumann, E.O., Levinson, W., O'Muircheartaigh, C.A., & Waite, L.J. (2007). A study of sexuality and health among older adults in the United States. *New England Journal of Medicine, 357*(8), 762–774.

Ménard, A.D., & Kleinplatz, P.K. (2008). 21 moves guaranteed to make his thighs go up in flames: Depictions of "Great sex" in popular magazines. *Sexuality & Culture, 12,* 1–20.

Metz, M.E., & McCarthy, B.W. (2012). The Good Enough Sex (GES) model: Perspectives and clinical applications. In P.J. Kleinplatz (Ed.), *New directions in sex therapy: Innovations and alternatives* (2nd ed., pp. 213–230). New York, NY: Taylor & Francis.

Morin, J. (1995). *The erotic mind: Unlocking the inner sources of sexual passion and fulfillment.* New York, NY: HarperCollins.

Moustakas, C. (1994). *Phenomenological research methods.* Thousand Oaks, CA: Sage.

Moynihan, R. & Mintzes, B. (2010). *Sex, lies, and pharmaceuticals: How drug companies plan to profit from female sexual dysfunction.* Vancouver: Greystone.

Neuman, W.L. (2004). *Basics of social research: Qualitative and quantitative approaches.* Boston, MA: Pearson Education.

Nicolosi, A., Laumann, E.O., Glasser, D.B., Brock, G., King, R., & Gingell, C. (2006). Sexual activity, sexual disorders and associated help-seeking behaviour among mature adults in five Anglophone countries from the Global Survey of Sexual Attitudes and Behaviours (GSSAB). *Journal of Sex and Marital Therapy, 32*(4), 331–342.

Ogden, G. (2006). *The heart and soul of sex: Making the ISIS connection.* Boston, MA: Shambhala/Trumpeter.

Polkinghorne, D.E. (1989). Phenomenological research methods. In R.S. Valle & S. Halling (Eds.), *Existential-phenomenological perspectives in psychology: Exploring the breadth of human experience* (pp. 41–62). New York, NY: Plenum Press.

Polkinghorne, D.E. (1994). Research methodology in humanistic psychology. In F. Wertz (Ed.), *The humanistic movement: Recovering the person in psychology* (pp. 105–128). Lake Forth, FL: Gardner.

Potts, A., Grace, V.M., Vares, T., & Gavey, N. (2006). 'Sex for life'? Men's counter-stories on 'erectile dysfunction', male sexuality and ageing. *Sociology of Health & Illness, 28*, 306–329.

Schnarch, D. (1991). *Constructing the sexual crucible.* New York, NY: Norton.

Schnarch, D. (1997). *Passionate marriage.* New York, NY: Henry Holt.

Shaw, J. (2012). Approaching your highest sexual function in relationship: A reward of age and maturity. In P.J. Kleinplatz (Ed.), *New directions in sex therapy: Innovations and alternatives* (2nd ed.; pp. 175–194). New York, NY: Taylor & Francis.

Simon, W., & Gagnon, J.H. (2003). Sexual scripts: Origins, influences and changes. *Qualitative Sociology, 26*(4), 491–497.

Sprinkle, A. (2005). *Dr. Sprinkle's spectacular sex — Make over your love life with one of the world's greatest sex experts.* New York, NY: Penguin.

Thomas, E., & Magilvy, J.K. (2011). Qualitative rigor or research validity in qualitative research. *Journal for Specialists in Pediatric Nursing, 16*, 151–155.

Vares, T. (2009). Reading the 'sexy oldie': Gender, age(ing) and embodiment. *Sexualities, 12*(4), 503–524.

Waite, L.J., Laumann, E.O., Das, A., & Schumm, L.P. (2009). Sexuality: Measures of partnerships, practices, attitudes, and problems in the National Social Life, Health, and Aging Project. *Journals of Gerontology: Social Sciences, 64B* (Suppl. 1), i56–i66.

Waltz, T. (2002). Crones, dirty old men, sexy seniors: Representations of the sexuality of older persons. *Journal of Aging and Identity, 7*(2), 99–112.

Wertz, F.J. (2005). Phenomenological research methods for counseling psychology. *Journal of Counseling Psychology, 52,* 167–177.

Woloski-Wruble, A.C., Oliel, Y., Leefsma, M., & Hochner-Celnikier, D. (2010). Sexual activities, sexual and life satisfaction, and successful aging in women. *Journal of Sexual Medicine, 7*, 2401–2410.

Zilbergeld, B. (1999). *The new male sexuality.* New York, NY: Bantam Books.

Zilbergeld, B. (2004). *Better than ever: Love and sex at midlife.* Norwalk, CT: Crown House.

The association of an open relationship orientation with health and happiness in a sample of older US adults

James R. Fleckenstein and Derrell W. Cox II

Department of Anthropology, University of Oklahoma, Norman, OK, USA

Sexual activity over the life course is strongly associated with better health and greater personal happiness, yet the sexuality of aging adults has been a neglected topic. There is a lack of research on those with a consensually non-exclusive sexual relationship style regardless of age. This research examines whether such an orientation has positive effects on sexual frequency, health and personal happiness, and how this might inform counselors and therapists providing services to older adults. The authors collected 502 responses via an online survey from individuals aged 55 and older residing in the United States who engage in consensually non-exclusive sexual relationships. Self-reported health and happiness, number of sexual partners, and sexual frequency were compared with 723 similar respondents from the nationally-representative 2012 United States (US) General Social Survey. Key findings were: irrespective of formal relationship status, the non-exclusive sample reported significantly more sexual partners, more sexual frequency, better health, and were much more likely to have had an HIV test than the general US population; the non-exclusive sample also reported being significantly happier than the general population, with the exception of married men, who reported being as happy as the general population sample; and regression analyses suggest that the factors which predict better health and happiness differ between the general population and those who participate in consensually non-exclusive sexual relationships. In summary, this study examines sexuality among the healthy aging population. Participation (or interest in participation), in consensual non-exclusive sexual relationship styles can be rewarding and contribute to personal health and happiness, as much as or more than monogamous marriages.

Introduction

Research shows that increased sexual activity is strongly associated with better health outcomes and greater personal happiness (Karraker, DeLamater, & Schwartz, 2011; Lindau & Gavrilova, 2010; Lindau et al., 2007; Whipple et al., 2007). This is true among older adults – especially men – where declining sexual frequency has been shown to be correlated with negative health (Laumann et al., 2004), increased risk of cardiovascular problems (Hall, Shackelton, Rosen, & Araujo, 2010), higher rates of depression (Ganong & Larson, 2011), and diminished general happiness (Laumann, Paik, & Rosen, 1999).

Sexual frequency has been found consistently to decline with age (Karraker et al., 2011; Waite, Laumann, Das, & Schumm, 2009). Research into the reasons for the decline has discovered a wide variety of causes and a consistent difference between men and women in both the degree of decline and stated reasons underlying the decline (DeLamater & Koepsel, 2014; Karraker et al., 2011). The most common causes for age-related declining sexual frequency are due to decreasing desire, changes in hormones, certain illnesses, specific medications, loss of an available partner, and a decline in the importance of sex (Aggarwal, 2013; Bradford & Meston, 2007; DeLamater, 2012; DeLamater & Sill, 2005; Kontula & Haavio-Mannila, 2009; Lindau et al., 2007; Matthias, Lubben, Atchison, & Schweitzer, 1997). While health issues are a significant factor for both men and women, these concerns manifest differently by gender. In several studies, attitudinal or psychosocial factors rather than physical factors, such as a "lack of interest in sex" (Lindau et al., 2007), rating sex "not an important part of life" (Waite et al., 2009), or "relationship concerns" (Wiley & Bortz, 1996) – especially, though not exclusively, among women – have been found to contribute consistently to reduced sexual activity and, in some cases, are the major contributors (DeLamater, 2012; DeLamater & Koepsel, 2014; DeLamater & Sill, 2005).

There is a correlation between sexual frequency and sexual and relationship satisfaction (McNulty & Fisher, 2008; Yucel & Gassanov, 2010), both of which are positively associated with relationship stability (Yeh, Lorenz, Wickrama, Conger, & Elder, 2006). Research has highlighted the importance of a positive and satisfying marital relationship for health outcomes, while demonstrating the deleterious health effects of negative and unsatisfying relationships (Bookwala, 2005; Donoho, Crimmins & Seeman, 2013). Dissatisfaction with sexual frequency has been shown to be a main contributor to relationship and sexual dissatisfaction (Smith et al., 2011). Sexual frequency is also associated with personal as well as relational happiness. Blanchflower and Oswald (2004), looking at data from the General Social Survey (GSS; Smith et al., 2011), noted: "The more sex, the happier the person...there is almost complete monotonicity in the way the frequency of sexual intercourse enters the equation" (2004, p. 402).

In spite of research findings supporting the beneficial effects of sexuality on personal health and well-being, there has been an ongoing neglect of sexuality among *healthy* aging adults in research and policy literature (DeLamater, 2012; DeLamater & Sill, 2005). This gap poses significant problems for both healthcare and counseling professions whose older clients may benefit from awareness of options for sexual expression. The present study aims to provide important and relevant information for health professionals, including sex educators, counselors, and therapists for determining appropriate counseling for older clients who seek an optimal sex life.

Previous research has suggested that marriage provides meaningful health benefits, that married individuals are happier and have more sex than single people, and better sex than cohabitors (Waite & Gallagher, 2000, p. 79). More recent research, however, indicates that, at least among older adults, married individuals are *not* necessarily getting more sex, are *not* being more sexually satisfied (Fisher, 2010, p. 1). Cohabiting adults appear to fare as well on most measures of emotional satisfaction, pleasure, openness, time spent together, and absence of criticism as do their legally married counterparts (Brown & Kawamura, 2010). Likewise, cohabiting partners appear to fare as well as married couples concerning depressive symptoms, time spent with friends, and the relationship with, and frequency of contact with one's parents (Musick & Bumpass, 2012).

Wiley and Bortz (1996) found that 92% of their sample of 118 male and female respondents desired sex at least once a week, but less than half attained that frequency. A similar percentage of the general population represented in the GSS (Smith, Marsden, Hout, & Kim, 2013) sample did not attain that level of frequency. Karraker and colleagues (2011) found similar results for the National Social Life, Health and Aging Project (NSHAP; Suzman, 2009) population, with mean sexual frequencies of 3.13 times per month for males and 1.74 times per month for females aged 57 and older.

The NSHAP revealed that significant pluralities of women in all age groups cited "lack of sexual interest" as their most frequent "sexual problem" (Waite et al., 2009). With much lower percentages of men reporting this as a "problem," the stage is set for discord within relationships between men and women based upon discordant sexual desire. This is reinforced by the NSHAP finding that nearly four times as many women (24.0%) as men aged 57–64 (6.2%) and about twice as many women (34.9% aged 65–74 and 52.3% aged 75 and older) as men (14.1% aged 65–74 and 25.9% aged 75 and older) agreed that "sex is not an important part of life" (Waite et al., 2009). Laumann and his co-researchers found similarly pronounced gender differences in rating the importance of sex across 29 nations studied (Laumann et al., 2006).

While sexual frequency declines with certain age-related illnesses, DeLamater and Sill (2005) found that attitudes were more significant than biomedical factors in determining sexual desire. Research indicates that sexual frequency positively correlates with physical and mental health (DeLamater, 2012). Nonetheless, significant majorities of men and women in the NSHAP agreed with the statement that married persons having sex outside of marriage was "always wrong," even when potentially mitigating factors such as dementia or serious physical illness were introduced (Waite et al., 2009). Among unpartnered female respondents to the NSHAP who reported no sexual activity, nearly one in five chose the answer, "religious beliefs prohibit sex outside of marriage," as a reason for their sexual inactivity (Lindau et al., 2007). These findings are not surprising given that sexually and emotionally exclusive monogamous marriages are the dominant relationship paradigm in the United States (Anderson, 2010). However, these ideological and practical factors place individuals in a catch-22 situation. There is a potential for relationship conflict as sexual frequency declines, especially within dyads experiencing discordant sexual desire. Yet, sociocultural values in the United States discourage pursuing relationship strategies that provide viable options for remaining in an otherwise satisfactory long-term relationship *and* remaining sexually active. For single and partnered adults who desire to remain sexually active in spite of these various obstacles, a non-exclusive strategy may provide an important alternative to address discrepancies of desire.

Researchers estimate that as many as 5% of the US population are engaged in consensually non-exclusive[1] relationships at any given time (Conley, as cited in Pappas, 2013). To date, no published research has considered the possible health and happiness effects of having multiple concurrent sexual and romantic partners in an open and consensual manner, regardless of age. As participation in, and public awareness of, the option of non-exclusive relationships increases, it is important to find out how individuals, both legally married and unmarried, and who adopt a relationally non-exclusive (RNE) orientation fare compared with adults in the general US population. The aim of this study is to investigate the relationship of sexual frequency with personal happiness and well-being among healthy aging individuals who practice non-exclusive relationships compared with the US general population.

It is to be expected that a population that has adopted a non-exclusive relationship orientation would have a greater number of sexual partners. Whether that would actually translate into greater sexual *frequency* is a question worthy of examination. Large-scale research with representative samples has found that older people rarely have multiple concurrent sexual partners. Waite et al. (2009), analyzing data from the NSHAP, found women reported multiple sexual partners in the last year at rates of 0.1% for ages 57–64,

0.8% for ages 65–74, and 0% for ages 75–85 (Waite et al., 2009, p. i58). For men, the rates were 3.4% for ages 57–64, 3.0% for ages 65–74, and 1.6% for ages 75–85 (Waite et al., 2009, p. i58). The significant disparity between men and women on this measure may be explained by the increasing sex-ratio imbalance as the population ages.

A frequently stated concern about sexually non-exclusive relationships is the increased potential risk for sexually transmitted infections (STIs). Many in the sexually or relationally non-exclusive population explicitly engage in concurrent sexual partnerships and sexual partnership concurrency is implicated as a risk factor for increased transmission of HIV (Eaton, Hallett, and Garnett, 2011). There is a legitimate concern about sexual health risks among the RNE group. In addition, it is well-documented that the aging population is at increased risk for STIs, including HIV (Bodley-Tickell et al., 2008; DeLamater & Koepsel, 2014; Pearline et al., 2010). According to the U.S. Centers for Disease Control, the estimated rates of persons living with diagnosed HIV infection who were aged 50 years or older increased 6.0%, from 15.0 to 15.9 per 100,000 from 2009 to 2010 (CDC, 2013, p. 18). In recent analyses of data from the 2008 Behavioral Risk Factors Surveillance System, it was found that only 20.0% ($n = 17,262$) of older adults (aged 55–64, $n = 86,194$) had ever been tested for HIV (Du, Camacho, Zurlo, & Lengerich, 2011). Among the 3.6% ($n = 6759$) of adults in the total sample (aged 18–64, $N = 281,826$) who identified as having been in any high-risk situations for HIV, 66.3% ($n = 4286$) had received at least one HIV test in their lifetime (Du et al., 2011). Clearly, routine STI testing is an important recommendation for sexually active adults, including older adults, and especially those who engage in behaviors that may place their sexual health at risk. Yet, Conley, Moors, Ziegler, and Karathanasis (2012) found significantly less overall and less consistent condom use, less frequent STI testing, and less frequent discussions about sexual health with partners among a comparison group of sexually unfaithful individuals than among an openly non-exclusive population being studied. This suggests a greater awareness of and commitment to safe sexual health practices in the latter group.

Theoretical orientation

Tornstam (2005) proposes a final stage in human psychological development called "gerotranscendence," adding to Erikson's (1950) stages of psychosocial development and similar to Kohlberg's (1981a; 1981b) sixth stage of moral development (universal principles). Gerotranscendence refers to a state of development where individuals transcend rigid sociocultural perspectives about the self, others, material things, and fundamental existential questions. Experiencing gerotranscendence results in a meta-perspective that is reflective, cosmic, transcendent, and typically, more personally satisfying (Tornstam, 2005). Gerotranscendence provides a theoretical and ethical framework for predicting adults' openness to the possibility of sexual non-exclusivity and greater satisfaction from sexuality, even as they age. Sexual and erotic gerotranscendence is not about a last mad dash to add notches on the bedpost, nor attempts to slake long-suppressed sexual lusts. It is a quest for optimal, transcendent sexuality.

Seeking to understand what things contribute to optimal sexual experience, Kleinplatz, Ménard, Paradis, et al. (2009) interviewed 20 sex therapists and 44 adults who reported having sustained "great sex" over the course of long-term relationships. Of the 44 adults who reported having "great sex," 25 were aged 60–82. Optimal sexual experience was described by the participants as consisting of authenticity, intense emotional connection, being present, deep sexual and erotic intimacy, extraordinary communication, vulnerability, interpersonal risk-taking and exploration, and transcendence (Kleinplatz,

Ménard, Paquet, et al., 2009). Kleinplatz, Ménard, Paquet, et al.'s (2009) (Kleinplatz, Ménard, Paradis, et al., 2009; Ménard et al., 2014) optimal sexual experience is very similar to what Schnarch (1991, 1997) has termed "wall-socket sex," a phenomenon experienced by couples during profoundly intense, fully-present, differentiation-enabled intimacy and erotic interaction that taps into a never-before-experienced erotic energy (pp. 462–466). Schnarch (2002) argues that resurrecting sexual desire and sexual frequency requires the optimization of individual physical health, physical stimulation, and the psychodynamics of sexual relating, including feelings, thoughts, and emotions experienced internally and in the relationship (pp. 79–97). Optimal sexual experience is also similar to Maslow's (1971) "peak experience" where sexual interaction unifies and becomes a mystical, "gates of heaven" experience.

A surprising finding among the older adults in long-term relationships from Kleinplatz, Ménard, Paradis, et al.'s (2009) study was that over half (13/25) reported being consensually non-monogamous, and some reported that the onset of their optimal sexual experiences emerged with the opening of their relationships. From a study conducted by Mazur (1973) of couples who were in open relationships in the 1960s and 1970s, one woman described that opening her marriage created a "continual excitement about our marital relationship and mutual growth," the antidote for emotional death, and a path to freedom from the "obscenity of possessiveness" (p. 10). Firestone, Firestone, & Catlett (2006) indicate that for some well-differentiated and emotionally-mature adults whose views of conventional marital arrangements have concomitantly matured, emotional and sexual relationships outside of the marriage can be healthy, loving, and growth-enabling for each partner, as well as relationship-revitalizing (pp. 220–222).

Consensual sexual non-exclusivity makes risk-taking more palatable when held in tension with the security of a long-term relationship where "negotiated safety" regarding sexual and psychological health can occur (Morin 1999; Nichols & Shernoff, 2007). Interpersonal negotiations regarding sexual health safety in the context of non-exclusivity, especially with the jealousy these discussions may invoke, require unusually effective communication skills. Extraordinary communication is widely considered the *sine qua non* of successful non-exclusive relationships (Anapol, 1997; Barker & Langdridge, 2010a; Bauer, 2010; Easton & Liszt, 1997; Sheff, 2014; Taormino, 2008). Extraordinary communication along with differentiation-enabled intimacy is a critical component of heightened sexual desire and pleasure (Schnarch, 1991).

Kleinplatz, Ménard, Paradis, et al. (2009) and Ménard et al. (2014) also found that for some of these older adults, time devoted to sexual intimacy, although not frequency, increased along with its quality even as they aged. This is consistent with Firestone et al. (2006) as well as Schnarch (1991, 1997, p. 78) who recognize that human sexual potential is rarely fully realized until middle age and beyond, as cellulite and grey hairs begin to emerge. Even with chronological maturity, the zenith of human sexual potential is likely realized by a small percentage of older adults. The implication of Kleinplatz, Ménard, Paradis, et al.'s (2009) findings concerning aging and open relationships suggests that these interrelated sexual experiences are far more than merely the sum of more partners, sexual conquests, or greater satiation. Each partner brings more of himself or herself into each interaction and their interaction forms a synergistic dynamic greater than the sum of its parts. Maslow (1971), Schnarch (1991, 1997), Firestone et al. (2006), Kleinplatz, Ménard, Paquet, et al. (2009), and Kleinplatz, Ménard, Paradis, et al. (2009) describe what can be characterized as a psychosexual dimension of gerotranscendence.

Drawing from the qualitative findings of these eminent psychologists, researchers, and theorists, we predicted that the adults from our subsample of adults 55 years and older would experience more frequent sex, with more sexual partners, and that these interactions would affect their general happiness and health in positive ways, at least enough to offset the stigma and shame associated with behaving counter to prevailing sociosexual norms (Goffman, 1963). These include non-hetero, non-monogamous counter-normative sexual relationships as well as simply being single, divorced, or never married (Barker & Langdridge, 2010b; Bauer, 2010; Sheff, 2010). Hence, we explored three main hypotheses: the non-exclusive sample would have a larger number of partners and a greater sexual frequency than the GSS sample; the non-exclusive sample as a whole would have self-reported health and happiness at least equal to the GSS sample; and the divorced, widowed, never-married, and separated among the non-exclusive sample would have self-reported health and happiness at least equal to the GSS sample.

Methods

Participants and recruitment

As part of a larger study examining attitudes, beliefs, and circumstances of individuals who self-identify as sexually or relationally non-exclusive, 4062 responses were collected via an Internet-based survey in February and March 2012. In order to compare our findings with those of the general US adult population, our survey questions mirrored those asked in the National Opinion Research Center's nationally representative, biennial GSS (Smith et al., 2013). The GSS is a full-probability survey conducted face-to-face with a representative sample of participants living in the United States. Participants in our study were recruited through various e-mail lists maintained by the Loving More non-profit organization. By means of a request to the list moderators, various local and regional list-serves of communities of "individuals who engage in consensual, nonexclusive intimate relationships, or who are philosophically open to doing so, regardless of their current relationship configuration" (Fleckenstein, 2012). As is common among researchers seeking access to hidden populations, in order to maximize exposure and possible participation, information about the survey and a request to forward a link to the survey webpage were sent to "gatekeepers" of several communication lists serving those who provide counseling to, conduct research among, advocate on behalf of, or those who may practice some form of relationship non-exclusivity. These included the American Association of Sexuality Educators, Counselors and Therapists' (AASECT) AltSex list (154 members); the PolyResearchers list (485 members); the National Coalition for Sexual Freedom's coalition partners list (representatives of the membership organizations that comprise NCSF) (50 members); and the Institute for Advanced Study of Human Sexuality's (IASHS) students and alumni list (139 members). We hoped that these gatekeepers would use their own networks and channels of communication to raise awareness of the survey among possible study subjects. This effort to leverage these individuals' access to the study population was successful, resulting in nearly 2000 additional responses. This large number reassured us that the increase in response was not solely due to the members of the gatekeeper lists responding themselves, though some percentage of them would likely qualify for inclusion. However, it is implausible that even a plurality of the members of these lists would meet the inclusion criteria, especially with respect to age. Nonetheless, we do wish to mention that professionals involved in sex education, counseling, therapy, and/or research are likely over-represented in our sample (RNE) compared to the sample from the general population (GSS).

While the General Social Survey (GSS) is comprised of statistically randomized samples of the general population, the RNE survey population is comprised of self-selected participants.This inherently biased sample is unavoidable as participants are part of a largely hidden segment of the general population. Such individuals are often closeted to avoid social stigma, hostile scrutiny from child protective services and other state authorities, and risks of socioeconomic harm due to employer discrimination and job loss (Barker & Langdridge, 2010b). Nevertheless, self-selection biases can affect the usefulness of surveys for analyses based upon the motivations of those who choose to participate, in ways that are difficult to ascertain (Ziliak & McCloskey, 2008). Properties of the data-set used for analyses conducted and described herein were reviewed by the University of Oklahoma Institutional Review Board and exempted from review of human subjects research, as the survey and derived data collected no identifiable information.

Of the more than 4000 respondents, 502 were 55 years of age or older and living within the United States. Based on our literature review, there was no clear consensus among researchers as to the onset of becoming part of the "aging adult population." We found that other research chose ages 50, 55, 57, 60, and 65 for lowest level inclusion. We selected 55 as our cut-off as it was consistent with prior research while retaining a large enough sample for comparison and statistical analyses. Data on these respondents' reported sex, educational attainment, age, marital status, marital happiness, health, happiness, and number of sexual partners and sexual frequency in the last 12 months were obtained. Due to our mirroring of the GSS question set, we cannot state whether those respondents who characterized themselves as "married" and who reported on their "martial" status were in same-sex or opposite-sex marriages. At the time of the survey (February–March 2012), only seven US states and the District of Columbia recognized same-sex marriages, with Washington State passing a law to recognize same-sex marriages during the course of the survey. Income was extracted by converting data from zip code median income in the RNE sample. Survey respondents' results were compared, using independent t-tests of the means, to 723 respondents, age 55 and over, from the 2012 GSS. Because of the self-selection bias of our RNE sample, we chose two-tailed tests of significance with an alpha (α) of .01 for this discussion. We also performed multivariable regression analyses of both populations for dependent variables of health and happiness with independent variables of frequency of sex, gender, marriage, age, number of partners, income, and either happiness or health (when happiness was the dependent variable, health was an independent variable and vice versa). In order to examine the factors that would increase or decrease the odds of ever having an HIV test, we performed binary logistic regressions with multiple variables.

The GSS did not ask a question about sexual orientation directly. However, the GSS did ask about the sex of the respondents' sexual partners in the past year. Unfortunately, we were not able to conduct analyses based upon this variable of behavioral sexual orientation, as the number of non-heterosexual respondents 55 years and over in the general population was too small for meaningful statistical analyses.

Table 1 describes the sociodemographic characteristics of the RNE and GSS population samples. Participants in the RNE sample had an average (mean) age of 62.36 (SD = 6.50, range = 55–92), which was significantly younger than the GSS sample that had an average age of 67.82 (SD = 9.67, range = 55–99). The majority of respondents in the RNE survey identified as male (65.9%, $n = 331$), 32.7% ($n = 164$) identified as female, and 1.4% ($n = 7$) identified outside of the gender binary. In the GSS sample, the majority of respondents identified as female (55%, $n = 398$) and 45% ($n = 325$) identified as male; there was not an option in the GSS survey to identify as other than male or female.

In the RNE sample, 46.0% ($n = 231$) of the respondents were currently married, 31.9% ($n = 160$) were divorced, and 22.1% ($n = 111$) were widowed (6.6%, $n = 33$),

Table 1. Description of the sociodemographic characteristics of the RNE and GSS groups.

Respondents (age 55 and older)	2012 RNE survey	2012 General Social Survey
Females n (%)	164 (33.1)	398 (55.0)
Males n (%)	331 (66.9)	325 (45.0)
Age, mean (SD)	62.36 (6.50)	67.82 (9.67)[***]
Married n (%)	231 (46.0)	341 (47.2)
Divorced n (%)	160 (3.9)	151 (20.9)
Widowed n (%)	33 (6.6)	150 (20.7)
Separated n (%)	40 (8.0)	24 (3.3)
Never married n (%)	38 (7.6)	57 (7.9)
Education, mean (SD)[a]	2.99 (1.023)[***]	1.57 (1.262)
Females BSO[b]		
Straight n (%)	101 (64.7)	150 (99.3)
Bisexual n (%)	51 (32.7)	0 (0.0)
Lesbian n (%)	4 (2.6)	1 (0.7)
Males BSO[b]		
Straight n (%)	256 (80.8)	165 (96.5)
Bisexual n (%)	52 (16.4)	3 (1.75)
Gay n (%)	9 (2.8)	3 (1.75)

Notes: Significant at $p \leq .10^{\dagger}$, $p \leq .05^{*}$, $p \leq .01^{**}$, $p < .0005^{***}$.
[a]0 = no degree, 1 = high-school diploma or GED, 2 = junior college or associate's degree, 3 = bachelor's degree, and 4 = graduate degree.
[b]BSO = behavioral sexual orientation – reflects the gender of the respondents' sex partner(s) during the previous 12 months.

separated (8.0%, $n = 40$), or never married (7.6%, $n = 38$). Currently married respondents comprised 47.2% ($n = 341$) of the GSS sample, 20.9% ($n = 151$) of the GSS respondents were divorced, and 32.0% were widowed (20.7%, $n = 150$), separated (3.3%, $n = 24$), or had never married (7.9%, $n = 57$). RNE respondents had completed significantly more education ($n = 502$, $M_{education} = 2.99$, SD = 1.02, range = 0–4), than the GSS respondents ($n = 723$, $M_{education} = 1.57$, SD = 1.26, range = 0–4), where 0 = no degree, 1 = high school diploma or GED, 2 = junior college or associate's degree, 3 = bachelor's degree, and 4 = graduate degree.

Measures

Sexual partners

Participants in the GSS and RNE surveys were asked: "How many sex partners have you had in the last 12 months?" Responses were coded as, "no partner" = 0, "1 partner" = 1, "2 partners" = 2, "3 partners" = 3, "4 partners" = 4, "5–10 partners" = 7, "11–20 partners" = 13.5, "21–100 partners" = 27, and "more than 100 partners" = 101.

Sexual frequency

In answer to the question on both surveys, "About how often did you have sex [as self-defined by the respondent] during the last 12 months?" Responses were coded as,

0 = "not at all," 1 = "once or twice," 2 = "once per month," 3 = "2−3 times per month," 4 = "weekly, 5 = "2−3 times per week," 6 = "four or more times per week." In both the GSS and the RNE surveys, respondents were left to determine what "having sex" meant for themselves.

Happiness

In order to assess general happiness, respondents in both surveys were asked: "Taken all together, how would you say things are these days? Would you say that you are very happy = 4, pretty happy = 3, not sure/don't know = 2, or not too happy = 1?" Responses were coded as indicated. Self-reported happiness is a valid and accepted measure for capturing "...a broader array of psychological well-being than merely happiness per se" (Karraker et al., 2011, p. 506).

Health

To assess general health, participants were asked: "Would you say your own health, in general, is excellent = 4, good = 3, fair = 2, or poor = 1?" Again, responses were coded as indicated. This question has been demonstrated to be a valid and robust indicator of respondents' true state of health (Benyamini, 2011).

Happiness in marriage

In order to assess married respondents' happiness with their marriages, they were asked: "Taking all things together, how would you describe your marriage—very happy, pretty happy, or not too happy?" Responses were coded as follows: not too happy = 1; pretty happy = 2; and very happy = 3. Please note that this is a different scale than the one used to assess general happiness.

Sexual health

In order to assess the rigor with which the RNE sample monitors their sexual health, participants were asked to report on whether or not they had ever been tested for human immunodeficiency virus (HIV). "Have you ever been tested for HIV? Do not count tests you may have had as part of a blood donation. Include oral tests (where they take a swab from your mouth)." Responses were coded as 1 = "yes," 0 = "no," and "not sure" was coded as system missing. Because the GSS only asked about HIV testing in its core question set, we were compelled to follow despite the limitation this imposed. We felt that this would at least offer a useful initial benchmark. Due to this limitation, no other questions were asked of the survey respondents regarding sexual health and testing.

Results

As previously discussed, the GSS sample used for comparative analyses in our research is from a nationally representative, in-person survey conducted in the United States on a regular basis (currently biennial). We used data from their 2012 survey. The RNE sample, also conducted in 2012, is based upon a self-selecting, online sample of a hidden population, that is, those who engage in consensual, non-exclusive intimate relationships, or are open to this as a possibility. Due to the self-selection bias of the RNE sample, the findings may have reduced generalizability. For this reason, we use a higher bar (alpha $(\alpha) = 0.01$) for reporting findings in the Results and Discussion sections below.

Number of sexual partners

The sexually or relationally non-exclusive sample reported statistically significantly more sexual partners in the past 12 months ($n = 499$, $M_{partners} = 3.24$, SD = 3.586) than the GSS sample ($n = 571$, $M_{partners} = 0.61$, SD = 0.648; $t = 16.145$, $p < .000$) (see Table 2). RNE women averaged 3.08 ($n = 163$, SD = 3.336) sexual partners over the previous year versus less than one sexual partner ($n = 312$, $M_{partners} = 0.49$, SD = 0.520) among GSS women, a statistically significant difference ($t = 9.861$, $p < .000$). RNE men averaged 3.37 ($n = 329$, $SD = 3.728$) sexual partners over the previous year versus less than one sexual partner among GSS men ($n = 259$, $M_{partners} = 0.77$, SD = 0.747), a statistically significant difference ($t = 12.329$, $p < .000$). Both married and unmarried individuals in the RNE sample reported having more sexual partners than did corresponding groups in the general population. Married RNE respondents indicated having 3.22 sexual partners on average ($n = 230$, SD = 3.684) versus 0.86 among the GSS sample ($n = 274$, SD = 0.422), also statistically significant ($t = 9.674$, $p < .000$). Unmarried RNE respondents indicated having 3.26 sexual partners on average ($n = 269$, SD = 3.508) versus 0.39 among the GSS sample ($n = 297$, SD = 0.732). Likewise, this difference is statistically

Table 2. Self-reported number of sex partners and frequency of sex (previous year).

Respondents	RNE 2012: mean (SD) n	GSS 2012: mean (SD) n	t (p)
Number of sex partners			
All	3.24 (3.586) 499[***]	0.61 (0.648) 571	16.145 (.000)
Males	3.37 (3.728) 329[***]	0.77 (0.747) 259	12.329 (.000)
Females	3.08 (3.336) 163[***]	0.49 (0.520) 312	9.861 (.000)
Married	3.22 (3.684) 230[***]	0.86 (0.422) 274	9.674 (.000)
Unmarried	3.26 (3.508) 269[***]	0.39 (0.732) 297	13.176 (.000)
Divorced	3.22 (1.653) 159[***]	0.56 (0.861) 127	9.736 (.000)
Widowed	3.14 (3.101) 31[***]	0.15 (0.406) 108	5.522 (.000)
Separated	2.99 (2.861) 40[***]	0.59 (1.064) 17	4.607 (.000)
Never married	3.84 (5.068) 37[***]	0.40 (0.654) 45	4.099 (.000)
Frequency of sex[a]			
All	3.69 (1.608) 478[***]	2.43 (1.411) 283	10.883 (.000)[†]
Males	3.67 (1.629) 317[***]	2.57 (1.318) 150	7.780 (.000)
Females	3.74 (1.574) 156[***]	2.28 (1.499) 133	8.026 (.000)[†]
Married	3.60 (1.529) 227[***]	2.27 (1.410) 200	9.295 (.000)[†]
Unmarried	3.76 (1.675) 251[***]	2.82 (1.345) 83	5.209 (.000)
Divorced	3.96 (1.653) 151[***]	2.90 (1.344) 50	4.107 (.000)[†]
Widowed	3.61 1.764) 31	3.23 (1.301) 13	.703 (.486)[†]
Separated	3.43 (1.632) 35	2.40 (1.342) 5	1.341 (.188)[†]
Never married	3.38 (1.670) 34[*]	2.33 (1.345) 15	2.142 (.037)[†]

Notes: Significant at $p \leq .10$[†], $p \leq .05$[*], $p \leq .01$[**], $p < .0005$[***].
[†]Levene's test for equal variances assumed; all others, equal variances not assumed.
[a]Sex frequency scale: 0 = not at all, 1 = once or twice, 2 = once per month, 3 = two to three times per month, 4 = weekly, 5 = two to three times per week, 6 = more than four times per week.

Table 3. Self-reported happiness, health, and happiness in marriage.

Respondents	RNE 2012: mean (SD) n	GSS 2012: mean (SD) n	$t\,(p)$
Happiness[a]			
All	3.23 (0.819) 502***	2.98 (0.963) 722	4.713 (.000)[†]
Males	3.18 (0.854) 331*	3.01 (0.939) 324	2.411 (.016)
Females	3.37 (0.727) 164***	2.96 (0.938) 398	4.720 (.000)
Married	3.34 (0.785) 231	3.23 (0.823) 341	1.583 (.114)[†]
Males	3.29 (0.753) 167	3.24 (0.802) 176	0.513 (.609)[†]
Females	3.48 (0.859) 63*	3.21 (0.847) 165	2.098 (.037)[†]
Unmarried	3.14 (0.838) 271***	2.77 (1.027) 381	5.160 (.000)
Males	3.07 (0.934) 164**	2.73 (1.014) 148	3.045 (.003)
Females	3.30 (0.625) 101***	2.79 (1.035) 233	5.512 (.000)
Divorced	3.16 (0.816) 160**	2.85 (0.983) 151	3.017 (.003)[†]
Widowed	3.21 0.857) 33*	2.83 (0.996) 149	2.030 (.044)[†]
Separated	2.95 (0.932) 40**	2.13 (1.227) 24	2.839 (.007)
Never married	3.21 (0.811) 38**	2.63 (1.046) 57	3.031 (.003)
Health[b]			
All	3.14 (0.734) 502***	2.74 (0.913) 474	7.417 (.000)
Males	3.15 (0.748) 331***	2.78 (0.965) 207	4.750 (.000)
Females	3.14 (0.708) 164***	2.72 (0.871) 267	5.482 (.000)
Married	3.13 (0.780) 231***	2.83 (0.914) 223	3.758 (.000)
Males	3.11 (0.784) 167*	2.84 (0.950) 113	2.472 (.014)
Females	3.19 (0.780) 63**	2.82 (0.880) 110	2.789 (.006)
Unmarried	3.15 (0.694) 271***	2.67 (0.907) 251	6.728 (.000)
Males	3.20 (0.708)164***	2.70 (0.982) 94	4.272 (.000)
Females	3.11 (0.662) 101***	2.65 (0.861) 157	4.824 (.000)
Divorced	3.12 (0.730) 160***	2.74 (0.983) 102	3.580 (.000)
Widowed	3.21 (0.600) 33***	2.56 (0.890) 93	4.685 (.000)
Separated	3.10 (0.591) 40**	2.26 (0.991) 19	3.404 (.002)
Never married	3.26 (0.724) 38	2.97 (0.799) 37	1.650 (.103)[†]
Happiness in marriage[c]			
All	2.52 (0.638) 231	2.59 (0.538) 340	−1.460 (.145)
Males	2.50 (0.620) 167	2.66 (0.476) 175*	−2.571 (.011)
Females	2.56 (0.690) 63	2.53 (0.590) 165	.308 (.758)

Notes: Significant at $p \leq .10^{\dagger}, p \leq .05^{*}, p \leq .01^{**}, p < .0005^{***}$.
[†]Levene's test for equal variances assumed; all others, equal variances not assumed.
[a]Happiness scale: 1 = not too happy, 2 = not sure, 3 = pretty happy, 4 = very happy.
[b]Health scale: 1 = poor, 2 = fair, 3 = good,4 = excellent.
[c]Happiness in marriage scale: 1 = not too happy, 2 = pretty happy, 3 = very happy.

significant ($t = 13.176, p < .000$). Table 3 describes the specific breakdown of the unmarried sample, with divorced ($n = 159$, $M_{partners} = 3.22$, SD $= 1.653$) and never-married ($n = 37$, $M_{partners} = 3.84$, SD $= 5.068$) persons reporting significantly more sexual partners than these groups in the general population ($n = 127$, $M_{partners} = 0.56$, SD $= 0.861$, $t = 9.736, p < .000$; $n = 45$, $M_{partners} = 0.40$, SD $= 0.654$, $t = 4.099, p < .000$, respectively). Likewise, widowed and separated persons reported similar trends between the RNE and GSS samples. RNE widowed persons reported having 3.14 ($n = 31$, SD = 3.101) partners on average, which was significantly more partners than GSS widowed persons reported ($n = 108$, $M_{partners} = 0.15$, SD = 0.406, $t = 5.522$, $p < .000$). RNE respondents who identified as being legally separated from their spouse indicated having significantly more sex partners ($n = 40$, $M_{partners} = 2.99$, SD = 2.861) than those in the GSS ($n = 17$, $M_{partners} = 0.59$, SD = 1.064; $t = 4.607$, $p < .000$).

Sexual frequency

In response to the question, "About how often did you have sex [as self-defined by the respondent] during the last 12 months?", the RNE sample reported significantly more sexual frequency (self-defined by survey respondents) than the GSS group (Table 2). The non-exclusive (RNE) population had a mean sexual frequency of almost weekly for men and women, which is significantly higher than that of the GSS population. GSS women averaged once or twice per month and GSS men, two to three times per month (RNE men: $n = 317$, $M_{sexfreq} = 3.67$, SD = 1.629; GSS men: $n = 150$, $M_{sexfreq} = 2.57$, SD = 1.318, $t = 7.780$, $p < .000$; RNE women: $n = 156$, $M_{sexfreq} = 3.74$, SD = 1.574; GSS women: $n = 133$, $M_{sexfreq} = 2.38$, SD = 1.499, $t = 8.026$, $p < .000$). Both married and unmarried individuals in the RNE sample reported having more frequent sex than did corresponding groups in the general population. Married RNE respondents indicated having sex nearly weekly ($n = 227$, $M_{sexfreq} = 3.60$, SD = 1.529) versus about once or twice per month among the GSS sample ($n = 200$, $M_{sexfreq} = 2.27$, SD = 1.410). Table 2 describes the specific breakdown of the unmarried sample, with divorced ($n = 151$, $M_{sexfreq} = 3.96$, SD = 1.653) RNE persons reporting significantly more sex than divorced individuals in the general population ($n = 50$, $M_{sexfreq} = 2.90$, SD = 1.344, $t = 4.107$, $p < .000$). Never-married RNE persons ($n = 34$, $M_{sexfreq} = 3.38$, SD = 1.670) approached significance of having more sex than the general population ($n = 15$, $M_{sexfreq} = 2.33$, SD = 1.345), but the results did not obtain our cutoff of $\alpha = .01$ ($t = 2.142$, $p = .037$). As with the never-married samples, widowed, and separated persons reported similar trends between the RNE and GSS samples, but the sample sizes for these groups were too small to indicate statistical significance.

Happiness

Consistent with previous research on the positive effects of increased sexual frequency, the RNE sample also reported significantly greater personal happiness ($n = 502$, M_{happy} = 3.23, SD = 0.819) than the GSS sample ($n = 722$, $M_{happy} = 2.98$, SD = 0.963, $t = 4.713$, $p < .000$). This held true for women (RNE: $n = 164$, $M_{happy} = 3.37$, SD = 0.727; GSS: $n = 398$, $M_{happy} = 2.96$, SD = 0.938; $t = 4.720$, $p < .000$), unmarried women (RNE: $n = 101$, $M_{happy} = 3.30$, SD = 0.625; GSS: $n = 233$, $M_{happy} = 2.79$, SD = 1.035; $t = 5.512$, $p < .000$), and approached significance for men (RNE: $n = 331$, $M_{happy} = 3.18$, SD = 0.854; GSS: $n = 324$, $M_{happy} = 3.01$, SD = 0.939; $t = 2.411$, $p = .016$), married women (RNE: $n = 63$, $M_{happy} = 3.48$, $SD = 0.859$; GSS: $n = 165$, $M_{happy} = 3.21$, SD = 0.847; $t = 2.098$, $p = .037$), and all other subgroups of unmarried (see Table 3 for details). In contrast to the other groups, married men among the RNE sample were no happier than men in the GSS sample (RNE: $n = 167$, $M_{happy} = 3.29$, SD = 0.753; GSS: $n = 176$, $M_{happy} = 3.24$, SD = 0.802; $t = 0.513$, $p = .609$).

Health

As detailed in Table 3, the RNE sample reported significantly better health than the GSS sample across all groups and subgroups, with the exception of those reporting as never married. The RNE sample reported being significantly healthier than the GSS sample (RNE: $n = 502$, $M_{health} = 3.14$, SD $= 0.734$; GSS: $n = 474$, $M_{health} = 2.74$, SD $= 0.913$; $t = 7.417$, $p < .000$). This was true for males (RNE: $n = 331$, $M_{health} = 3.15$, SD $= 0.748$; GSS: $n = 207$, $M_{health} = 2.78$, SD $= 0.965$; $t = 4.750$, $p < .000$), females (RNE: $n = 164$, $M_{health} = 3.14$, SD $= 0.708$; GSS: $n = 267$, $M_{health} = 2.72$, SD $= 0.871$; $t = 5.482$, $p < .000$), and all but one subgroup of unmarried, the never married. Married males (RNE: $n = 167$, $M_{health} = 3.11$, SD $= 0.784$; GSS: $n = 113$, $M_{health} = 2.84$, SD $= 0.950$; $t = 2.472$, $p = .014$) and married females (RNE: $n = 63$, $M_{health} = 3.19$, SD $= 0.780$; GSS: $n = 110$, $M_{health} = 2.82$, SD $= 0.880$; $t = 2.789$, $p = .006$) approached significantly better reported health. The never married (RNE, $n = 38$; GSS, $n = 37$) trended towards significant differences, but the sample size was small (see Table 3 for details).

Happiness in marriage

Married men in the RNE sample reported being less happy with their marriages than married men in the general GSS population, but these differences were just short of the cutoff point for significance (RNE: $n = 167$, $M_{hapmar} = 2.50$, SD $= 0.620$; GSS: $n = 175$, $M_{hapmar} = 2.66$, SD $= 0.476$; $t = -2.571$, $p = .011$). Participants in the RNE sample were asked: "If it were legal, would you be open to being legally married to more than one person concurrently?" The majority of men (69.2%, $n = 229$) and women (66.5, $n = 109$) responded "yes," while 30.8% of men ($n = 102$) and 33.5% of women ($n = 55$) responded "no" or "not sure" to this question. When married men in the RNE sample who did not desire to marry multiple partners was controlled for, then the differences were erased (RNE: $n = 24$, $M_{hapmar} = 2.67$, SD $= 0.482$; GSS: $n = 175$, $M_{hapmar} = 2.66$, SD $= 0.476$; $t = 0.091$, $p = .928$). It appears that men in the RNE sample who want to be married concurrently to more than one partner, but are unable to do so, are less happy with their marriage, or perhaps, are less happy with marriage in general (RNE: $n = 134$, $M_{hapmar} = 2.49$, SD $= 0.634$; GSS: $n = 175$, $M_{hapmar} = 2.66$, SD $= 0.476$; $t = -2.626$, $p = .009$). There were no significant differences in marital happiness among women regarding their perspective on legal marriage to multiple concurrent partners.

As can be seen in Table 3, there was no difference in reported marital happiness among the total groups (RNE: $n = 231$, $M_{hapmar} = 2.52$, SD $= 0.638$; GSS: $n = 340$, $M_{hapmar} = 2.59$, SD $= 0.538$; $t = -1.460$, $p = .145$) or between RNE women and GSS women (RNE: $n = 63$, $M_{hapmar} = 2.56$, SD $= 0.690$; GSS: $n = 165$, $M_{hapmar} = 2.53$, SD $= 0.590$; $t = 0.308$, $p = .758$).

Sexual health HIV testing

The RNE sample reported being significantly more likely to have ever had an HIV test than the GSS sample across all groups analyzed. RNE respondents (77.9%) were over three times as likely to have ever had an HIV test as the GSS respondents (25.0%, Pearson $X^2 = 295.104$, df $= 1$, $p < .000$). Table 4a reports on the findings across the groups using a mean score. Married women in the RNE sample were just as likely (80.7%) to have had an HIV test as were unmarried females (81.0%, $X^2 = .003$, $p = .955$), while married

Table 4a. Self-reported sexual health monitoring (ever had an HIV test).

Respondents	RNE 2012: mean (SD) n	GSS 2012: mean (SD) n	$t\,(p)$
Sexual health[a]			
All	.779 (0.415) 493***	.250 (0.433) 565	20.269 (.000)
Males	.765 (0.424) 324***	.280 (0.450) 257	13.239 (.000)
Females	.809 (0.395) 162***	.224 (0.418) 308	14.700 (.000)[†]
Married	.727 (0.447) 227***	.202 (0.402) 272	13.667 (.000)
Males	.701 (0.459) 164***	.206 (0.406) 141	10.007 (.000)
Females	.807 (0.398) 62***	.195 (0.400) 131	9.867 (.000)[†]
Unmarried	.823 (0.382) 266***	.294 (0.456) 293	14.931 (.000)
Males	.831 (0.376) 160***	.371 (0.485) 116	8.537 (.000)
Females	.810 (0.394) 100***	.243 (0.430) 157	11.122 (.000)
Divorced	.835 (0.372) 158***	.349 (0.479) 126	9.368 (.000)
Widowed	.781 (0.420) 32***	.178 (0.384) 107	7.636 (.000)[†]
Separated	.775 (0.423) 40**	.353 (0.493) 17	3.281 (.002)
Never married	.861 (0.351) 36***	.395 (0.495) 43	4.880 (.000)

Notes: Significant at $p \leq .10^{†}, p \leq .05^{*}, p \leq .01^{**}, p < .0005^{***}$.
[†]Levene's test for equal variances assumed; all others, equal variances not assumed.
[a]Sexual health/HIV test scale: 0 = no, 1 = yes.

women in the GSS were significantly less likely (19.5%) than were unmarried women in the GSS sample (24.3%, $X^2 = 8.593, p = .003$) to have had an HIV test.

Regression analyses

Regression analyses uncovered differences in the factors predicting health and happiness between those who engage in non-exclusive relationships and the general population. Table 5 describes the predictive relationships between sex, age, sex frequency, number of partners, presence of minors in the home, marriage, income, and either health or happiness with the dependent variables of happiness or health among older adults from the RNE and GSS samples. Sexual frequency is significantly correlated with both health and happiness among the RNE sample. In the GSS sample, only income and general happiness were significant predictors of health, and health was the only significant predictor of happiness for the GSS sample. In addition, they highlight the differences of predictors for these dependent variables, suggesting different life goals and orientations between the RNE and GSS samples. Multiple regression analyses were performed, as given in Table 5.

Table 5 compares the standardized regression coefficients (β), the mean standard errors (SE), and t statistics, as well as the R^2 and F statistics for the whole models between the RNE and GSS samples with happiness, and then with health, as the dependent variable. For the RNE sample, being female ($\beta = .152$, SE $= .078, t = 3.218, p = .001$), having more frequent sexual interaction (where "sex frequency" was self-defined by the respondents in both surveys) ($\beta = .217$, SE $= .025, t = 4.344, p < .000$), being married ($\beta = .142$, SE $= .074, t = 3.029, p = .003$), and reporting better health ($\beta = .184$, SE $= .051, t = 3.843, p < .000$) all significantly predicted greater happiness. Being older approached significance as a predictor for greater happiness ($\beta = .110$, SE $= .006, t = 2.324, p = .021$), and having minor children present in the home trended towards having a significant negative effect ($\beta = -.086$, SE $= .116, t = -1.832, p = -.068$) in this

Table 4b. Binary regression odds ratios for ever having an HIV test.

Nagelkerke $R^2(-2LL$, df$) X^2$	.124 (360.353, 8) 32.362***	.211 (193.382, 8) 29.065***
Predictors	RNE: B (SE) Wald (OR)	GSS: B (SE) Wald (OR)
Gender	.066 (.292) .052 (1.069)	−.470 (.365) 1.663 (.625)
Age	−.030 (.020) 2.290 (.970)	−.008 (.024) 0.116 (.992)
Sex frequency	.232 (.089) 6.731 (1.261)**	.136 (.137) 0.992 (1.146)
Number of partners	.118 (.063) 3.454 (1.125)‡	.744 (.436) 2.906 (2.104)‡
Education	.143 (.133) 1.154 (1.154)	.101 (.167) 0.368 (1.107)
Married	−.631 (.275) 5.274 (.532)*	−.962 (.419) 5.268 (.382)*
Income	.000 (.000) 2.355 (1.000)	.000 (.000) 1.198 (1.000)
Health	.034 (.184) 0.035 (1.035)	−.450 (.216) 0.493 (.638)*

Notes: Significant at $p \leq .10^\ddagger, p \leq .05^*, p \leq .01^{**}, p < .0005^{***}$.

model ($F(8,399) = 9.273, p < .000, R^2 = .14$). For the GSS sample of older adults, only reporting better personal health was a significant predictor of happiness ($\beta = .223$, SE = .073, $t = 2.857, p = .005$) in this model ($F(8,173) = 2.216, p = .028, R^2 = .093$).

With health as the dependent variable, more frequent sexual activity ($\beta = .170$, SE = .024, $t = 3.302, p = .001$) and greater personal happiness ($\beta = .194$, SE = .047, $t = 3.843, p < .000$) significantly predicted better health in the RNE sample in this model ($F(8,399) = 6.449, p < .000, R^2 = .115$). Concerning personal health among the GSS sample, income ($\beta = .334$, SE = .000, $t = 4.418, p < .000$) and general happiness ($\beta = .202$, SE = .076, $t = 2.857, p = .005$) were the only statistically significant predictors in this model ($F(8,173) = 4.716, p < .000, R^2 = .179$).

When we examined the odds ratios (OR) for ever having had an HIV test using binary logistic regression (Table 4b), we found that only frequency of sex was a significant factor in increasing the odds and only among the RNE sample ($\beta = .118$, SE = .089, Wald = 6.731, OR = 1.261, $p = .009$). Being in poor health also approached significance for improving the odds of having had an HIV test among the GSS sample ($n = 723$, $\beta = -.450$, SE = .216, Wald = 0.493, OR = .638, $p = .037$), but not the RNE sample. Being married approached significance of reducing the likelihood of having had an HIV test among both samples (RNE: $n = 495$, $\beta = -.631$, SE = .275, Wald = 5.274, OR = .532, $p = .022$; GSS: $n = 723$, $\beta = -.962$, SE = .419, Wald = 5.268, OR = .382, $p = .022$). Interestingly, income, educational attainment, gender, age, and number of partners did not significantly affect the probability of ever having had an HIV test.

Discussion

Our first hypothesis, which predicted that the RNE sample would have more sexual partners and more sexual frequency as compared to the GSS sample, was supported by our findings. As noted in Table 2, the non-exclusive population had a mean sexual frequency of almost weekly for men and women, which is significantly higher than that of the GSS population, which averaged between two and three times per month.

The second hypothesis, that the sample of non-exclusive respondents would report at least equal levels of self-reported health and personal happiness to those of the GSS population, was also supported strongly. As seen in Table 3, both males and females in the

Table 5. Regression coefficients for happiness and health.

Happiness R^2 (df) F	.140 (8,399) 9.273***	.093 (8,173) 2.216*
Predictors	RNE 2012: β (SE) t	GSS 2012: β (SE) t
Gender	.152 (.078) 3.218*	.086 (.126) 1.138
Age	.110 (.006) 2.324*	−.073 (.008) −0.949
Sex frequency	.217 (.025) 4.344***	−.078 (.046) −1.029
Number of partners	−.004 (.011) −0.090	−.062 (.142) −0.805
Minors present in home	−.086 (.116) −1.832‡	−.084 (.196) −1.140
Married	.142 (.074) 3.029**	.110 (.155) 1.331
Income	.003 (.000) 0.068	−.044 (.000) −0.528
Health	.184 (.051) 3.843***	.223 (.073) 2.857**
Health R^2 (df) F	.115 (8,399) 6.449***	.179 (8,173) 4.716***
Gender	−.018 (.076) −0.370	.068 (.129) .938
Age	.087 (.006) 1.788‡	.132 (.008) 1.822‡
Sex frequency	.170 (.024) 3.302**	.141 (.047) 1.960‡
Number of partners	.063 (.010) 1.271	.088 (.145) 1.202
Minors present in home	−.036 (.112) −0.760	.010 (.202) 0.140
Married	−.054 (.072) −1.104	−.056 (.160) −0.706
Income	.071 (.000) 1.472	.334 (.000) 4.418***
Happiness	.194 (.047) 3.843***	.202 (.076) 2.857**

Note: Significant at $p \leq .10^{‡}$, $p \leq .05^{*}$, $p \leq .01^{**}$, $p < .0005^{***}$.

non-exclusive sample reported greater happiness than their GSS counterparts. The effect was especially dramatic for women. Regression analysis clearly identified sexual frequency as a main contributor to the increased personal happiness of the non-exclusive sample, with marriage and *increasing* age approaching significance as additional contributors (Table 5). Interestingly, number of partners was not a significant contributor in and of itself towards personal happiness. These findings suggest that, in line with previous research, sexual frequency matters a great deal to maintaining higher levels of personal happiness. It is possible, and would be consistent with our theoretical predictions, that the quantitative aspects of sexual frequency are driven, in part, by the qualitative aspects of these sexual experiences. In other words, optimal sexual experiences are worth wanting and having more of. Though the relationship is complex, the causal relationships between sexual frequency and happiness appear to be bidirectional, meaning that more frequent sex leads to more personal happiness, and more personal happiness is conducive to more frequent sex. Other factors, unavailable for our analyses, also contribute to, or take away from, personal happiness and health. The findings for self-reported health were equally robust, with males and females in the non-exclusive sample reporting dramatically better health than the GSS counterparts. Regression analysis showed a clear positive contribution from personal happiness and sexual frequency to positive health outcomes for the non-exclusive sample. Only income showed a strong positive contribution, with a lesser contribution from personal happiness, to health for the GSS group. We found no support for the conventional position, and some previous research findings, that suggest exclusive marriage is the best predictor of health, happiness, and sexual frequency, at least when compared to a consensually non-exclusive lifestyle.

One of the most significant findings is that the currently unmarried members of the non-exclusive sample reported such high levels of sexual frequency, health, and happiness in comparison with the general population sample. This finding supports our third hypothesis that those who currently identify as unmarried would report at least as good health and happiness as the GSS sample. This stands in stark contrast to much of the existing literature about health outcomes for unmarried individuals. Due to limitations imposed by small sample sizes, statistical analysis performed on the various subgroups of the unmarried portions of the samples has limited utility. For informational purposes, these breakdowns are included in Table 3.

Although having concurrent sexual partners has been identified as a risk factor for sexually transmitted infections among certain populations, this outcome has generally been associated with the presence of substance abuse and inconsistent condom use. Allowing for the limitation that the GSS imposed by asking only a single question regarding sexual health (HIV testing), the magnitude of the difference between the RNE and GSS respondents' rates of HIV testing suggests that the RNE population are concerned about and monitor their sexual health more closely than do those in the general population (Du et al., 2011). These differences were not explained by education, income, or gender (Table 4b).

The finding that married men in the non-exclusive sample were less happy with their marriages was unexpected. Some prior research into *non-consensual* extramarital sexuality (EMS) has found that marital unhappiness is a less important factor for men than for women in choosing EMS (Glass & Wright, 1992; Mark, Janssen, & Milhausen, 2011). More research is required to ascertain the cause of this finding.

For the RNE sample, frequent sexual activity is the most significant predictor of health and happiness. Frequent sexual activity approaches significance among the general population as a predictor of better general health, but only income and personal happiness are statistically significant in the full model used in these analyses. The differences in the importance of sexual frequency between the GSS and the RNE samples suggests that sexual interaction may be more important to the RNE respondents, but also that the sexual interactions they share may be qualitatively different (akin to optimal sexual experiences) from those commonly shared among the GSS sample. The strength of the correlation and apparent bidirectional causal relationship between health and sexual activity suggests that steps to maintain sexual activity over the life course are well-taken, especially as sexual activity is a principal contributor to sexual satisfaction and indirectly, relationship satisfaction and stability. Additionally, sexual frequency is correlated with personal happiness and health. Our findings are consistent with earlier research into these connections (Deacon, Minichiello, and Plummer, 1995; McNulty & Fisher, 2008; Smith et al., 2011; Weeks, 2002; Yeh et al., 2006; Yucel & Gassanov, 2010).

Given these realities, the salutary effect of frequent sex (and likely qualitatively better sex) on these important quality-of-life measures is realized more commonly by older adults who have adopted a non-exclusive sexual relationship orientation. However, the relationship is complex, and more frequent sexual interaction among the RNE population is likely driven by factors that make the sex they are having, *worth* having more frequently. Many other unknown and unaccounted factors also contribute to quality of life among older adults, but these were not in the data collected and thus could not be added into the regression models. For healthy, older adults dissatisfied with their current sexual frequency, whether due to unavailability of a partner or the effects of illness and aging (Gott & Hinchliff, 2003), a non-exclusive relationship strategy may be a viable option for maintaining a healthy and robust sex life. No research to date has examined that notion. This study represents an important initial look at this possibility.

The findings reveal that open consensual relationships are one viable pathway to increased healthy sexual activity. Our findings suggest that many of those who choose this pathway report better health and greater personal happiness, consistent with our predictions based on previous research (e.g. Firestone et al., 2006; Kleinplatz, Ménard, Paquet, et al. 2009; Kleinplatz, Ménard, Paradis, et al. 2009). The multivariable regression analyses suggest significant differences in the factors that predict happiness and health among the RNE and GSS populations. These differences suggest that a mere change in sexual relationship style may not contribute to greater happiness for older adults in the general population, but the differences are consistent with expectations for psychosexual gerotranscendence among the RNE sample. Likewise, for individuals whose general happiness is dependent upon the frequency of warm human connections, especially as expressed through sexual activity with a partner who is emotionally available, a consensually non-exclusive relationship strategy may be of significant benefit.

Utility/limitations/risks

The RNE sample was from an Internet-based, cross-sectional, self-selected convenience sample of a hidden population which was compared to the randomized and statistically sophisticated GSS survey, so results may have limited generalizability. Potential respondents who practice some form of consensual sexual non-exclusivity, but who do not have access to online services, are most likely not represented in these findings. The relatively small sample size imposed limitations on the ability to conduct finer analysis of the data in ways (such as by sexual orientation) that would produce statistically valid results. Respondents to the RNE survey were not asked about race or ethnicity, so differences across cultures or among those who identify with one of the many minority populations could not be assessed with the available data.

Compared to the GSS group, the sample had a relatively high educational attainment, which has been correlated with more liberal sexual attitudes (Fischtein, Herold, & Desmarais, 2007; Laumann, Gagnon, Michael, & Michaels, 1994). However, our findings indicate that educational attainment was not a significant predictor of happiness for the RNE or GSS sample. Neither was educational attainment a predictor of health for the RNE sample, but was, along with income, for the GSS sample. Our sample was skewed towards male respondents, whom research has shown tend to remain sexually active at higher rates than women (Karraker et al., 2011). Yet, in our samples of older adults, there were no significant differences between women and men regarding sexual frequency. An indeterminable percentage of our sample may be comprised of sexuality professionals among our "gatekeeper" lists who also happened to be 55 or over, personally identified as non-exclusive, and chose to participate. Given the small absolute number of these individuals who received the request to forward the survey link, we do not believe that their potential presence in the respondent population had any statistically meaningful effect on the survey findings, but we wish to mention this as another possible limitation. The RNE sample had significantly more representation from individuals who reported having sex with persons of the same sex and both sexes in the previous 12 months. Unfortunately, there were not enough like respondents in the GSS sample to make comparisons. Finally, the R^2s in our regression analyses indicate that our models from the available data did not predict very much of the variability, More research is needed to understand more completely the factors driving health and happiness in both the RNE and the GSS populations. Likewise, future research is necessary to assess the quality of these more frequent sexual interactions and the motives for engaging with more sexual partners, as was found among the RNE sample, to determine if these individuals are enjoying optimal sexual experiences and perhaps, psychosexual gerotranscendence.

Conclusions

Across all age categories, in all types of relationships, the non-exclusive sample generally outscored the relevant comparison group of the general population on sexual frequency, number of sexual partners, and self-reported health and personal happiness. These findings were especially significant for the portion of the sample that identified as other than currently legally married. This apparent prophylactic effect, if confirmed in future research, represents a very important finding for the health and well-being of millions of unpartnered older adults.

Continued sexual activity as one ages is consistently and robustly associated with better health and happiness. The results of our regression analyses support a bidirectional causality between greater sexual frequency and positive self-reported health. The strength of these results suggests that steps to maintain or increase one's opportunity for sexual activity over the life course are well taken. These findings also provide evidence that, for some older adults, one pathway to maintain an active and healthy sex life may be found through a consensually non-exclusive relationship style, and that those who have chosen this pathway report greater health and personal happiness than their peers in the general population.

Given the strength and prevalence of attitudes inimical to non-exclusive relationships, counselors face formidable barriers to raising the possibility for clients to consider a non-exclusive relationship as one possible solution to declining sexual frequency and its concomitant negative relational and health outcomes. Yet, the ethics of evidence-based counseling suggest that, given the findings of this research, such a conversation is one that may have merit, regardless of the potential obstacles.

Acknowledgements

The authors express gratitude to Curtis R. Bergstrand, PhD, who provided advice and counsel for the initial survey design. Likewise, the authors express gratitude to Robyn Trask, Executive Director of Loving More Nonprofit, Inc., who requested that the lead author undertake the larger research project to ascertain answers to questions concerning marriage equality for those practicing some form of non-exclusive committed relationship. The questions under analyses in this article were drawn from the General Social Survey by the lead author and combined with the questions initiated by Loving More to create the survey from which these results are extracted. The only support provided by Loving More was the use of its Survey Monkey account for the collection of data. This was important to the success of the project. However, Loving More had no involvement in the substance of the research, the formulation of questions, tabulation or analysis of the data, or the decision to publish. The lead author serves as an unpaid volunteer member of the board of directors of the National Coalition for Sexual Freedom and the NCSF Foundation. There are no financial relationships to disclose.

The second author, who is responsible for the theoretical orientation section, statistical analyses, and write-up of the results in this article, has no affiliation with any of the above-mentioned organizations, and has received no compensation from any source for this project or for publication of this article.

Note

1. This term is preferred over "non-monogamous" by many in the community who may also identify as polyamorous, relationship anarchist, in an open marriage, in a designer relationship, swingers, and others, including those who identify as non-monogamous. Many people who identify as

polyamorous (and other relationship styles) are also married to only one person, and are, therefore, by strict definition, monogamous, yet not sexually or intimately exclusive. There are also those, monogamously married and not, who identify with this community who remain sexually exclusive, but engage in emotionally-intimate relationships with more than one person.

References

Aggarwal, K.K. (2013). Sexual desire and sexual activity of men and women across their lifespan. *Indian Journal of Clinical Practice, 24*(3), 207–210.

Anapol, D. (1997). *Polyamory: The new love without limits: Secrets of sustainable intimate relationships*. San Rafael, CA: IntiNet Resource Center.

Anderson, E. (2010). "At least with cheating there is an attempt at monogamy": Cheating and monogamism among undergraduate heterosexual men. *Journal of Social and Personal Relationships, 27*(7), 851–872.

Barker, M., & Langdridge, D. (2010a). Introduction. In M. Barker & D. Langdridge (Eds.), *Routledge research in gender and society: Understanding non-monogamies* (pp. 3–8). New York, NY: Routledge.

Barker, M., & Langdridge, D. (2010b). Whatever happened to non-monogamies? Critical reflections on recent research and theory. *Sexualities, 13*(6), 748–772

Bauer, R. (2010). Non-monogamy in queer BDSM communities: Putting the sex back into alternative relationship practices and discourse. In M. Barker & D. Langdridge (Eds.), *Routledge research in gender and society: Understanding non-monogamies* (pp. 142–153). New York, NY: Routledge.

Benyamini, Y. (2011). Why does self-rated health predict mortality? An update on current knowledge and a research agenda for psychologists. *Psychology & Health, 26*(11), 1407–1413.

Blanchflower, D.G., & Oswald, A.J. (2004). Money, sex and happiness: An empirical study. *The Scandinavian Journal of Economics, 106*(3), 393–415.

Bodley-Tickell, A.T., Olowokure, B., Bhaduri, S., White, D.J., Ward, D., Ross, J.D., ... Goold, P. (2008). Trends in sexually transmitted infections (other than HIV) in older persons: Analysis of data from an enhanced surveillance system. *Sexually Transmitted Infections, 84*, 312–317.

Bookwala, J. (2005). The role of marital quality in physical health during the mature years. *Journal of Aging and Health, 17*(1), 85–104.

Bradford, A., & Meston, C.M. (2007). Senior sexual health: The effects of aging on sexuality. In L. VandeCreek, F.L. Peterson, & J.W. Bley (Eds.), *Innovations in clinical practice: Focus on sexual health* (pp. 35–45). Sarasota, FL: Professional Resource Press.

Brown, S., & Kawamura, S. (2010). Relationship quality among cohabiters and marrieds in older adulthood. *Social Science Research, 39*(5), 777–786.

Centers for Disease Control and Prevention. (2013). *Diagnoses of HIV infection among adults aged 50 years and older in the United States and dependent areas, 2007–2010* (HIV Surveillance Supplemental Report) (Vol. 18, Issue 3). Retrieved from http://www.cdc.gov/hiv/library/reports/surveillance/2010/surveillance_Report_vol_18_no_3.html. Published February 2013.

Conley, T.D., Moors, A.C., Ziegler, A., & Karathanasis, C. (2012). Unfaithful individuals are less likely to practice safer sex than openly nonmonogamous Individuals. *Journal of Sexual Medicine, 9*(6), 1559–1565.

Deacon, S., Minichiello, V., & Plummer, D. (1995). Sexuality and older people: Revisiting the assumptions. *Educational Gerontology, 21*(5), 497–513.

DeLamater, J. (2012). Sexual expression in later life: A review and synthesis. *Journal of Sex Research, 49*(2–3), 125–141.

DeLamater, J., & Koepsel, E. (2014). Relationship and sexual expression in later life: A biopsychosocial perspective. *Sexual and Relationship Therapy.* doi:10.1080/14681994.2014.939506

DeLamater, J.D., & Sill, M. (2005). Sexual desire in later life. *Journal of Sex Research, 42*(2), 138–149.

Donoho, C.J., Crimmins, E.M., & Seeman, T.E. (2013). Marital quality, gender, and markers of inflammation in the MIDUS Cohort. *Journal of Marriage and Family, 75*(1), 127–141.

Du, P., Camacho, F., Zurlo, J., & Lengerich, E.J. (2011). Human Immunodeficiency Virus testing behaviors among US adults: The roles of individual factors, legislative status, and public health resources. *Sexually Transmitted Diseases, 38*(9), 858–864.

Easton, D., & Liszt, C.A. (1997). *The ethical slut: A guide to infinite sexual possibilities.* San Francisco, CA: Greenery Press.

Eaton, J., Hallett, T., & Garnett, G. (2011). Concurrent sexual partnerships and primary HIV infection: A critical interaction. *AIDS and Behavior, 15*(4), 687–692.

Erikson, E.H. (1993 [1950]). *Childhood and society.* New York, NY: W.W. Norton.

Firestone, R., Firestone, L.A., & Catlett, J. (2006). *Sex and love in intimate relationships* (1st ed.). Washington, DC: American Psychological Association.

Fischtein, D.S., Herold, E.S., & Desmarais, S. (2007). How much does gender explain in sexual attitudes and behaviors? A survey of Canadian adults. *Archives of Sexual Behavior, 36*(3), 451–461.

Fisher, L.L. (2010). *Sex, romance, and relationships: AARP survey of midlife and older adults.* Washington, DC: AARP Knowledge Management.

Fleckenstein, J.R. (2012). *Polyamory and marriage survey.* Manassas, VA: Lovemore.com and NCSFreedom.org.

Ganong, K., & Larson, E. (2011). Intimacy and belonging: The association between sexual activity and depression among older adults. *Society and Mental Health, 1*(3), 153–172.

Glass, S.P., & Wright, T.L. (1992). Justifications for extramarital relationships: The association between attitudes, behaviors, and gender. *Journal of Sex Research, 29*(3), 361–387.

Goffman, E. (1963). *Stigma: Notes on the management of spoiled identity.* Englewood Cliffs, NJ: Prentice-Hall.

Gott, M., & Hinchliff, S. (2003). How important is sex in later life? The views of older people. *Social Science & Medicine, 56*(8), 1617–1628.

Hall, S.A., Shackelton, R., Rosen, R.C., & Araujo, A.B. (2010). Sexual activity, erectile dysfunction, and incident cardiovascular events. *The American Journal of Cardiology, 105*(2), 192–197.

Karraker, A., DeLamater, J., & Schwartz, C.R. (2011). Sexual frequency decline from midlife to later life. *The Journals of Gerontology Series B: Psychological Sciences and Social Sciences, 66*(4), 502–512.

Kleinplatz, P.J., Ménard, A.D., Paquet, M.-P., Paradis, N., Campbell, M., Zuccarino, D., & Mehak, L. (2009). The components of optimal sexuality: A portrait of "great sex". *Canadian Journal of Human Sexuality, 18*(1–2), 1–13.

Kleinplatz, P.J., Ménard, A.D., Paradis, N., Campbell, M., Dalgleish, T., Segovia, A., & Davis, K. (2009). From closet to reality: Optimal sexuality among the elderly. *The Irish Psychiatrist, 10*(1), 15–18.

Kohlberg, L. (1981a). *Essays on moral development* (1st ed.). San Francisco, CA: Harper & Row.

Kohlberg, L. (1981b). *The meaning and measurement of moral development.* Worcester, MA: Clark University Press.

Kontula, O., & Haavio-Mannila, E. (2009). The impact of aging on human sexual activity and sexual desire. *The Journal of Sex Research, 46*(1), 46–56.

Laumann, E.O., Gagnon, J.H., Michael, R.T., & Michaels, S. (1994). *The social organization of sexuality: Sexual practices in the United States.* Chicago, IL: University of Chicago Press.

Laumann, E.O., Nicolosi, A., Glasser, D.B., Paik, A., Gingell, C., Moreira, E., & Wang, T. (2004). Sexual problems among women and men aged 40–80 y: Prevalence and correlates identified in the Global Study of Sexual Attitudes and Behaviors. *International Journal of Impotence Research, 17*(1), 39–57.

Laumann, E.O., Paik, A., Glasser, D.B., Kang, J.H., Wang, T., Levinson, B., ... Gingell, C. (2006). A cross-national study of subjective sexual well-being among older women and men: Findings from the Global Study of Sexual Attitudes and Behaviors. *Archives of Sexual Behavior, 35*(2), 143–159.

Laumann, E.O., Paik, A., & Rosen, R.C. (1999). Sexual dysfunction in the United States: Prevalence and predictors. *Journal of the American Medical Association, 281*(6), 537–544.

Lindau, S.T., & Gavrilova, N. (2010). Sex, health, and years of sexually active life gained due to good health: Evidence from two US population-based cross sectional surveys of ageing. *British Medical Journal, 340*(7746), 580.

Lindau, S.T., Schumm, L.P., Laumann, E.O., Levinson, W., O'Muircheartaigh, C.A., & Waite, L.J. (2007). A study of sexuality and health among older adults in the United States. *New England Journal of Medicine, 357*(8), 762–774.

Mark, K.P., Janssen, E., & Milhausen, R.R. (2011). Infidelity in heterosexual couples: Demographic, interpersonal, and personality-related predictors of extradyadic sex. *Archives of Sexual Behavior, 40*(5), 971–982.

Maslow, A.H. (1971 [1967]). *The farther reaches of human nature.* San Francisco, CA: Esalen Institute.

Matthias, R.E., Lubben, J.E., Atchison, K.A., & Schweitzer, S.O. (1997). Sexual activity and satisfaction among very old adults: Results from a community-dwelling medicare population survey. *The Gerontologist, 37*(1), 6–14.

Mazur, R.M. (1973). *The new intimacy; open-ended marriage and alternative lifestyles.* Boston, MA: Beacon Press.

McNulty, J.K., & Fisher, T.D. (2008). Gender differences in response to sexual expectancies and changes in sexual frequency: A short-term longitudinal study of sexual satisfaction in newly married couples. *Archives of Sexual Behavior, 37*(2), 229–240.

Ménard, A.D., Kleinplatz, P.J., Rosen, L., Lawless, S., Paradis, N., Campbell, M., & Huber, J.D. (2014). Individual and relational contributors to optimal sexual experiences in older men and women. *Sexual and Relationship Therapy, 30*(1).

Morin, J. (1999). When hot monogamy isn't happening, consider plan B. *In the family: A Magazine for Lesbians, Gays, Bisexuals, & Their Relations, 4*, 12.

Musick, K., & Bumpass, L. (2012). Reexamining the case for marriage: Union formation and changes in well-being. *Journal of Marriage and Family, 74*(1), 1–18.

Nichols, M., & Shernoff, M. (2007). Therapy with sexual minorities: Queering practice. In S.R. Leiblum (Ed.), *Principles and practice of sex therapy* (4th ed., pp. 379–415). New York, NY: Guilford Press.

Pappas, S. (2013, February 14). New sexual revolution: Polyamory may be good for you. *LiveScience.* Retrieved from http://www.livescience.com/27129-polyamory-good-relationships.html

Pearline, R.V., Tucker, J.D., Yuan, L.F., Bu, J., Yin, Y.P., Chen, X.S., & Cohen, M.S. (2010). Sexually transmitted infections among individuals over fifty years of age in China [Letter to the Editor]. *AIDS Patient Care and STDs, 24*(6), 345–347.

Schnarch, D.M. (1991). *Constructing the sexual crucible: An integration of sexual and marital therapy.* New York, NY: W.W. Norton.

Schnarch, D.M. (1997). *Passionate couples: Love, sex, and intimacy in emotionally committed relationships* (1st ed.). New York, NY: W.W. Norton.

Schnarch, D.M. (2002). *Resurrecting sex: Resolving sexual problems and rejuvenating your relationship* (1st ed.). New York, NY: HarperCollins.

Sheff, E. (2010). Strategies in polyamorous parenting. In M. Barker & D. Langdridge (Eds.), *Routledge research in gender and society: Understanding non-monogamies* (pp. 169–181). New York, NY: Routledge.

Sheff, E. (2014). *The polyamorists next door: Inside multiple-partner relationships and families.* Lanham, MD: Rowman & Littlefield.

Smith, A., Lyons, A., Ferris, J., Richters, J., Pitts, M., Shelley, J., & Simpson, J.M. (2011). Sexual and relationship satisfaction among heterosexual men and women: The importance of desired frequency of sex. *Journal of Sex & Marital Therapy, 37*(2), 104–115.

Smith, T.W., Marsden, P.V., Hout, M., & Kim, J. (2013). *General Social Surveys, 1972—2012* [machine-readable data file]. Chicago, IL: National Opinion Research Center.

Suzman, R. (2009). The national social life, health, and aging project: An introduction. *The Journals of Gerontology Series B: Psychological Sciences and Social Sciences, 64B*(suppl 1), i5–i11.

Taormino, T. (2008). *Opening up: A guide to creating and sustaining open relationships* (1st ed.). San Francisco, CA: Cleis Press.

Tornstam, L. (2005). *Gerotranscendence: A developmental theory of positive aging.* New York, NY: Springer Pub. Co.

Waite, L., & Gallagher, M. (2000). *The case for marriage: Why married people are happier, healthier, and better off financially.* New York, NY: Doubleday.

Waite, L.J., Laumann, E.O., Das, A., & Schumm, L.P. (2009). Sexuality: Measures of partnerships, practices, attitudes, and problems in the National Social Life, Health, and Aging Study. *The Journals of Gerontology Series B: Psychological Sciences and Social Sciences, 64*(Suppl 1), i56–i66.

Weeks, D.J. (2002). Sex for the mature adult: Health, self-esteem and countering ageist stereotypes. *Sexual and Relationship Therapy, 17*(3), 231–240.

Whipple, B., Knowles, J., Davis, J., Koch, P.B., Moglia, R.F., Owens, A.F., . . . Golub, D. (2007). *The health benefits of sexual expression white paper.* New York, NY: Planned Parenthood Federation of America: Katharine Dexter McCormick Library; Society for the Scientific Study of Sexuality.

Wiley, D., & Bortz, W.M. (1996). Sexuality and aging—usual and successful. *The Journals of Gerontology Series A: Biological Sciences and Medical Sciences, 51*(3), M142–M146.

Yeh, H.C., Lorenz, F.O., Wickrama, K.A.S., Conger, R.D., & Elder Jr, G.H. (2006). Relationships among sexual satisfaction, marital quality, and marital instability at midlife. *Journal of Family Psychology, 20*(2), 339–343.

Yucel, D., & Gassanov, M.A. (2010). Exploring actor and partner correlates of sexual satisfaction among married couples. *Social Science Research, 39*(5), 725–738.

Ziliak, S.T., & McCloskey, D.N. (2008). *The cult of statistical significance: How the standard error costs us jobs, justice, and lives.* Ann Arbor: University of Michigan Press.

Sex, desire and pleasure: considering the experiences of older Australian women

Bianca Fileborn[a], Rachel Thorpe[a], Gail Hawkes[b], Victor Minichiello[a], Marian Pitts[a] and Tinashe Dune[c]

[a]Australian Research Centre in Sex, Health and Society, La Trobe University, Melbourne, Australia; [b]School of Behavioural and Cognitive Sciences, University of New England, Armidale, Australia; [c]School of Science and Health, University of Western Sydney, Campbelltown, Australia

Older age is often associated with asexuality. That is, older individuals are not viewed as desiring of sex, nor as sexually desirable to others. Broader social and cultural norms that downplay women's sexual desire and agency further compound these phenomena. Whether this popular image accurately reflects older women's sexual desires, behaviour and capacity to experience pleasure is unclear. Drawing on semi-structured interviews with 43 partnered Australian women aged 55–81, this article considers women's sexual experiences and desires in older age. The findings of our research confirm that older women's experiences of sex and sexual desire are diverse and fluid. Some of the factors that influenced participants' sexual behaviour and desire will be considered in this article, as will their understandings of what "counts" as sexual satisfaction and "successful sex". The factors affecting sexual behaviour and desire also influence the way in which women are able to negotiate sexual interaction with their partners. Participants expressed a need for education and resources in order to gain greater control and to make autonomous choices over their sexual experiences, desire and ability to give and receive pleasure. The implications of these findings for practitioners are also considered.

Introduction

Older women's embodied experiences of sexuality are considerably under-explored in existing research. This can be attributed, in part, to the association between ageing and asexuality. In Western cultures, older individuals are often seen as sexually undesirable or as not desiring sexual activity (Dixon, 2012; Drummond et al., 2013; Hinchliff & Gott, 2008; Hurd Clarke & Korotchenko, 2011; Sandberg, 2013a). A considerable body of research has discredited this popular assumption. It is well established that many individuals desire sexual intimacy and continue to engage in various forms of sexual activity throughout their later years (Gray & Garcia, 2012; Hinchliff, Gott, & Ingelton, 2010; Hurd Clarke & Korotchenko, 2011; Kleinplatz, Ménard, Paradis, Campbell, & Dalgleish, 2013; Lindau et al., 2007; Minichiello, Plummer, & Loxton, 2004; Schick et al., 2010).

As a result of this shift, a new norm of sexuality in older age has been established: which Hinchliff and Gott (2008) refer to as the "sexy oldie". A representation of "successful" ageing as maintenance of a "youthful" sexual performance (see also Marshall, 2012; Sandberg, 2013a). Within this new norm, sexual performance still adheres to a heteronormative framework of sex, with penetration positioned as the "ultimate", desirable sexual act. Biomedical models of sexuality which focus on sexual "dysfunction" and age often reinforce this with a fixation on restoring penetrative capacity through the facilitation of erections and remedies for vaginal dryness (Mamo & Fishman, 2001; Marshall, 2012; Sandberg, 2013a, 2013b).

Whether this binary view of elder sexuality as asexual or "sexy oldie" accurately reflects practices, experiences or desires of older people remains unclear (Marshall, 2012). Indeed, a more notable finding emerging from recent qualitative studies is the heterogeneity of older women's sexual lives (Hinchliff et al., 2010; Howard, O'Neill, & Travers, 2006; Kontula & Haavio-Mannila, 2009). Definitions of sex based around penetration and "youthful" models of sex obscure the broader range of practices, and the greater focus on intimate touch and affection that older people actually do desire and engage in (Drummond et al., 2013; Helmes & Chapman, 2012; McCarthy, Farr, & McDonald, 2013; Willert & Semans, 2000; Yee, 2010). While it is clear that older individuals do still engage in and desire sexual interaction, there is also a range of health, social and cultural barriers that can limit or alter older individuals' abilities to engage in sexual activity (Bitzer, Platano, Tschudin, & Alder, 2008; Hinchliff & Gott, 2008; Kontula & Haavio-Mannila, 2009; Trudel, Turgeon, & Piché, 2010). Traditional gender roles, and social and cultural views of later life sexuality, can also shape sexual activity and desire in older age (DeLamater, 2012; Drummond et al., 2013; Kontula & Haavio-Mannila, 2009; Lodge & Umberson, 2012; Montemurro & Gillen, 2013; Sandberg, 2013b).

Attitudes towards sex, and their subsequent influence on sexual behaviour, can be related to an individual's particular generational cohort (Bentrott & Margrett, 2011; Kontula & Haavio-Mannila, 2009; Lodge & Umberson, 2012). Having grown up during the sexual revolution, the "Baby Boomer" generation are renowned for challenging and disrupting stereotypes in relation to both sex and ageing. There is evidence supporting the assertion that a cultural shift in relation to ageing and sex is occurring (DeLamater, 2012; Kingsberg, 2002; Kirkman, Kenny, & Fox, 2013).

A question arises as to how older individuals negotiate their sexual subjectivity within this competing binary framework. There is a considerable dearth of research on later life sexuality that is informed by the voices of older people themselves, and in particular by those of older women. Despite the "Baby Boomers" representing the vanguard of the sexual revolution there is little research that takes account of the specific sexual subjectivities of women who came of age in this cohort. Because women's sexual behaviour is most frequently subject to a range of formal and informal social controls, the shift in sexual mores observed at this time has had an arguably greater impact on the sexual subjectivities of women. Decades on from this period of rapid social, cultural and sexual change, it is important to ask how women from this cohort are experiencing their sexual selves as they age. Drawing on the findings of a qualitative research project, this article explores the position of older Australian women in relation to their experiences and negotiation of sex, sexuality and desire in their relationships.

Producing sexual difference: a theoretical perspective

A key challenge in researching and discussing the sexual subjectivity of older women is to do so in a way that avoids re-creating the asexual/"sexy oldie" binary. We use the term "sexual subjectivity" here to refer to women's individual, subjective understandings of sex and sexual desire, and the meanings they ascribe to sex. Instead, a theoretical position is required that acknowledges the diversity of later life sex, and avoids (re)creating hierarchies of sex/sexuality, which reinforces heteronormativity.

Sandberg (2013a) provides an alternative framework for thinking about later life sexuality that has informed this paper. Rather than positioning later life sex as either in decline, dysfunctional or absent (or, conversely, "successful", penetrative and youthful), we can instead realign the sexual changes that accompany the ageing process as the "continuous production of difference" (2013, p. 19). This approach avoids the (re)creation of binaries, such as decline/success, dysfunctional/functional, while still creating space to acknowledge "the material specificities of the ageing body" (Sandberg, 2013a, p. 14). Sandberg's work provides an appropriate framework for discussing older women's sexual experiences and subjectivity that can account for the diversity of women's experiences, whilst avoiding the (re)creation of sexual hierarchies and norms.

Methods

Interview data from 43 partnered women aged 55–81 (mean 64.4; sd 5.9) forms the basis of the following analysis and discussion.[1] Participants were primarily recruited from three locations in Australia: Melbourne and regional Victoria; the mid-north coast region of New South Wales and the New England tablelands region of New South Wales. A similar number of participants were recruited from each region. Smaller numbers of participants were also recruited from Brisbane and Sydney. Recruitment efforts involved a combination of snowballing and advertisements. Significant interest in the project was generated on a major Australian radio programme. All interviews were audio recorded with the participant's consent. The recordings were transcribed by an external service. Quality checks and data cleaning of the transcripts were carried out by the first two authors.

This sample includes women who are married, in long-term de facto relationships, and in newly formed romantic partnerships (see Table 1). One participant referred to in this paper was in a same-sex relationship, but identified as bisexual, while all other women were in heterosexual partnerships. The women participated in semi-structured, in-depth interviews that explored their body image and sexual subjectivity as they aged. Qualitative, in-depth interviews were used to capture the voices of women that spoke directly about their sexual experiences, and to ensure that the researchers did not restrict the dialogue to preconceived notions about sexualities. The interviews varied in length, depending upon the particular experiences of each woman; however, the majority ran for between one and two hours. The women were interviewed in their homes or in public locations of their choice. Pseudonyms referred to in this paper were chosen by the participants or assigned by researchers.

Table 1. Participant relationship status by location.

Location	Married	In a relationship	Total
New South Wales	14	6	20
Victoria	13	6	19
Brisbane/Sydney	3	1	4
Total	30	13	43

Data coding and analysis was completed by the first and second authors. The first author was responsible for the coding and analysis of the New South Wales, Sydney and Brisbane data, while the second author was responsible for the Victorian data. Each researcher coded the data independently. An initial reading of the transcripts was undertaken to identify the key themes emerging from the data: that is, an inductive coding approach was taken. The researchers were particularly concerned with identifying key themes relating to participants' body image, their current sexual desire and sexual activity, and the ways in which experiences of ageing shaped participants' sexual subjectivities. A series of codes and sub-codes were designed on the basis of the more prominent themes, and additional codes were developed throughout this process as further themes were identified through a closer reading of the transcripts. Particular attention was paid to both the similarities of participants' experiences, but also to the diversity of experience. The researchers then compared codes to ensure consistency and agreement on the significant emerging themes. Interview data was initially coded by hand, and then again in NVivo, with this approach lending itself to a thorough reading and analysis of the data.

Results

In the following section, we provide an overview of the key themes and findings of this research in relation to our participants' experiences of sex and their sexual subjectivity within relationships. Specifically, we consider participants' experiences of sexual activity within their current relationships; the factors which influenced their current sexual desire and sexual activity; and participants' need for information and resources on sex and sexuality in older age.

Partnered women's sexual activity and experiences

A particularly striking finding was the diversity of sexual experience and desire amongst this group of women. Participants ranged from having ceased sexual activity completely to still engaging in regular sexual activity of various forms. The following comments from participants illustrate the range of sexual activity that the women currently engaged in, and the importance of sexual satisfaction to them:

No, we don't have it. It doesn't worry me. No...

Do you have cuddles [hugging]? [Italics are used here to denote when the interviewer is talking.]

Oh yeah. Yeah. Cuddle, sit on the lounge and hold hands and all that stuff. (Jessica, age 67)

Really important. With my partner it's very good, very satisfying. But yeah, it's really important and it's a lot of fun achieving it too. (Rolly, age 63)

Many participants remained intimate in the absence of penetrative sex; however, this interaction was not always overtly identified as a form of sexual intimacy. Direct questioning of older individuals about their sexual behaviour might not elicit a complete picture of their experiences. For instance, Jessica responded that she did not have sex with her partner anymore, yet when prompted she revealed that they did still engage in some forms of sexual interaction. This may reflect the influence of cultural norms in which "sex" is defined as limited to penetration at the expense of other forms of sexual intimacy.

Respondent Anna distinguished ideas of sexual satisfaction and sensual satisfaction:

> I'm quite happy to have what you might call a fuck, I mean it's great and to feel horny and to have somebody else feel attracted and passionate...But I also probably desire more whole body intimacy. I love to be touched, to be stroked, to be massaged. (Anna, age 69)

Anna related this focus on sensuality to her previous sexually disappointing and unfulfilling relationship. This indicates that the context of a relationship and the individual trajectories of women's lives are fundamental to understanding how they negotiate their sexual subjectivity.

For individual women, sexual desire was often fluid across their lifetimes. That is, rather than desire for sex being static or uni-directional (i.e. traversing towards a decline and eventual cessation of sexual desire), women's desire ebbed and flowed according to contextual factors and events. Common influences on desire included entering into a new relationship, physiological changes and the women's partners. For example, participant Joy (age 59) experienced a dramatic increase in both her sexual desire and activity following a significant period of celibacy. During this period, Joy indicated that her desire for sex waned due to sexual incompatibilities with her partner. Her desire for sex returned with a new casual sexual partner, and the ability to negotiate a non-traditional relationship arrangement with her partner greatly improved Joy's sexual satisfaction. Other participants experienced a decline in sexual desire as they aged:

> I just don't have a sexual urge anymore. (Connie, age 60)

For some participants, this shift in sexual desire was a welcome one; however, for others, it was discussed with a sense of loss or grief. Participant Joy, for example, described her lowered libido and sexual response as "disappointing".

Desire for sex did not always relate to sexual activity. Some participants expressed various levels of desire for sex, yet were unable to translate this desire into action:

> *How important is sexual satisfaction to you?*
>
> Very important and I don't feel very satisfied. Well, it's not very important. Oh no, I'm going to burst into tears. (Rusty, age 57)
>
> *So do you miss it [penetrative partnered sex]?*
>
> At times. I get a bit kind of cross [answering back quickly]. But generally, I was thinking there was almost a time when you didn't have a cuddle just in case he wanted it and you didn't want that. So now you can have a cuddle whenever you want to because the other is not necessary. (Janet, age 74)

For some participants, a level of ambivalence was apparent in relation to whether sexual satisfaction was important to them. Rusty's comments provide an example of this. In other instances, the gap between participants' sexual desire and sexual activity was paradoxically experienced as both limiting because they still desired partnered sex, and liberating because the expectation of sex was removed. The possibility for other forms of intimacy, such as cuddling, was often opened up for participants in the absence of a (presumably penetrative) sexual imperative.

Yet, other women engaged in regular sexual activity in the absence of any sexual desire:

I just don't have a sexual urge anymore…You know my husband and I are still sexually active. (Connie, age 60)

One participant discussed her friend's continued engagement in sex with her husband in the absence of any desire:

She's pleasing her husband, which is always done, but in pleasing your husband you often get a lot of pleasure yourself. (Susie, age 68)

Many participants discussed sexual acts in a way that constructed a sexual hierarchy. These hierarchies tended to privilege partnered, penetrative sex, with 'alternative' forms of sex, such as masturbation, relegated to the bottom of the sexual heap:

Do you ever self-satisfy yourself?

No not really.

Did you ever?

When I was a teenager. Before I knew boys. (Janet, age 74)

Similarly, participant Sally constructed "other" forms of intimacy and closeness as lesser forms of sexuality:

Do you find substitutes for it?

There's not a real substitute. You're just close, that's all. (Sally, age 64)

However, other participants held more inclusive definitions of sexual intimacy:

I think basically we care for each other. We sleep together, and we curl up together. We touch each other, all these things, which is basically what intimacy is. (Tabitha, age 78)

Other participants welcomed masturbation as part of their sexual repertoire:

There's not a lot of sex anymore and it doesn't really worry me. You know masturbation is still perfectly available. (Greta, age 61)

Participants' views towards masturbation must also be viewed in terms of the social and cultural context these women grew up in:

Not supposed to masturbate?

Oh god no! No, no. And that's one of the issues with me was, growing up as a good Catholic girl. You know you certainly didn't do that. (Jeffa, age 64)

Many of the women in this study reported growing up in a social context where sex was not openly discussed, and masturbation was taboo and shameful, although this was increasingly challenged throughout the 1960s and 1970s as many of our participants were coming of age. It is thus difficult to separate the influence of social and cultural context and the influence of ageing on women's attitudes towards masturbation.

Are you in the mood? What factors influence women's experiences of, and desire for, sex?

Life stage

For many participants, their particular stage of life increased both their desires for sex and abilities to engage in it. Being free from the pressures of raising a young family, work and the risk of pregnancy, opened up opportunities to engage in and enjoy sex. Additionally, many (though certainly not all) women had a strong sense of what worked for them sexually at this point in their lives and were confident in asking for or negotiating what they wanted with their partners:

> The women I've known, like in this stage of my life, are not frightened of sex. I reckon it's probably the best time in your life actually because you're not going to have kids, you don't have to think about a house. (Rosie, age 57)

For some women, the ability to negotiate pleasurable sex came after involvement in sexually disappointing relationships earlier in their lives. This was occasionally accompanied by general dissatisfaction with the relationship, and less commonly by physically and emotionally abusive behaviour. Many women commented that they were no longer willing to compromise or "put up with" unsatisfying relationships later in life.

Partners

Women's sexual lives were also shaped, influenced, and at times limited, by the attitudes and behaviours of their partners. A number of women indicated that their partners displayed minimal insight into their sexual needs and desires, leading to an unsatisfactory partnered sexual life:

> He couldn't see that I had sexual needs. He couldn't see that I didn't need a penis. . .Because once he'd done his bit that was it. He'd roll over and go to sleep. And I'd be left going "what the fuck"? (Jeffa, age 64)

Women's attempts to negotiate sex with their partners were met with varying levels of success. Some partners were resistant to discussing their sexual techniques and women's attempts to raise problems fell on deaf ears:

> And as I say I have tried to talk to [partner] and to do it differently or, whatever, and I felt that he was like a bull in a china shop sometimes, and he'd just roll over. (Rusty, age 57)

Rusty believed her partner felt "undermined" whenever she raised issues regarding sex, particularly if she had suffered in silence for some time with her partner believing that she was sexually satisfied. Participant Kim (age 56) also indicated that her husband was reluctant to develop new sexual techniques in order to adapt to the physiological changes she had experienced during menopause. Kim described her partner as a "man who does not do intimacy". His unwillingness to expand his sexual horizons left Kim feeling sexually dissatisfied.

When partners constructed sex only in the limited terms of penetration, the end of women's partnered sexual life was signalled when their partners could no longer maintain erections and the women were unable or unwilling to leave their relationships or initiate alternative sexual arrangements, for example, by having a casual sexual partner:

I have another girlfriend whose husband had prostate cancer, and so he can't get an erection anymore...she wishes that he would find another way to satisfy her, but he won't because he can't have sex at all. He won't engage in any sex with her. (Toohey, age 63)

Erectile dysfunction (ED), associated with age or resulting from major health problems, such as prostate cancer and diabetes, was commonly identified as influencing women's sexual practices later in life. However, this did not signal the end of partnered sex for all women. Some adjusted their sexual repertoires to accommodate for their partners, for example, some participants engaged in mutual masturbation, while others discussed using drugs, such as Viagra, in order for their partners to achieve erections:

Things have changed in our life because my husband has had a prostate cancer. So he was operated on...He got nervous because of the operation and so yes, we managed to have a nice time, but quite different and so that's it. But there's lots more cuddles and things. (Janet, age 74)

Health, well-being and medication

Women's general health and well-being was a significant feature mediating their desire for sex. Depleted libido, caused by the side effects of medications, was mentioned by a number of participants:

And I wonder too about the Zoloft[2] because...I'm not sort [of] interested much [since] I've been on those. I think it really has killed a lot of that. (Suki, age 55)

However, major health incidents did not always result in decreased sexual desire. Indeed, for one participant, having a hysterectomy, in conjunction with additional life circumstances, enhanced her sexual desire:

Actually I think on our part the sex is better. It has got better since the kids have left home. And I had a hysterectomy five years ago and now that's [sex] all I want. (Macca, age 57)

Menopause had a highly variable influence on the sexual desire and activity of our participants:

There is a tenderness and a sensitivity that is unfortunate but undeniable and unavoidable. (Greta, age 61)

I've been very fortunate...with menopause...I've sort of breezed through that and the physiological things haven't really, not like the dryness and all that sort of thing. I really haven't had that. (Narelle, age 67)

One participant discussed the dual impact of menopause and having an sexually transmitted infection (STI):

Herpes, for example, has affected the skin down there. It is very thin, and it means that as things are changing down there just through natural progression of ageing, it is much more tender. I have to be really careful. (Kim, age 56)

Kim also experienced additional complications from past surgeries on her vagina and vulva, which in conjunction with herpes and her menopausal symptoms compounded the effects of a lack of "natural" lubrication and sensitive skin. A common theme amongst women's experiences of medication, surgery or other health interventions was the lack of information or advice provided by doctors in relation to how the intervention would affect their sexual functioning or desire. Participants commented that this lack of information made it difficult to predict how these interventions would affect them, and prevented them from taking steps to minimise or prevent subsequent problems.

Need for education and resources

Participants highlighted the lack of available resources on ageing and sexuality:

> I thought this was really important to bring up with you; there are no books about sexuality for older people. (Joy, age 59)

In particular, participants wanted information on how to cope with the effects of ageing on sexual activity:

> You can find books on arthritis, diabetes. . .but where is it about how to discover what's still good about your body and how to pleasure yourself and your partner? Issues that arise for older people. It doesn't exist. (Joy, age 59)

Some participants expressed a need for information that allowed them to create opportunities for sexual pleasure in a way that accommodates for changing, ageing bodies. However, the lack of available advice and resources restricted the ability of some participants to adjust their sexual practices accordingly. Other women discussed the fact that the notion of older women experiencing sexual pleasure and desire was a taboo even among their peers. The silence around these issues further entrenched the belief that older women do not desire sexual pleasure. Several participants expressed a wish to know if their experiences were "normal". Despite still having sexual desire, a lack of knowledge around ageing and sex meant that participants lacked autonomy and control over their sexual subjectivities. This point is encapsulated in Sally's experience of her husband's surgery for prostate cancer:

> I don't think he was given any counselling or any information or anything because I believe there's rehabilitation or something but that certainly wasn't offered to him. . .we weren't given enough information because at the time you are quite shocked and you think. . .that's it. . .that's both of us that that operation affected. (Sally, age 64)

Sally felt that a lack of discussion, information and advice from health care professionals prevented her partner from having the choice to undergo rehabilitation to maintain the ability to have an erection, leading to the cessation of their partnered sex life. Another participant argued that older women need information exposing them to, and normalising, the diversity of sexual practices:

> I don't think anyone has ever educated us as women to think that we don't need a penis. Until such time, you know with women seeking out female partners, I think it's only then that you go, well most of us go, well how does that work? (Jeffa, age 64)

Participants also identified a lack of information relating to safe-sex practices targeted towards older individuals:

> It doesn't matter what age you are. If you don't take precautions then if you get the consequences you have to deal with it, and if it's HIV it's bad luck. . . [Sex education is] mostly in

regard to young people getting started, not older people. I suppose we're expected to know better. (Rolly, age 63)

Discussion

This study sought to explore the sexual subjectivities of older Australian women. The sexual desires and activities of the older women in this study were reportedly diverse and fluid across the life course. They were influenced by a broad range of social, cultural and medical factors. Indeed, these women's accounts defy simplistic definitions of later life sex as either absent or "youthfully" sexual and instead were heterogeneous. These findings support recent qualitative research that has also demonstrated the diversity of older women's sexual practices and desires (Hinchliff et al., 2010; Howard et al., 2006; Kontula & Haavio-Mannila, 2009). The emergent findings of this project suggest that limited, binary models of elder sexuality ultimately obscure and prevent a better understanding of the range and diversity of older women's sexual experiences.

Our participants' sexual practices and sexual desires were influenced by a broad range of factors. Relationship context and life events, such as children leaving home, were a key influence on women's sexual lives. The social and cultural context that our participants grew up in also played a role in shaping their sexual subjectivities. Many of the women in this study reported growing up in a social context where sex was not discussed openly, and masturbation in particular was considered taboo and shameful. It is subsequently difficult to separate the influence of social and cultural factors and the influence of ageing on participants' attitudes towards sex. Participants' sexual practices were also shaped by heteronormative notions of sex, with penetrative sex often positioned as 'real' sex. However, women in this study also challenged this sexual hierarchy by privileging broad and inclusive understandings of sex. This further highlights the diversity in older women's understandings of sex.

Significant life changes, such as menopause or surgery, had highly variable impacts on our participants. This diversity in experience makes it difficult to fully account for the role that menopause plays in influencing women's sexual desires and sexual practices. Such findings are in line with research challenging the influence of menopause on women's sexual desire and "function" (Hinchliff & Gott, 2008; Kingsberg, 2002; Ringa, Diter, Laborde, & Bajos, 2013; Trudel et al., 2010). The lack of open discussion and information provided by health care providers in relation to the impacts of medical interventions and health changes on women's sexual function was identified by participants and is of particular concern. The reluctance of health care providers to discuss issues pertaining to sexuality with older clients has been well documented in existing research. This silence contributed at least in part towards practitioners' ageist assumptions that older individuals are asexual (Gott, 2001, 2005; Gott & Hinchliff, 2003; Gott, Hinchliff, & Galena, 2004; Hinchliff & Gott, 2004, 2011; Slinkard & Kazer, 2011). The lack of information provided to our participants is perhaps unsurprising in light of this. Reluctance, by health care providers, to discuss sexual issues affected the participants' ability to anticipate and negotiate the effects of healthcare interventions on their sexual lives and ultimately limited sexual autonomy.

Women's sexual desire, and the sexual practices they engaged in, and their need for information on adjusting to sex in older age have also been highlighted. Our findings present clear implications for practitioners working with older women in relationships. Noticeably, our participants highlighted the lack of information and discussion around sexual pleasure and ageing. There is a clear role for practitioners and health care providers in initiating conversations with clients about their sexual lives and desires, and in providing

information for those women who wish to receive it. It is imperative that practitioners recognise the diversity in women's sexual desires and practices. Practitioners should avoid
imposing normative views about how older women's sex lives "should look", allowing
women to give their own meanings to sexual desires and practices. Cultural norms around
sex influence the choices that individuals are able to make. It is problematic to assume that
education and information alone will open up the sexual choices available to women if
these resources merely reinforce narrow understandings of sex and sexuality.

In addition, women's partners represented a significant influence on our participants'
sexual lives. There is little point in designing resources for women in heterosexual relationships to assist them in negotiating sex in older age unless similar resources for older
men are not also developed. These issues should be considered in the context of the partnership. In particular, there is a need to open up a discussion around diversity in sexual
practice, and to challenge understandings of sex that privilege penetration. Practitioners
may need to discuss and explore how alternative forms of pleasure can be made more
readily available to women. This could include, for example, considering open or casual
sexual relationships, the use of sex toys and aids, the use of pornography which is specifically designed to meet the needs and demands of women, or the use of commercial sex
workers (see Law, 2014). Providing older women and their partners with the tools to
negotiate their sexual lives will ultimately afford women greater autonomy over their sexual subjectivities and sexual trajectories into and throughout older age.

Given that STI rates have risen dramatically amongst older age groups in recent years
(The Kirby Institute, 2012; Minichiello, Rahman, Hawkes, & Pitts, 2012), it is particularly timely that resources be developed to encourage safer sexual practices in older age
groups. The precise reasons for this lack of safer sex education for older age groups
remain unclear; however, it seems plausible that the contradictory views of older people
as asexual, and baby boomers as sexually liberated and knowledgeable (and, thus, not
needing sexual education) may both contribute towards this silence.

Limitations

There are some limitations associated with this research. Participant sample sizes were
small, and the overwhelming majority of participants were heterosexual and Caucasian.
Additionally, many of the women participating in this study were university educated or
professionally employed during their working lives, and largely stemmed from middle to
upper class socio-economic background. The findings of this research are subsequently
not generalisable to more diverse groups of women. As such, the research team has developed daughter-projects using principles and methods similar to those of this study which
explore the sexual subjectivities amongst ageing African migrants living in Australia as
well as Aboriginal and Torres Strait Islanders. In doing so, ongoing research aims to draw
on more diverse samples of women. We aim to explore the influence of socio-demographic factors such as class and educational background on women's sexual subjectivities. Given the centrality of women's male partners in this study, it would also be
worthwhile to extend this research by including male participants. Lastly, this discussion
has focused on the experiences of older women who were in committed relationships,
which may indeed differ from older women who are single or dating casually.

Conclusion

Limitations aside, this research represents an important contribution to a growing discussion on older women's sexual subjectivity. It has highlighted and reaffirmed the diversity

and fluidity of older women's sexual practices and desires, while challenging simplistic characterisations of elder sex as either asexual or as the "sexy oldie". In order to support older women's sexual autonomy, it is imperative to create and provide women with the resources that allow them to make informed choices over their sexual and bodily practices, while avoiding making normative assumptions about or prescriptions of older women's sexual lives.

Acknowledgements

The authors wish to thank the anonymous reviewers and Catherine MacPhail for their insightful feedback on earlier versions of this article. The research was approved by the La Trobe University Human Ethics Committee on 12 October 2011 (UHEC 11-049).

Funding

This research was funded by the Australian Research Council [grant number DP110101199].

Notes

1. These interviews represent a subset of interviews from a larger research project.
2. Zoloft, also known as Sertraline, is a selective serotonin reuptake inhibitor. This class of antidepressants may cause, contribute to, or exacerbate sexual dysfunction.

References

Bentrott, M., & Margrett, J. (2011). Taking a person-centered approach to understanding sexual expression among long-term care residents: Theoretical perspectives and research challenges. *Ageing International, 36*, 401–417.

Bitzer, J., Platano, G., Tschudin, S., & Alder, J. (2008). Sexual counselling in elderly couples. *Journal of Sexual Medicine, 5*(9), 2027–2043.

DeLamater, J. (2012). Sexual expression in later life: A review and synthesis. *Journal of Sex Research, 49*(2–3), 125–141.

Dixon, J. (2012). Communicating (St)ageism: Exploring stereotypes of age and sexuality in the workplace. *Research on Aging, 34*, 654–669.

Drummond, J.D., Brotman, S., Silverman, M., Sussman, R., Orzeck, P., Barylak, L., & Wallach, I. (2013). The impact of caregiving: Older women's experiences of sexuality and intimacy. *Affilia: Journal of Women and Social Work, 28*, 415–428.

Gott, M. (2001). Sexual activity and risk-taking in later life. *Health and Social Care in the Community, 9*(2), 72–78.

Gott, M. (2005). Are older people at risk of sexually transmitted infections? A new look at the evidence. *Reviews in Clinical Gerontology, 14*(1), 5–13.

Gott, M., & Hinchliff, S. (2003). Barriers to seeking treatment for sexual problems in primary care: A qualitative study with older people. *Family Practice, 20*, 690–695

Gott, M., Hinchliff, S., & Galena, E. (2004). General practitioner attitudes to discussing sexual health issues with older people. *Social Science & Medicine, 58*, 2093–2103.

Gray, P., & Garcia, J. (2012). Ageing and human sexual behaviour: Biocultural perspectives – a mini-review. *Gerontology, 58*, 446–452

Helmes, E., & Chapman, J. (2012). Education about sexuality in the elderly by healthcare professionals: A survey from the Southern Hemisphere. *Sex Education, 12*(1), 95–107.

Hinchliff, S., & Gott, M. (2004). Perceptions of well-being in sexual ill health: What role does age play? *Journal of Health Psychology, 9*, 649–660

Hinchliff, S., & Gott, M. (2008). Challenging social myths and stereotypes of women and aging: Heterosexual women talk about sex. *Journal of Women and Aging, 20*(1/2), 65–81.

Hinchliff, S., & Gott, M. (2011). Seeking medical help for sexual concerns in mid- and later life: A review of the literature. *Journal of Sex Research, 48*(2–3), 106–117.

Hinchliff, S., Gott, M., & Ingelton, C. (2010). Sex, menopause and social context: A qualitative study with heterosexual women. *Journal of Health Psychology, 15*, 724–733.

Howard, J.R., O'Neill, S., & Travers, C. (2006). Factors affecting sexuality in older Australian women: Sexual interest, sexual arousal, relationships and sexual distress in older Australian women. *Climacteric, 9*, 355–367.

Hurd Clarke, L., & Korotchenko, A. (2011). Aging and the body: A review. *Canadian Journal on Aging, 30*, 495–510.

Kingsberg, S. (2002). The psychological impact of aging on sexuality and relationships. *Journal of Women's Health and Gender-Based Medicine, 9*(Suppl 1), s33–s38.

The Kirby Institute (2012). *HIV, viral hepatitis and sexually transmissible infections in Australia.* Annual Surveillance Report 2012. Sydney: The Kirby Institute, the University of New South Wales.

Kirkman, L., Kenny, A., & Fox, C. (2013). Evidence of absence: Midlife and older adult sexual health policy in Australia. *Sexuality Research and Social Policy, 10*, 135–148.

Kleinplatz, P., Ménard, D., Paradis, N., Campbell, M., & Dalgleish, T. (2013). Beyond sexual stereotypes: Revealing group similarities and differences in optimal sexuality. *Canadian Journal of Behavioural Science, 45*, 250–258.

Kontula, O., & Haavio-Mannila, E. (2009). The impact of aging on human sexual activity and sexual desire. *Journal of Sex Research, 46*(1), 46–56.

Law, B. (2014, February 1). The business of pleasure. *The Sydney Morning Herald.* Retrieved from http://www.smh.com.au/lifestyle/the-business-of-pleasure-20140127-31hjs.html

Lindau, S.T., Schumm, P., Laumann, E.O., Levison, W., O'Muircheartaigh, C.A., & Waite, L.J. (2007). A study of sexuality and health among older adults in the United States. *The New England Journal of Medicine, 357*, 762–774.

Lodge, A., & Umberson, D. (2012). All shook up: Sexuality of mid- to later life married couples. *Journal of Marriage and Family, 74*, 428–443.

Mamo, L., & Fishman, J. (2001). Potency in all the right places: Viagra as a technology of the gendered body. *Body and Society, 7*, 13–35.

Marshall, B. (2012). Medicalization and the refashioning of age-related limits on sexuality. *Journal of Sex Research, 49*, 337–343.

McCarthy, B., Farr, E., & McDonald, D. (2013). Couple sexuality after 60. *Journal of Family Psychotherapy, 24*(1), 38–47.

Minichiello, V., Plummer, D., & Loxton, D. (2004). Factors predicting sexual relationships in older people: An Australian study. *Australasian Journal on Ageing, 23*(3), 125–130.

Minichiello, V., Rahman, S., Hawkes, G., & Pitts, M. (2012). STI epidemiology in the global older population: Emerging challenges. *Perspectives in Public Health, 132*(4), 178–181.

Montemurro, B., & Gillen, M. (2013). Wrinkles and sagging flesh: Exploring transformations in women's sexual body image. *Journal of Women and Aging, 25*, 3–23.

Ringa, V., Diter, K., Laborde, C., & Bajos, N. (2013). Women's sexuality: From aging to social representations. *Journal of Sexual Medicine, 10*, 2399–2408.

Sandberg, L. (2013a). Affirmative old age – the ageing body and feminist theories on difference. *International Journal of Ageing and Later Life, 8*(1), 11–40.

Sandberg, L. (2013b). Just feeling a naked body close to you: Men, sexuality and intimacy in later life. *Sexualities, 16*, 261–282.

Schick, V., Herbenick, D., Reece, M., Sanders, S., Dodge, B., Middlestadt, S., & Fortenberry, J.D. (2010). Sexual behaviors, condom use, and sexual health of Americans over 50: Implications for sexual health promotion for older adults. *Journal of Sexual Medicine, 7*(Suppl 5), 315–329.

Slinkard, M., & Kazer, M. (2011). Older adults and HIV and STI screening: The patient perspective. *Geriatric Nursing, 32*, 341–349.

Trudel, G., Turgeon, L., & Piché, L. (2010). Marital and sexual aspects of old age. *Sexual and Relationship Therapy, 25*, 316–341.

Willert, A., & Semans, M. (2000). Knowledge and attitudes about later life sexuality: What clinicians need to know about helping the elderly. *Contemporary Family Therapy, 22*, 415–435.

Yee, L. (2010). Aging and sexuality. *Australian Family Physician, 39*, 718–721.

Social connection, relationships and older lesbian and gay people[1]

Catherine Barrett[a], Carolyn Whyte[a], Jude Comfort[b], Anthony Lyons[a] and
Pauline Crameri[a]

[a]Australian Research Centre in Sex, Health and Society, La Trobe University, Melbourne,
Australia; [b]School of Public Health, Faculty of Health Sciences, West Australian Centre for Health
Promotion Research, Curtin University, Perth, Australia

This paper presents data from a small study exploring the impacts of homophobia on
the lives of older lesbian and gay Australians. Eleven in-depth interviews were
conducted with older lesbians (6) and gay men (5) ranging in age from 65 to 79 years.
The study found that participants' sense of self was shaped by the dominant medical,
legal and religious institutions of their youth that defined them as sick, immoral or
criminal. Participants described enforced "cure" therapies, being imprisoned, having
employment terminated and being disowned and disinherited by family. In this
context, intimate relationships and social networks provided refuge where trust was
rebuilt and sexuality affirmed. Many created safe spaces for themselves. This
equilibrium was threatened with increasing age, disability and the reliance on health
and social services. Participants feared a return to institutional control and a need to
"straighten up" or hide their sexuality. In response, partners stepped into the role of
caregiver, at times beyond their capacity and at a cost to their relationship. The study
describes the importance of understanding social connections in the lives of older
lesbians and gay men. It highlights the need for inclusive services to ensure that social
networks are supported and that health and well-being are promoted.

Introduction

Many older lesbians and gay men have lived through a time when their only protection
against heterosexist violence and discrimination was to make themselves invisible, to
publicly deny their sexual orientation and pass as heterosexuals (Barrett, 2008). Disclosure could result in imprisonment, enforced medical interventions and "cures," or the loss
of employment, family and friends (Barrett, 2008; Leonard, Duncan, & Barrett, 2012).
Prior to the gay liberation movement, the experience of coming out or disclosing their
sexual orientation had a detrimental impact on their sense of self, relationships and social
connections. Older lesbians and gay men are less likely than their post-liberation peers to
have had their sexual orientation affirmed or celebrated, are less likely to have developed
positive self-image and self-esteem (Cronin & King, 2014) and more likely to have experienced fracturing of significant relationships.

The discrimination experienced by older lesbians and gay men has also affected their
health adversely and their willingness to access health services (Fredriksen-Goldsen

---

[1]This paper describes research conducted by the Australian Research Centre in Sex, Health and
Society at La Trobe University in Melbourne and Curtin University in Perth, Australia.

et al., 2011). They have higher rates of disability, depression and loneliness than their heterosexual counterparts (Fredriksen-Goldsen et al., 2011). They have fewer social networks, are more likely to be single and live alone (Guasp, 2011) and are at greater risk of social isolation (Fredriksen-Goldsen et al., 2011). Friendships are integral to building social networks and have been shown to be a key factor in positive mental health (Lyons, Pitts, & Grierson, 2013). However, many older lesbians and gay men report that their sexuality is a barrier to building friendships in the broader community (Cronin & King, 2014). The social isolation this creates further diminishes their health and well-being (Fredriksen-Goldsen et al., 2011).

Despite these disparities, older lesbians and gay men are less likely to access services they feel are needed, because they fear discrimination (Guasp, 2011). They are also more likely to be reliant on partners and friends for support as they age (Fredriksen-Goldsen et al., 2011), which is attributable in part to the fact that they are less likely to have children and less likely to have regular contact with their biological families (Guasp, 2011).

To address these disparities, service providers must understand the historical experiences and needs of older lesbians and gay men (Barrett, Turner, & Leonard, 2013). However, until recently, older lesbians and gay men were almost completely ignored in gerontology, policy development and legal reform (Harrison, 2006). This created a cycle of invisibility (Harrison, 2001). Sexuality was hidden because it was not safe − fostering an illusion that reforms were not required. In turn, the absence of reforms meant that older lesbians and gay men continued to believe it was unsafe to disclose their sexual orientation. Research demonstrates that many service providers do not believe that they need to be inclusive because it does not occur to them that they have any lesbian or gay clients (Barrett, Harrison, & Kent, 2009; GLBTI Retirement Association Inc. [GRAI], 2010). There is also a commonly held myth that older people are asexual and therefore cannot be sexually diverse (Barrett, 2011). The failure to address the needs of older lesbians and gay men is an indirect form of discrimination (Hughes, 2006, 2007) that is currently being addressed in a number of countries around the world.

This paper describes a small ethnographic study documenting the effects of discrimination on older lesbians and gay men in Australia. The project was funded in response to a growing body of research, linking higher rates of depression and anxiety to the experiences of homophobic discrimination (Corboz et al., 2008). Funding was provided by *beyondblue*, a national organisation working to address issues associated with depression, anxiety and related disorders in Australia. The study was conducted by Val's Café at the Australian Research Centre in Sex, Health and Society at La Trobe University, in collaboration with the Western Australian Centre for Health Promotion Research at Curtin University between 2012 and 2013. The study documented the effects of discrimination on relationships and social connections and highlighted the need for improved services and further research.

Aims of the research

The aims of the research were to document older lesbian, gay, bisexual, transgender and intersex people's experiences of discrimination, particularly with regard to its impact on their relationships with partners, friends and family, and to understand how these experiences are implicated in higher than average rates of depression and anxiety. The study was largely exploratory. We did not specify hypotheses. However, we expected that accounts from participants would focus strongly on the impact of discrimination on their relationships and psychological well-being given the growing body of research, linking higher rates of depression, anxiety and related disorders among lesbians, gay, bisexual, transgender and intersex (LGBTI) Australians to their experiences of homophobic and transphobic discrimination (Corboz et al., 2008), as well as evidence for a strong protective effect of social support (Lyons et al., 2013).

Method

Study design

In-depth interviews were conducted to explore participants' experiences of discrimination, the effects of discrimination, the experience of anxiety and depression and whether participants felt that there was a connection between discrimination and their depression or anxiety. Ethics approval for the project was granted by the La Trobe University Human Research Ethics Committee.

Procedure for recruitment

A recruitment flyer was developed and circulated to LGBTI groups and service providers in Victoria, Western Australia and Queensland. The study was restricted to three Australian states because of the limited resources and small scale of the study. The flyer clarified that the researchers were seeking to interview LGBTI people aged 65 years or more who had experienced homophobic or transphobic discrimination and depression or anxiety.

Participants

Twelve interviews were conducted with participants from Victoria ($n = 5$), Western Australia ($n = 6$) and Queensland ($n = 1$). Six participants identified as lesbian/gay women, five as gay men and one as transgender. No intersex or bisexual people were recruited. This paper focuses on interview data from the 11 lesbians and gay men who participated. The age range of participants was 65–79 years with a mean age of 70 years (SD = 4.7 years).

Procedure

Nine interviews were conducted face-to-face in participants' homes. Two of these were conducted in nursing homes. Further three interviews were conducted by phone. Each interview lasted between 40 and 90 minutes. Participants were asked about their experiences of homophobic discrimination and the effects on their lives, particularly in relation to depression and anxiety. They were invited to share an image to help complement their spoken account and explore experiences that they might find difficulty to talk about (Eisner, 2008; Frawley, Barrett, & Dyson, 2013). Participants were invited to select an image that would not identify them and, in the case of phone interviews, to email or post the image to the researcher. Given the sensitive and potentially distressing nature of the experiences that were being recounted, participants were provided with details of professional support services and invited to identify strategies for self-support before the interview was conducted.

The interviews were audio recorded and transcribed using a professional transcription service approved by La Trobe University Human Research Ethics Committee. The draft narratives and full transcripts were returned to participants for verification and to provide participants with the opportunity to make changes to protect their identity. Feedback from participants was considered important to maximise the report's credibility (Patton, 2002) and authenticity (Winter, 2002). It was also considered important to maximise participants' control over how their lives were represented given the historical pathologising of lesbian and gay sexuality. To ensure anonymity, all participants' names were replaced with pseudonyms when reporting findings in this article.

Data analysis

The interview transcripts were analysed thematically adapting Ritchie and Spencer's "framework" to identify common themes and significant differences (Ritchie & Spencer, 1994). Analysis was independently undertaken by two of the authors of this article and then discussed with the broader team to identify key themes. In addition, individual narratives were constructed from the transcripts. This involved ordering events into a chronological sequence, editing some data and providing thematic headings within each narrative.

Findings

Many of the participants' responses in interviews involved recounting the devastating impacts of homophobia on their lives, their health and their relationships. Narratives about discrimination and its effects included strong themes around the effects of discrimination on relationships and social connections. Three major themes were identified, each of which revolved around key relationships: early relationships with biological family; intimate relationships; and friendships and the broader community. A fourth theme was further identified, which centred on ageing, disability and support services and how these changed relationships and social networks.

Early relationships with biological family

Participants described the heartache of rejection by their biological families and the consequences on their lives. Pam (not her real name) reported that her family gave her "the flick" after she came out; adding that her sister-in-law "could not even bear to be in the same room ... I was persona non grata." In response, Pam recalled, I had to "distance myself from my family completely" in order to maintain her mental health. Relationships with family were often irreparably damaged. Gerri recounted, my mother said I was "in the gutter and that's where I'd stay while I chose to live this life. ... It's not a good feeling when you are told that by your mother. I'll never forgive mum for that."

While some participants severed contact with family, others tried to build rapport in the hope that their sexual orientation would be accepted over time. Larry described being placed in a psychiatric institution and given shock therapy at the age of 14 after his parents became aware that he was gay. He later joined the army to get away from his father, but was discharged after disclosing to the army chaplain that he was gay. Larry felt that his mother embraced his sexuality but his father continued to reject him and later disinherited him.

Rejection by family was also experienced by Dawn when she left her husband and children to be in a lesbian relationship. Dawn felt pressured to leave her hometown and to withdraw contact from her children because her family believed that the children "would become ... corrupted by our relationship ... that I would corrupt the children and they would be[come] deviants or something." Dawn missed key milestones in her children's lives, including her daughter's wedding and was not reconciled with her son until 30 years later. She listed the losses she experienced: "I had a loss of identity for a start, a loss of children, a loss of home, a loss of income, a loss of parenting, a loss of friends." Dawn's parents removed her images from family photo albums and she described how "the rejection by so many people really broke my spirit." In the immediate period after leaving her husband, she took an overdose of sleeping pills in an attempt to kill herself.

These early experiences of rejection by biological family members shaped participants' sense of self, social connection and future relationships. The impacts of this lack of family support were noted by Patrice who said, "the bottom line is [if] you get support first off from your family it does make things a little easier for you ... it gives you that extra support, that extra confidence, you know." In narratives about family support, participants described their appreciation for even small gestures of recognition, particularly in their teenage years when they were still dependent on family.

The importance of family support was highlighted by participants who described significant efforts to regain family support. They also demonstrated a great capacity to forgive family members when they were rejected. For example, Dawn assisted her siblings to care for her father after her mother died and he was diagnosed with Alzheimer's disease. During this time her father apologised and Dawn noted, "he was instantly forgiven." Expectations of family were lowered; participants did not expect unconditional love and often worked hard at getting families on their side.

Rejection by biological family has significant effects on the lives of older lesbians and gay men (Barrett, 2008; Leonard et al., 2012). As a result, they missed the opportunities for affirming and celebrating sexual orientation (Cronin & King, 2014) and this had enduring effects. For example, Larry described how the view of homosexuality as deviant or disordered "burns its little tentacles into your brain and it stays there, believe me it stays there."

Intimate relationships

A lack of affirmation from family, and society more broadly, appeared to influence perceptions and experiences of intimate relationships in later life. Intimate relationships were described as the first and sometimes the only place where sexual orientation was affirmed and valued. Larry recalled how he believed his sexuality was "a sickness" until he met his first partner who affirmed his sexuality by saying there was "nothing wrong with me." Intimate relationships also provided a safe space, free from discrimination. In reflection on this Pam noted, "the effect that [discrimination] has [is that] there is **you** and the **rest of them** and you are trying to make your own little space." Similarly, Gerri said: "you feel like you've come home. ... this is what I want, I'm safe here and love grows, it definitely grows." In these ways, intimate relationships appeared to help heal the rejection of biological families (Smalley, 1987) and at times provided the only place where it was safe to be gay or lesbian.

In the longer term, intimate relationships provided an important source of psychological support to manage the everyday experience of homophobia. Cliff reflected, "sometimes it's my partner who understands what I might be going through ... a person who's experienced something can certainly relate it much better."

It may not be surprising then that intimate partners were greatly valued and often referred to as "soul mates." They provided a significant mediating factor against marginality (Cronin & King, 2014; Heaphy, 2009) that enabled many older lesbians and gay men to survive extraordinary experiences of discrimination. As other studies show, the positive effects of such relationships for lesbians and gay men tend to be sustained over time with those in long-term relationships having more positive attitudes towards ageing than those who are single (Heaphy, 2009).

Although intimate relationships were an important source of social connection, being in a relationship also meant that sexual orientation was more visible, increasing the likelihood of rejection and discrimination. Pam recounted that when she disclosed her sexuality, "my family didn't want to have anything to do with me ... because I had a relationship it made it so much worse. If I wasn't in a relationship they could have glossed over it." The responses of family and the broader community meant that some participants felt the need to hide their relationships to be safe.

The pressure to hide relationships to avoid discrimination created tension (Smalley, 1987) and social isolation. Gerri described declining an invitation to her niece's wedding because she was not sure how people would respond to her partner. She reflected that not being able to share her partner "pisses you off. It does make you angry and sad at the same time and I think if you let yourself dwell on it too much it can be very hard." The consequences of this for Gerri were that she felt, "boxed in, you can't open up. It is very sad that you have to hide when it's so natural to you and the horrible things that people say and do because you are not like them."

The decision to straighten up or hide a relationship was at times a point of dissonance in relationships. Larry described how his partner was "ashamed of being found out he was a homosexual so ... I could not tell anybody I was a homosexual because I didn't want to hurt him." While Larry understood his partner's fear, he lamented the lack of recognition of his own sexuality adding "I have lived all my life wanting to be recognised."

Having an intimate partner also changed the interaction that some participants had with service providers. When Pam's partner became ill, they moved to a rural area to reduce costs and Pam became her partner's full-time caregiver. Pam described how her partner "wanted to jump right into the closet again to the point of telling me off that we shouldn't do things like holding hands. I had to mind 'p's and 'q's and not be so obvious." As others have found (Jordan & Deluty, 2000), having to hide their sexual orientation again after so many years led to dissatisfaction in some relationships.

The hidden nature of some intimate relationships created difficulties around the death of a partner. Gerri described her family's surprise at the extent of her grief when her partner died, believing that she and her partner were just two women "living together and sharing expenses." Gerri experienced significant difficulty at work because she had not disclosed the nature of her relationship, describing how it was "hell at work ... I had to hold [the grief] in." The lack of relationship recognition resulted in disenfranchised grief (Westwood, 2013), with the loss not being openly mourned, supported or acknowledged (Doka, 1989). For some other participants, the funeral of a partner was the first time their relationship received recognition. After decades of rejection by family, Larry described that at his partner's funeral "... there was all my family, nephews, nieces, all our friends and there must have been about 200 people in there and I send him out with Shirley Bassey singing Hey Big Spender...[he] didn't go out alone."

Friendships and the broader community

A broad range of friendships and social groups provided important support networks and a sense of social connection. Tim reflected that he joined a gay social group that "provides friendship ... you know it's doing us a service, that's something we require, you can't just sort of isolate yourself." Similarly, Cliff noted that friendships were important to "help you through" difficult times.

The capacity to embrace friendships and the characteristics of friends were debated. Amanda suggested that some lesbians enter relationships thinking, "okay I am safe here, let's put up the wall," having little engagement with the broader heterosexual community. Amanda reported that this often led to a "very claustrophobic relationship where you start to rely on each other just too much. . . . You just cannot get everything you want and need in life from one person." Amanda believed that "in relationships you should get out and grow. You don't want to become inward looking because you just won't survive." In her own life, Amanda engaged a broad range of people beyond her circle of lesbian friends. She reported that lesbians who did not do this were at risk of depression if their relationships ended because "there is nothing else . . . working" in their life.

Although Amanda engaged successfully with the broader community, others had more mixed experiences of heterosexual friendships. Noel was imprisoned at the age of 17 for the "abominable crime of buggery" and described losing heterosexual friends who were concerned that they could be seen as "consorting with a known criminal." Larry described his close friendship with a heterosexual couple that was severed after the couple became pregnant and did not want gay men near their child. The potential homophobic tension in relationships was highlighted by Gerri who described that by coming out, you "know who your true friends are . . . some of them think it's a disease and they might catch it, so you don't hear from them, they disappear."

For participants in this study, heterosexuality was not an exclusion criterion in relationships; rather it was the capacity to value and affirm sexual orientation that determined whether or not friendships were formed and sustained. This phenomenon has been described elsewhere by older lesbians and gay men as "My People" or social networks of supporters who value and affirm sexual diversity (Barrett, 2008). These friendship networks may include ex-lovers (Cook-Daniels, 1997) and may be afforded the status of family (Guasp, 2011) sometimes referred to as "families of choice" (Dewaele, Cox, Van den Berghe, & Vincke, 2011). It has been argued that traditional conceptions of friendship inadequately describes the range and depth of these relationships (Almack, Seymour, & Bellamy, 2010), with some relationships not easily fitting into a "friend–lover" binary classification system (Roseneil & Budgeon, 2004, p. 138).

Friendships appear to be a greater source of support for older lesbians and gay men compared with their heterosexual counterparts (Weeks, Heaphy, & Donovan, 2003), and serve as a possible protective factor against the effects of homophobia and is linked with greater psychological well-being (Lyons et al., 2013; Masini & Barrett, 2008). For some participants in this study, friendships were very important, particularly for those who had lost partners or who were not in intimate relationships. Participants described how their small social networks provided places where they felt valued, affirmed and safe.

Ageing, disability and support services

Many participants described the protection and support provided by intimate partners and social networks as being jeopardised with increasing age and disability. As participants aged, many lost partners and friends and found that their friendship networks diminished with few opportunities to meet other older lesbians and gay men. They feared that accessing services for older people would see a return to the institutional control of their youth. Accessing services was conceptualised as stepping outside of existing social networks where they were safe and affirmed and stepping into a heteronormative world where there was little choice but to hide their sexual orientation to escape homophobic abuse from staff and other clients.

To illustrate these potential losses, Patrice described her perspective on accessing a senior citizens group and how she felt she had little in common with the heterosexual people accessing this service. She said:

> I've been gay all my life, why am I now at 68 going to a group of people who've been married, have children and join their conversations and their life? I've got nothing in common with them. . . . We have nothing in common other than the fact we breathe the same air and we eat food and we are human beings. . . . They've got no concept of my life.

Similarly, Gerri expressed concern that in a retirement village she would have little in common with other residents who would be "looking down their noses because they would be of an age when it was taboo." Pam also noted that while all older people were vulnerable when accessing services, "you add a different sexuality and it's much, much worse." Many participants like Cliff believed that there would be few choices other than to go back into the closet.

Given these perspectives it is not surprising that older lesbians and gay men often stepped into the role of caregiver if their partner needed support, rather than access services. At times this support was provided beyond their capacity and at cost to their relationship. Pam, whose partner became seriously ill, described her partner's reluctance to access home services because she was concerned about discrimination. As a consequence, she gave up work to become her partner's full-time caregiver. Pam described how she was a "24/7 carer and it was a big mistake. I think that taking on the carer's role led to the destruction of our relationship. I overdid it." The change in their relationship dynamic and her partner's health placed a significant burden on their relationship, which later ended.

Intimate relationships were also viewed as a buffer against the challenges of ageing. Larry described how he was able to care for his dying partner and how his partner "was lucky I was here for him ... gays die a very, very lonely life." Where social networks were limited to an intimate relationship, participants felt they had little to live for after their partner died. Some felt isolated and alone, surrounded by services and people who did not understand or value them.

Discussion

Experiences of relationships appear to be different for older lesbians and gay men compared to their heterosexual counterparts. Many participants in this study described growing up and coming out in a world where institutionalised homophobia was sanctioned and how this led to fractured social supports and a detrimental impact on relationships with families, friends and other forms of social connectedness. Despite these challenges, many found ways to build social networks and to create safe, affirming spaces to enjoy their lives, particularly within their intimate relationships.

Family support has been shown to be a factor in mitigating the effects of discrimination (Masini & Barrett, 2008). However, many of the older lesbians and gay men in this study described having been rejected by family when they disclosed their sexual orientation. While some walked away from families to protect their health, others worked at rebuilding relationships with family over decades. Some scaled back their expectations of family, not expecting full support, and treasured even small gestures of support. On the whole, the frequently negative responses from families appeared to have eroded self-esteem, confidence and trust. They also appeared to influence the ways in which future relationships were negotiated and valued, and how these relationships often became refuges from the hostile world of their youth.

For some older lesbians and gay men, being in intimate relationships was their only source of social support. However, being in an intimate relationship appeared to be a double-edged sword for some participants, with the presence of a partner making sexual orientation more public and increasing the likelihood of discrimination. To avoid discrimination, relationships were often hidden, exacerbating social isolation and placing burden on the relationship. Considerable grief was expressed about the lack of opportunities for recognition of intimate relationships, particularly around the death of a partner. The fact that intimate relationships were seldom acknowledged or celebrated reinforced to some older lesbians and gay men that their sexual orientation was not valued. The many conflicting issues around intimate relationships are perhaps some reasons why friendships were given considerable importance.

However, there was significant divergence in experiences and views relating to heterosexual friendships. Experiences with homophobic heterosexuals resulted in some older lesbians and gay men dismissing the capacity of heterosexuals to genuinely understand and value their sexual orientation. For others, it was about the characteristics of friends, rather than their sexuality. A friend was someone who valued and affirmed their sexuality and the capacity to achieve this was not always considered to be dependent on whether a friend was lesbian, gay or straight. Friendships were negotiated and some were lost when it was apparent that these friends were not accepting of their sexuality. On the whole, participants appeared to be very discerning about who entered and remained in their networks.

The safe and affirming places created by intimate relationships and broader social networks were threatened with increasing age and disability. Over time, partners and friends were lost and social networks diminished. Increasing levels of disability made it difficult to get out and meet other like-minded people. The opportunities to engage with other older lesbians and gay men are also inhibited by geography and by the fact that there are no dedicated spaces in which this engagement can occur (Cronin & King, 2014). Many believed that their safe spaces and affirming networks would be undermined by service providers and other clients who were homophobic and with whom they had nothing in common. A more distressing fear for participants was that they would have to "straighten up" their lives, or hide their sexual orientation if they required residential aged care. Many considered that they would no longer be safe and would lose the possibility of expressing their sexual orientation. Unfortunately, while many services are now embracing strategies to become more inclusive, evidence also shows that older lesbians and gay men receive a lesser standard of care in some services (Barrett, 2008; Barrett et al., 2009; The Equal Rights Center, 2014).

The narratives from this small sample highlight the importance of service providers' understanding and addressing the needs of older lesbians and gay men. They demonstrate how history and life experiences shape the way that relationships are valued and negotiated and how this potentially affects social networks, health and well-being. They also emphasised the importance of providing culturally safe services, or service providers' understanding history and institutional discrimination, analysing power imbalances and reflecting on how their own values and beliefs influence service delivery (Nursing Council of New Zealand, 2002).

The study also highlights the need for further research. This study was small, limited to three Australian states, only recruited one transgender person and failed to recruit any bisexual or intersex people. Data was not collected about levels of education, socioeconomic status or other factors that may influence participant's social connectedness, health and well-being. The results cannot be generalised, but rather emphasise that a more substantial body of evidence is required to influence legislation, policy and service delivery. Such research could involve a survey of health and well-being, social connections, caregiving responsibilities, access to services and older people's perspectives on what changes need to occur.

At the time of writing significant reforms occurred in Australia that recognised the social support needs of older lesbians, gay, bisexual, transgender and intersex (LGBTI) people. Reforms include an amendment to the Aged Care Act (Australian Government, 2012) to afford older LGBTI people special needs group status and the development of a National LGBTI Ageing and Aged Care Strategy (Department of Health and Ageing [DoHA], 2012). These reforms have been supported by the allocation of funding for community visiting schemes, or programmes to provide visitors for socially isolated older LGBTI people. Community visitors will be volunteers who value older LGBTI people and have the capacity to build social networks and reduce the fear of social isolation and vulnerability to discrimination. This important reform recognises the challenges to social networks addressed in this paper. The authors hope that further research will identify other strategies to build social networks for older LGBTI people.

Acknowledgements

We would like to acknowledge the older lesbians and gay men who bravely shared their stories — many for the first time.

Funding

We wish to thank *beyondblue* [grant number 6615:10635] for funding this research; *beyondblue* is a national organisation addressing issues associated with depression, anxiety and related disorders in Australia.

References

Almack, K., Seymour, J., & Bellamy, G. (2010). Exploring the impact of sexual orientation on experiences and concerns about end of life care and on bereavement for lesbian, gay and bisexual older people. *Sociology, 44*(5), 908–924. doi:10.1177/0038038510375739

Australian Government. (2012). Allocation amendment (people with special needs) principles 2012 – F2012L01469. Retrieved from http://www.comlaw.gov.au/Details/F2012L01469

Barrett, C. (2008). *My people: Exploring the experiences of gay, lesbian, bisexual, transgender and intersex seniors in aged care services.* Melbourne: Matrix Guild Victoria and Vintage Men.

Barrett, C. (2011). Auditing organisational capacity to promote the sexual health of older people. *Electronic Journal of Applied Psychology, 7*(1), 31–36.

Barrett, C., Harrison, J., & Kent, J. (2009). *Permission to speak. Towards the development of gay, lesbian, bisexual, transgender and intersex friendly aged care services.* Melbourne: Matrix Guild Victoria and Vintage Men.

Barrett, C., Turner, L., & Leonard, L. (2013). *Beyond a rainbow sticker. A report on How2 create a gay, lesbian, bisexual, transgender and intersex (GLBTI) inclusive service 2012–2013.* Melbourne: Gay and Lesbian Health Victoria.

Cook-Daniels, L. (1997). Lesbian, gay male, bisexual and transgendered elders: Elder abuse and neglect issues. *Journal of Elder Abuse & Neglect, 9*(2), 35–49.

Corboz, J., Dowsett, G., Mitchell, A., Couch, M., Agius, P., & Pitts, M. (2008). *Feeling queer and blue: A review of the literature on depression and related issues among gay, lesbian, bisexual and other homosexually-active people* (a report prepared for beyondblue: the national depression initiative). Melbourne: Australian Research Centre in Sex, Health and Society, La Trobe University.

Cronin, A., & King, A. (2014). Only connect? Older lesbian, gay and bisexual (LGB) adults and social capital. *Ageing & Society, 34*(02), 258–279. doi: 10.1017/S0144686×12000955

Department of Health and Ageing [DoHA]. (2012). *National LGBTI ageing and aged care strategy.* Canberra: Commonwealth of Australia.

Dewaele, A., Cox, N., Van den Berghe, W., & Vincke, J. (2011). Families of choice? Exploring the supportive networks of lesbians, gay men, and bisexuals1. *Journal of Applied Social Psychology, 41*(2), 312–331. doi: 10.1111/j.1559-1816.2010.00715.x

Doka, K.J. (1989). *Disenfranchised grief: Recognizing hidden sorrow.* Lexington, MA: Lexington Books.

Eisner, E. (2008). Art and knowledge. In J. Knowles & A. Cole (Eds.), *Handbook of the arts in qualitative research* (pp. 3–12). London: Sage.

The Equal Rights Center. (2014). *Opening doors: An investigation of barriers to senior housing for same-sex couples.* Washington, DC: The Equal Rights Center.

Frawley, P., Barrett, C., & Dyson, S. (2013). *Real people, core business: Evaluation of the living safer sexual lives peer education project for people with intellectual disabilities.* Melbourne: The Australian Research Centre in Sex, Health and Society.

Fredriksen-Goldsen, K.I., Kim, H.-J., Emlet, C.A., Muraco, A., Erosheva, E.A., Hoy-Ellis, C.P., . . . Petry, H. (2011). *The aging and health report: Disparities and resilience among lesbian, gay, bisexual, and transgender older adults.* Seattle, WA: Institute for Multigenerational Health.

GLBTI Retirement Association Inc. (2010). *We don't have any of those people here: Retirement accommodation and aged care issues for non-heterosexual populations.* Perth: GRAI (GLBTI Retirement Association Inc) and Curtin Health Innovation Research Institute, Curtin University.

Guasp, A. (2011). *Lesbian, gay & bisexual people in later life.* London: Stonewall.

Harrison, J. (2001). 'It's none of my business': Gay and lesbian invisibility in aged care. *Australian Occupational Therapy Journal, 48*(3), 142–145. doi:10.1046/j.0045-0766.2001.00262.x

Harrison, J. (2006). Coming out ready or not! Gay, lesbian, bisexual, transgender and intersex ageing and aged care in Australia: Reflections, contemporary developments and the road ahead. *Gay and Lesbian Issues and Psychology Review, 2*(2), 44–53.

Heaphy, B. (2009). Choice and its limits in older lesbian and gay narratives of relational life. *Journal of GLBT Family Studies, 5*(1–2), 119–138. doi:10.1080/15504280802595451

Hughes, M. (2006). Queer ageing. *Gay and Lesbian Issues and Psychology Review, 2*(2), 54–59.

Hughes, M. (2007). Older lesbians and gays accessing health and aged-care services. *Australian Social Work, 60*(2), 197–209.

Jordan, K.M., & Deluty, R.H. (2000). Social support, coming out, and relationship satisfaction in lesbian couples. *Journal of Lesbian Studies, 4*(1), 145–164.

Leonard, W., Duncan, D., & Barrett, C. (2012). What a difference a gay makes: The constitution of the 'older gay man'. In A. Kampf, B. Marshall, & A. Petersen (Eds.), *Aging men: Masculinities and modern medicine* (pp. 105–120). London: Routledge.

Lyons, A., Pitts, M., & Grierson, J. (2013). Factors related to positive mental health in a stigmatized minority: An investigation of older gay men. *Journal of Aging and Health, 25*(7), 1159–1181. doi:10.1177/0898264313495562

Masini, B.E., & Barrett, H.A. (2008). Social support as a predictor of psychological and physical well-being and lifestyle in lesbian, gay, and bisexual adults aged 50 and over. *Journal of Gay & Lesbian Social Services, 20*(1–2), 91–110. doi:10.1080/10538720802179013

Nursing Council of New Zealand. (2002). *Guidelines for cultural safety, the treaty of Waitangi, and Maori health in nursing and midwifery education and practice*. Wellington: Nursing Council of New Zealand.

Patton, M. (2002). *Qualitative research and evaluation methods*. London: Sage.

Ritchie, J., & Spencer, L. (1994). 'Qualitative data analysis for applied policy research'. In B. Alan & B. Robert (Eds.), *Analyzing qualitative data*. London: Routledge.

Roseneil, S., & Budgeon, S. (2004). Cultures of intimacy and care beyond 'the family': Personal life and social change in the early 21st century. *Current Sociology, 52*(2), 135–159.

Smalley, S. (1987). Dependency issues in lesbian relationships. *Journal of Homosexuality, 14*(1–2), 125–135. doi:10.1300/J082v14n01_10

Weeks, J., Heaphy, B., & Donovan, C. (2003). *Same sex intimacies*. London: Routledge.

Westwood, S. (2013). 'My friends are my family': An argument about the limitations of contemporary law's recognition of relationships in later life. *Journal of Social Welfare and Family Law, 35*(3), 347–363. doi:10.1080/09649069.2013.801688

Winter, R. (2002). Truth or fiction: Problems of validity and authenticity in narratives of action research. *Educational Action Research, 10*(1), 143–154.

To date or not to date, that is the question: older single gay men's concerns about dating

Yiu Tung Suen

Department of Sociology, Chinese University of Hong Kong, Hong Kong, China

Previous research with older gay men has overlooked their concerns about dating. This paper addresses the gap by analysing in-depth interviews conducted with 25 self-identified single gay men over the age of 50, who lived in England. The paper focuses on the research question: "What factors do older, single gay men consider when they contemplate dating?". Five factors were identified which affected their decisions about whether to date. Because the same factors operated simultaneously to encourage and to discourage them to contemplate dating, feelings of tension and ambivalence were reported by participants. Although some of these issues are similar to the ones older straight people considered, some of the concerns identified in this study were distinctively different for older gay men. The findings can help to make therapists aware that being single among older gay men is not only a personal experience, but is heavily influenced by social ideals and historical development of gay rights. It also can inform therapists of the factors that encourage and discourage older gay men from contemplating dating. This awareness can help therapists with developing effective strategies for working with clients on the topic of relationships.

Introduction

The therapeutic needs of older, gay men, who live at the intersection of ageism and homophobia, have gained increasing attention during the past decades (e.g., Friend, 1987; Frost 1997; McDougall, 1994). The recognition that therapists must be culturally competent, coupled with a growing interest in the needs of the ageing population, has contributed to this shift (Garnets & Kimmel, 2003; Shannon & Woods, 1991).

Older, gay men may have distinctive concerns about internalized homophobia, sexual identity and self-esteem, which they bring to the therapeutic encounter. In addition, the literature has identified the social isolation experienced by older gay men (Jacobs, Rasmussen, & Hohman, 1999). The gay community's youth-oriented culture excludes this group from "a world in which being old equates to being unattractive and being attractive is a precondition for entry" (Jones & Pugh, 2005, p. 258). Older, gay men have stated that their wish to "locate a setting that was not dominated by younger men" was difficult to realize (Christian & Keefe, 1997, p. 69). They also expressed worries over care provisions in later life, if their capacity for independence is compromised. There is a perception among older gay men that healthcare providers, particularly personal care assistants, may reject or neglect them on the grounds of their sexual and gender identities. They also feel that, should they require residential care, they may not be accepted and respected by other residents, thus forcing them "back into the closet" (Barrett, Whyte, Comfort, Lyons, & Crameri, 2014; Stein, Beckerman, & Sherman, 2010). Administrative and care staff, as well as residents of retirement care facilities were all perceived as potential sources of discrimination (Johnson, Jackson, Arnette, & Koffman, 2005).

Relatively, little is known about older gay men's needs for intimacy and relationship formation, their dating patterns, preferences and experiences (Brown & Shinohara, 2013; Bulcroft & Bulcroft, 1991). Even less is known of their views about dating. As single status amongst gay men is relatively common, it is imperative that this gap in the research is addressed. A review of data from surveys conducted between the 1970s and 1990s identified that at any given time approximately 45–80 per cent of lesbians were in committed relationships. In a corresponding sample of gay men, only 40–60 per cent were reported to be in similar relationships (Hostetler, 2009). These rates did not appear to vary much by age (Hostetler, 2009, p. 500).

Although the research on older people and dating is limited (Sassler, 2010), work has been undertaken to establish whether or not older people want to date (Calasanti & Kiecolt, 2007; Davidson, 2002; Dickson, Hughes, & Walker, 2005). These studies identified that, among older people, those who are younger and male are more likely to express a desire to repartner. Older people attributed their desires to date to: (1) prestige or an enhanced sense of identity or esteem from peers; (2) emotional affection or intimacy; (3) perceived companionship and social connection; and (4) physical affection (Watson & Stelle, 2011). Many older people considered exploring more diverse and alternative forms of dating and relationship formation (e.g. Kleinplatz et al., 2009). In previous studies, older people discussed the importance of looking for relationships that are based on emotional and sexual equality, but not necessarily on cohabitation or monogamy. Many older widows were opposed to remarriage or considered it impossible (Talbott, 1998). Consistent with that, they were keen to remain independent (Dickson et al., 2005). They often associated dating with loss of independence because the men they dated wanted marriage (Calasanti & Kiecolt, 2007; Dickson et al., 2005). They expressed concern that a potential remarriage might entail an unequal division of labour (Davidson, 2002, p. 57). In contrast, they associated widowhood with freedom. They enjoyed what they termed their "selfish" abilities to do what they wanted (Davidson, 2001). As a result, widows were more open to experimenting with different forms of relationship without cohabitation (Talbott, 1998). In some cases, they made the effort to separate emotional closeness, physical proximity and geographical distance (Koren, 2014).

Assumptions about relationships based on the values and experiences of heterosexual people may however not necessarily apply to gay and lesbian couples (Peplau & Cochran, 1990, p. 323). The needs of older, non-heterosexual people are not adequately addressed in the literature. The aim of this paper is to consider the views of older, single, gay men on the subject of dating. In addition, this includes gaining an insight into the decision-making processes undertaken by this group of people when they think about dating. The focus is on the research question "What factors do older, single gay men consider when they contemplate dating?". The findings have the potential to increase awareness of older, gay men's needs for intimacy and relationship formation amongst therapists.

Methods

The data in this article are drawn from a larger study of older gay men's experiences of singlehood. Twenty-five, self-identified, gay, single men over the age of 50 who lived in England were interviewed. Qualitative methodology, which has a particular capacity to generate novel understandings of "how the social world is interpreted, understood, experienced, produced or constituted" (Mason, 2002, p. 3), was employed to understand the many ways in which the participants interpreted their single status. Ethical clearance and approval was obtained from the University of Oxford Social Sciences and Humanities Inter-divisional Research Ethics Committee. Before each interview, written informed consent from the research participants was sought. The participants were recruited through different organizations that worked with older lesbian, gay, bisexual and transgender (LGBT) people and through recruitment in online general classified websites. Recruitment was supplemented by snowballing, which involved asking participants to refer to the researcher any other persons who might fit the criteria and may be interested to take part in the study. Of the 25 participants, an overwhelming majority (80 per cent) were recruited through social groups that work with either gay men or LGBT people. Two participants were recruited through snowballing. One participant was recruited through posting on a general classified website, one through an organization that works with men and another by word of mouth. It can be argued that because most of the participants were recruited through social groups, the sample may be more socially active and socially connected than average.

The participants ranged from 52 to 73 years of age (mean age = 59.6, SD = 5.8). Twelve of the participants were in their 50s, 11 were in their 60s, and one was in his 70s. All of the participants were white. Despite considerable effort to recruit participants from diverse groups, advertising failed to attract participants from ethnic minority groups. More than half of the participants (n = 15) were educated to at least undergraduate level. Most of the participants lived in south-east England. All the names employed in this paper are pseudonyms.

The interviews made use of the funnelling approach of "grand tours and mini tours" (Plummer, 2001, p. 145), sequencing the questions to start deliberately broadly. Initially, the participants were invited to share their life stories via an open-ended question "Would you mind telling me a bit about your life story?". Then, questions on topics such as relationship history, the participants' views about ageing, being single and dating were introduced. Towards the end of the interviews, the participants were asked if there were any significant people, events or aspects in their lives that they thought were relevant, but which had not yet been discussed. The purpose of this question was to create a space for the viewpoint of the participants uninfluenced by the researcher's questioning strategy. In general, the interviews took between two and six hours. They were recorded with informed consent. The interviews were transcribed in full rather than summarized. Guided by the grounded theory approach (Glaser & Strauss, 1967), the themes were derived inductively from repeated readings of the participants' narratives. The technique of constant comparison (Glaser, 1965) was employed to seek out differences as well as similarities among the participants' views about dating. The process of analysis involved the following stages: first, open coding of the data line by line, exploring emergent concepts; second, collapsing similar concepts and highlighting contrasts between the concepts; and third, axial coding through which categories are linked and connections were made among the data. Analytical memos and concept maps were used throughout the process to aid the analysis, noting reflections and other remarks. Coding of the data was facilitated by the software NVivo, a computer program for qualitative analysis.

Findings

Five factors were identified which affected participants' decisions about whether to contemplate dating (see Table 1). These five factors will be discussed below.

Table 1.   Key factors in older single gay men's concerns about dating.

Factors that encouraged contemplation of dating	Factors that discouraged contemplation of dating
Social pressure	Rejecting the social norm
Social companionship	Personal freedom and independence
Emotional needs	Avoiding having to deal with the emotional needs of a partner
Difficulties in taking care of oneself	Ease with taking care of oneself
Sexual needs	Sexual exploration

Factors that encouraged contemplation of dating

Social pressure

The older gay men's perceptions were that their surrounding social climate both privileged couple relationships and marginalised being single. The participants stated repeatedly that those surrounding them, including family members, friends, colleagues and acquaintances, constantly questioned them about being single. Strikingly, very few participants mentioned that they did not experience any social pressure. People who did not know about the participants' sexual orientation assumed that the participants were heterosexual and asked them why they were not married. Some of the participants' parents were concerned that no one would take care of the participants in later life. Participants' friends assumed that forming a relationship would be more desirable for the participants. For example, Patrick recalled that when he came out to his friends, their first response was to offer to introduce a potential boyfriend to him so that he could "settle down". Hence, the participants were surrounded by concerns about their partnership status and this put pressure on them to contemplate dating.

Social companionship

Some participants thought that being single influenced their social lives. Some participants found that not having a partner made them less inclined to attend social events, and, as a result, they became less socially connected. There were several reasons for this. First, some felt a lack of motivation to plan social activities just for themselves. For example, Philip said that he was less inclined to go to the theatre on his own because he needed someone else to provide the incentive for planning social events. Second, some participants found it difficult to arrive at social events without a companion. They thought that a couple could at least talk to each other should they be unable to find anyone of interest with whom to socialize. The participants believed that for singles, there was "no one to sort of fall back onto" if they found no one to interact with. Third, some participants felt that they were being invited to fewer social occasions because they did not have a partner. They felt that "couples thought couples" and "families thought families", which meant that singles could be excluded from the guest lists for some events. They sometimes felt that the hosts might ask them to bring another person with them. That could also be challenging because if not handled well, they could be sending the wrong signals to the persons they asked to accompany them, implying that they were interested in developing romantic relationships.

Emotional needs

Some participants felt a lack of emotional fulfilment. They thought they were missing out on the aspects of relationships, which involve openness, the sharing of thoughts and the expression of feelings. Cuddling, sharing and watching television together could all sound very trivial — but these activities were exactly what many of the participants said that they missed. Some participants stated explicitly that sexual desires were relatively easier to meet — as Laurence said: "If I really want to have sex, I can pay for it" — but the need for intimacy was more difficult to satisfy:

> What's important is not having the warmth of a fellow human being beside you, and waking up in the middle of the night, and just cuddling in. I mean, you can masturbate if you want a climax. You can masturbate; it's not a big deal. It's the intimacy and the warmth that's what I really miss. I mustn't sound like a grumpy old man. (Henry)

> When you hit a psychological or physical setback, not having someone make you a cup of tea and tell you how good you are. . . that's an obvious disadvantage to me. (Harry)

Norman also said he found having no one to "offload" his worries and troubles onto affected his mental health significantly. He said partly because of that he was suicidal the year before the interview:

> Mental health? I would say I am completely mental, screwed-up at the moment. Because I do not want to be on my own. There's nobody to offload things to. . . on two occasions I was seriously suicidal last year. (Norman)

For some participants, being single meant a lack of attachment and gave them a feeling of floating around without an anchor. For example, Laurence said he sometimes felt almost "too free" being on his own, "a bit like a ghost, really".

Difficulties in taking care of oneself

Some participants found taking care of themselves difficult. First, some participants thought being single brought about practical problems. Being single meant that there was not a pair of helping hands when the car broke down, or when there was a leaky tap. Second, some participants felt a lack of incentive to take care of themselves. For example, Norman believed that in a relationship, partners could "police" each other: "[O]ne probably has tolerance level that's lower than the other person's". The interview with Norman was conducted at his home. He said that not having a partner lessened his motivation to keep the place in a better state:

> Look at the state of this house. You know it could be cleaner, it could be more modern. If I have somebody who I care about, I care for myself more. Whereas being single, I'll sit here tonight, I won't sort of dust or hoover or anything. I'll just say, forget it, I am going off for a drive. Whereas if I have somebody to focus on, who I needed to dust the house for, it is different . . . I can't do things just for myself. I have to have somebody to do it for. (Norman)

Laurence also said that he needed a partner's nagging to help him take care of himself better:

> I think it would have helped, because I do need to be nagged. If I leave myself to myself, I just sort of carry on doing what I want to do . . . if I want to eat a big meal, I would go and eat a big meal, because nobody says I can't do it. (Laurence)

Sexual needs

A few participants found lack of regular sex problematic:

> I kind of felt the need, when I wasn't in a relationship, to be looking for sex. In a relationship I didn't need to be spending a lot of time going to bars or so on. (Justin)

> Okay, the aspect I least enjoy is waking up in the morning when I am in the mood for sex. Other times I can go out and find it [laughs], but it would have been nice in the morning with a hunk body next to me that I could have sex with. (Malcolm)

The five factors identified above encouraged older gay men to contemplate dating. However, it was found that these factors also served to discourage them to contemplate dating, as will be illustrated below.

Factors that discouraged contemplation of dating

Rejecting the social norm

The older gay men in this study were aged between 50 and 73, and were therefore born between 1937 and 1960. They have had a chance to experience the influences of gay liberation, coupled with second wave feminism in the 1960s and 1970s that began to challenge the notion of coupledom in society. Malcolm, for example, mentioned that gay liberation affected his attitudes towards forming relationships, because the white, middle-class, heterosexual, monogamous relationship as the hegemonic ideal was challenged:

> There was this feeling about fucking for gay liberation, that you want to go from one guy to another, rather than imitating straight people and getting into a relationship. I do think there was that kind of spirit out there, sleeping around as much as possible just in opposition to being straight. I think I was liberated to do that . . .

Similarly, Justin was a teenager at the start of gay liberation and he felt that the changing social atmosphere lessened the pressure he felt about forming relationships:

> When I was young there was gay liberation politics, the feeling was that we shouldn't imitate heterosexual relationships. So, you know, having open relationships, being single, and having multiple partners were seen by a certain proportion of people as the way to be. To be in a monogamous, quasi-marriage was seen as selling out. I think it was good that I didn't feel I had to be in a relationship.

Therefore, these societal attitudes influenced the participants' ideas about whether relationships were supposed to be the ideal to aspire to and hence, whether they wanted to date. Changing social attitudes planted in them the seed of liberation and the desire to achieve a greater degree of freedom from the monogamous, reproductive ideals of a conventional relationship.

Personal freedom and independence

Many participants perceived being single meant that they could go where they wanted and do what they liked, as their decisions only needed their sole approval. They did not have to negotiate with partners, thereby avoiding the likelihood of having to give up their preferences or make compromises:

> Being your own boss, and certainly when you're retired, you decide what you're going to do. (Hector)

> I like being able to get up in the morning what I am like. I like to go and get on a train and do what I like. That is freedom. Not "shall we do this or shall we do that?" (Ben)

> I do like the notion of being able to decide what I am going to do and what I am not going to do, what I am going to eat and what I am not going to eat, which television programme I am going to watch or not watch . . . (Nic)

The participants talked about the flexibility of using their time as they chose as a positive aspect of being single. For them, this meant that they could do things and change their timetables at short notice. They thought that it was something that people who were partnered, especially those with children, could not afford to do. Vincent, for example, said he had never been envious of couples:

> I thought they are stuck, really. They do not have the freedom that I have. I consider myself very lucky to have the freedom and independence to do what I want to do. I think I am extremely lucky. (Vincent)

The participants who enjoyed spontaneity or impulsiveness found such freedom to be especially compatible with their lifestyles. For some participants, the independence and freedom also meant that they could focus more on work. Jason, for example, said that he was able to take up research posts, which required focus and concentration, something he probably would not have done had he been married with children.

It may sound as if singles take into account only their own wishes and preferences. Does that mean they are as "selfish" as their sometime stereotype? Not necessarily. The single people interviewed made use of their freedom and independence in a variety of ways. For example, after retirement, Ben took up a part-time job, doing shift work. He found that being single gave him the chance to "help people out" and to "be supportive to people" because his schedule was flexible. For example, he described that he was going to cover a shift for a colleague whose wife was not feeling well on the coming Saturday:

> His wife is not very well. And he's gonna stay with her and I said I would do your shift on Saturday. I have booked off that Saturday but I am going to do it for you. I am able to do that. That's good being able to do that. (Ben)

This flexibility made some participants feel that they could lead less restricted social lives. In some instances, their previous partners controlled their social lives and wanted all their attention. For some, being single meant that they could spend more time with their friends:

> I find it delightful to have a small circle of close friends that I see as regularly as I can. That's really important to me. What I generally experience in my friends is they find a boyfriend, and I see far less of them. (Victor)

At the time of interview Stanley, for example, said that his experience of being single was very positive. He was the chairman of a gay men's social group. He was also the secretary of an outdoor activity group and an active member of a campaign group. He held a season ticket for the theatre and said he usually had someone to accompany him there. He said that his social life was quite full. He then talked for some time about the lectures that he attended and the speakers' funny titles. In the end, he spent more time talking about the decline of membership in the social group he chaired than about single-hood itself.

Avoiding having to deal with the emotional needs of a partner

While some participants found that being single meant that their emotional needs remained unfulfilled, others found that being single meant they were freed from having to deal with their partners' emotional troubles. In other words, they thought that a partner could, in part, fulfill their emotional needs, but also, and conversely, that a partner could, on occasions, be problematic. A few participants mentioned that especially when they were tired or stressed, being single allowed them access to a quiet space which they would not have if they had to deal with someone else's emotions:

> When I am tired, a bit of me loves being on my own. Especially when I am knackered from work, when I open the door I know exactly how it's going to be like. There isn't somebody else's emotions to deal with. [laughs] (Dan)

For participants who felt scarred by their previous relationships, avoiding the need to care for a partner's emotional demands was especially salient. Not long after Malcolm started his first serious relationship, he discovered that his boyfriend "was having sex with other boys". When he thought he had met his second lover, he discovered that he was seeing somebody else and he felt "devastated". Finally, he thought "third time lucky" when he met another man. He started seeing more of him and eventually fell in love. At this point he discovered, just as before, his partner was "unfaithful". When questioned about whether these relationships had, in any way, changed his feelings towards relation-ships, he said that he had "his fingers burned": "I am sceptical about what love means. If you can tell me what love means, I would be most grateful to you . . .". Some participants had learned through their previous experiences that relationships did not always end posi-tively. Realizations about the negative aspects of relationships – the possibilities of being cheated, feeling lonely, trapped and restricted – taught the participants that being in a relationship may not be a panacea promising happiness. Being single was not necessarily a bad idea. As a result, some participants either became more cautious or less interested in entering new relationships. Distancing themselves from relationship involvement, per-ceived as a possible source of pain, was seen by some participants as a way to "protect oneself" emotionally, to "keep one safe" or to "prevent the harm". Ben described this phe-nomenon as preventing himself from getting "emotionally smacked" again after his first two relationships: "I just got hurt, it's not my idea of fun. It's too heart-ragingly horrify-ing, do you know what I mean?".

Ease with taking care of oneself

Although some participants mentioned that taking care of themselves without a partner is difficult, others found it easier to take care of themselves alone. For example, some partic-ipants said that if they only needed to cook for one, they only had to cater to their own tastes. One participant said that even if his cooking did not go well, he was the only one to eat it and there would be no one else to judge him.

Some found that having been single for a long time they developed an increased awareness of the need to take care of themselves. As Malcolm said, having been single for a long time prepared him for taking care of himself. He went on to describe his mother's experience of widowhood. He described how devastating it was for her to be on her own after his father died. In comparison, he said he was preparing himself for old age and thought he would be "more prepared" for being on his own than someone used to being in a relationship. He noted that he was on a very healthy diet and he exercised a lot. Although he was not following a weight loss diet, he would go to street markets to buy fresh produce and create his own recipes. Referring to his health and the need to take care of himself, he said: "I am very aware of it":

> Well, being single makes you self-sufficient. It makes you self-sufficient physically, mentally, and emotionally. Emotionally I don't need to be in a relationship and intellectually I don't have to be talking with somebody else. And then physically I am independent and I also take care of my own health. (Malcolm)

Sexual exploration

Although some participants saw the lack of a regular partner as a downside of being single, many others saw being single as giving them greater freedom for sexual exploration. Patrick, for example, said being single allowed him to have multiple sex partners. He said that he was not interested in having sex with the same man too frequently, no matter how attractive he might be:

> I remember one particular guy who actually used to be an upmarket rent boy... he was extremely good, had a fantastically good body, in his early 30s. But I think after the third time having sex with him, I wasn't interested in him anymore. I wanted to be his friend. (Patrick)

Contrary to some others, who missed having a regular sex partner because they were single, he saw the freedom for sexual exploration as a positive aspect of being single:

> I want to have sex with different people. One of my ambitions is to have sex with men from every country in the world. Since 2002 I have slept with men from 35 countries. (Patrick)

He went on to describe how easy it was to access casual sex because of the increasing convenience of using the Internet to set-up sexual encounters. He had mainly used the *Gaydar* website to find casual sex encounters. He said that for him, sex was readily available. He recalled his experience of chatting to someone on the website with whom he was trying to set up a meeting. This man replied at 9:00 am in the morning: "I just live round the corner and my parents have just gone off to work so just pop by...". Being single meant the possibility of having all these different casual sexual encounters. It meant that he was released from the pressure to conform to monogamy. It seemed his sexual needs were fulfilled, and without much difficulty. What was afforded him by singlehood was excitement and freedom to play in the sexual arena.

Thus, the very same older gay man himself may not be sure whether he sees a certain issue as an encouraging or discouraging factor; he may not be sure whether he wants to date or not. Victor, for example, said he was very fortunate that except for a friend or two who would approach the subject very gently out of concern, his family and friends and neighbours and acquaintances did not really exert any pressure on him to form relationships, or "if they did, they did a great job of hiding it". However, towards the end of the interview he said that there was one person who still brought the question up from time to time:

> One obvious person that fairly regularly brings it up and checks it out with me is of course... me, myself. He asked, "Are you sure? Are you sure this is right for you? Are you happy? Is this really what you want?" (Victor)

Discussion

This paper contributes to the research literature by analysing the accounts of 25 self-identified, older, single gay men whose experiences of being single have previously received minimal attention.

This paper focused on answering the research question "What factors do older, single gay men consider when they contemplate dating?". This paper illustrates that participants considered dating concerns as relevant and important. There was no option for participants to gloss over the topic of being single when people around them asked personal questions. This echoes the suggestion that the dominant ideology "bestows a range of social, economic and symbolic rewards on those who couple, leaving those who do not in a position to account for their marginalized condition" (Budgeon, 2008, p. 309). Singles continuously face pressure from families and peers, and because of that, some may "use marital status to evaluate their lives, and based on this measure, wonder if there is something lacking" (Schwartzberg, Berliner, & Jacob, 1995, p. 4). The social pressure that older single gay men face must not be underestimated.

There are factors that both encouraged and discouraged participants in this study to contemplate dating. It is noteworthy that the same factors often simultaneously created both positive and negative attitudes towards entering into a relationship. For example, while the social climate privileging couple status was seen by some participants as a reason to date, so that they could conform to societal expectations, they also actively questioned the social norm that centres only on conjugal couples. While some saw having a partner as providing them with companionship, they also enjoyed the freedom and independence that being single brings. Some participants believed that a partner could fulfill their emotional needs; simultaneously, they were worried that they might need to deal with the emotional needs of their partners. Some found it difficult to take care of themselves alone, but they also found it easier to do so than to also take care of their partners. Some felt that their sexual needs were unfulfilled because they were single, at the same time that they found that it gave them more opportunities for sexual exploration. Thus, the same older gay man may feel ambivalent in his stance towards the advantages and disadvantages that being single brings, and thus, he may not be sure whether he wants to date or not. That is, "moments of ambivalence" prevailed in singles' stories (Budgeon, 2008, p. 317). Whether a single older gay men is "single by choice" is thus difficult to define (Hostetler, 2009).

Some of the issues participants considered in deciding whether to date are similar to the ones older straight people considered, as suggested by previous research. However, some of these concerns were distinctively different for older gay men. Life course approaches suggest that "no period of life can be understood in isolation from people's prior experiences, as well as their aspirations for the future" (Mortimer & Shanahan,

2003, p. xi). These approaches are especially helpful for contextualizing why some participants drew on gay liberation and an ideological attack on the monogamous, conjugal couple as a reason to reject dating. When the cohort of participants in this study was growing up, the social climate allowed and encouraged more diverse understandings of relationship norms. Future research about older single gay men's concerns, or indeed any singles' experiences, should take into account how the constantly changing social attitudes towards singlehood may have an impact on singles' lives. Particularly, the move towards wider recognition of same-sex relationships (see Harding, 2008; Kitzinger & Wilkinson, 2004), in the form of civil partnership or same-sex marriage, in an increasing number of countries at the time of writing, may have an impact directly or indirectly on singles' lives.

Participants were also ready to engage in casual sexual encounters and saw sexual exploration as a positive aspect of being single. This is in line with the suggestion that lesbians and gay men can be seen as exemplars of self-fashioned identities (Giddens, 1992). They have to construct their own life course without ready-made role models because they are socialized within a heterosexist society, where such models are not available (D'Augelli, 1994, p. 127). The views that some participants held towards being single point to gay men's creativity and agency in redefining heterosexist notions in relationship formation (Heaphy, 2008).

This study provides insights into how participants experienced and understood their single status, which can make therapists more aware of the life situation of older, gay male clients. In particular, it can help to make therapists aware that being single is not only a personal experience, but is heavily influenced by social ideals and historical development of gay rights. It can also inform therapists of the factors that encourage and discourage older gay men from contemplating dating.

This awareness can help therapists to develop effective strategies for working with clients on the topic of relationships. First, the findings highlight the necessity both for therapists and their clients to question the dominant messages in society and to be aware of their impact on the meanings single clients give to their lives (Schwartzberg et al., 1995, p. ix). If single clients bring up self-blaming statements, therapists may remind them how their feelings about being single have been influenced by larger powers at work in society (Lewis & Moon, 1997). This can steer singles away from (unfairly and unjustifiably) blaming or criticizing themselves. New perspectives can allow them to think of singlehood as more than "a troubled category" (Reynolds & Wetherell, 2003) and a "deficit identity" (Reynolds & Taylor, 2005). The therapeutic encounter should move away from reinforcing couple relationships as being normative or necessarily preferable. Instead, the therapeutic encounter should be hosted as a non-judgemental thinking space for older single gay men to ponder their struggles with their relationship status. It requires the therapeutic encounter, as well as the therapist and the client themselves, to remove themselves from viewing couples and heterosexuality as the golden rules of society.

Second, therapists can draw on the competing factors and the associated feelings of tension and ambivalence identified in this study, to work with singles on their experiences of being single as complex and multi-dimensional in the ways suggested by this study. By framing single life in this way, it provides the possibility for the clients to re-evaluate their perceptions of their experience as singles, and question whether they have evaluated all the aspects of their lives honestly. Therapists can work with the client, whether gay or straight, to explore the various possibilities in the life of a single person, through an enhanced shared understanding of how particular aspects of a single's life can be narrated and experienced in dramatically different ways and from different perspectives.

This paper has limitations. The sample lacks diversity in terms of ethnic background. Also, the participants were relatively young: it may be the case that single gay men who are older and thus experience more intense health and mobility problems might experience their singlehood differently. Further research is warranted and may explore the therapeutic needs of older, gay men in different domains of their lives.

Acknowledgements

I would like to thank Mr Christopher Fallon for his continuous support and inspirations, and Professor Mike Baynham, Dr Walter Pierre Bouman, and Professor Peggy Kleinplatz, for their constructive comments and feedback that have significantly improved this paper.

References

Barrett, C., Whyte, C., Comfort, J., Lyons, A., & Crameri, P. (2014). Social connection, relationships and older lesbian and gay people. *Sexual and Relationship Therapy*. doi:10.1080/14681994.2014.963983

Brown, S.L., & Shinohara, S.K. (2013). Dating relationships in older adulthood: A national portrait. *Journal of Marriage and Family, 75*(5), 1194–1202.

Budgeon, S. (2008). Couple culture and the production of singleness. *Sexualities, 11*(3), 301–325.

Bulcroft, R.A. & Bulcroft, K.A. (1991). The nature and functions of dating in later life. *Research on Aging, 13*(2), 244–260.

Calasanti, T., & Kiecolt, K.J. (2007). Diversity among late-life couples. *Generations, 31*(3), 10–17.

Christian, D.V., & Keefe, D.A. (1997). Maturing gay men. *Journal of Gay & Lesbian Social Services, 6*(1), 47–78.

D'Augelli, A.R. (1994). Lesbian and gay male development: Steps toward an analysis of lesbians' and gay men's lives. In B. Greene & G.M. Herek (Eds.), *Lesbian and gay psychology: Theory, research, and clinical implications* (pp. 118–132). Newbury Park, CA: Sage.

Davidson, K. (2001). Late life widowhood, selfishness and new partnership choices: A gendered perspective. *Ageing & Society, 21*(03), 297–317.

Davidson, K. (2002). Gender differences in new partnership choices and constraints for older widows and widowers. *Ageing International, 27*(4), 43–60.

Dickson, F.C., Hughes, P.C., & Walker, K.L. (2005). An exploratory investigation into dating among later-life women. *Western Journal of Communication, 69*(1), 67–82.

Friend, R.A. (1987). The individual and social psychology of aging. *Journal of Homosexuality, 14*(1–2), 307–331.

Frost, J. (1997). Group psychotherapy with the aging gay male: Treatment of choice. *Group, 21*(3), 267–285.

Garnets, L.D., & Kimmel, D.C. (2003). *Psychological perspectives on lesbian, gay, and bisexual experiences* (2nd ed.). Chichester, NY: Columbia University Press.

Giddens, A. (1992). *The transformation of intimacy: Sexuality, love and eroticism in modern societies*. Cambridge: Polity.

Glaser, B.G. (1965). The constant comparative method of qualitative analysis. *Social Problems, 12*(4), 436–444.

Glaser, B.G., & Strauss, A.L. (1967). *Discovery of grounded theory: Strategies for qualitative research*. Chicago, IL: Aldine.

Harding, R. (2008). Recognizing (and resisting) regulation: Attitudes to the introduction of civil partnership. *Sexualities, 11*(6), 740–760.

Heaphy, B. (2008). The sociology of lesbian and gay reflexivity or reflexive sociology? *Sociological Research Online, 13*(1), 9.

Hostetler, A.J. (2009). Single by choice? Assessing and understanding voluntary singlehood among mature gay men. *Journal of Homosexuality, 56*(4), 499−531.

Jacobs, R.J., Rasmussen, L.A., & Hohman, M.M. (1999). The social support needs of older lesbians, gay men, and bisexuals. *Journal of Gay & Lesbian Social Services, 9*(1), 1−30.

Johnson, M.J., Jackson, N.C., Arnette, J.K., & Koffman, S.D. (2005). Gay and lesbian perceptions of discrimination in retirement care facilities. *Journal of Homosexuality, 49*(2), 83−102.

Jones, J., & Pugh, S. (2005). Ageing gay men: Lessons from the sociology of embodiment. *Men and Masculinities, 7*(3), 248−260.

Kitzinger, C., & Wilkinson, S. (2004). Social advocacy for equal marriage: The politics of "rights" and the psychology of "mental health". *Analyses of Social Issues and Public Policy, 4*(1), 173−194.

Kleinplatz, P.J., Ménard, A.D., Paradis, N., Campbell, M., Dalgleish, T., Segovia, A., & Davis, K. (2009). From closet to reality: Optimal sexuality among the elderly. *The Irish Psychiatrist, 10*(1), 15−18.

Koren, C. (2014). Together and apart: A typology of re-partnering in old age. *International Psychogeriatrics, 26*, 1327−1350.

Lewis, K.G., & Moon, S. (1997). Always single and single again women: A qualitative study. *Journal of Marital and Family Therapy, 23*(2), 115−134.

Mason, J. (2002). *Qualitative researching* (2nd ed.). London: Sage.

McDougall, G.J. (1994). Therapeutic issues with gay and lesbian elders. *Clinical Gerontologist, 14*(1), 45−57.

Mortimer, J.T., & Shanahan, M. (2003). *Handbook of the Life Course*. New York, NY: Springer.

Peplau, L.A., & Cochran, S.D. (1990). A relationship perspective on homosexuality. In D.P. McWhirter & J.M. Reinisch (Eds.), *Homosexuality/heterosexuality: Concepts of sexual orientation* (pp. 321−349). New York, NY: Oxford University Press.

Plummer, K., (2001). *Documents of Life 2: An invitation to a critical humanism* (2nd ed.). London: Sage.

Reynolds, J., & Taylor, S. (2005). Narrating singleness: Life stories and deficit identities. *Narrative Inquiry, 15*(2), 197−215.

Reynolds, J., & Wetherell, M. (2003). The discursive climate of singleness: The consequences for women's negotiation of a single identity. *Feminism & Psychology, 13*(4), 489−510.

Sassler, S. (2010). Partnering across the life course: Sex, relationships, and mate selection. *Journal of Marriage and Family, 72*(3), 557−575.

Schwartzberg, N., Berliner, K., & Jacob, D. (1995). *Single in a married world: A life cycle framework for working with the unmarried adult*. New York, NY: W.W. Norton.

Shannon, J.W. & Woods, W.J. (1991). Affirmative psychotherapy for gay men. *The Counseling Psychologist, 19*(2), 197−215.

Stein, G.L., Beckerman, N.L., & Sherman, P.A. (2010). Lesbian and gay elders and long-term care: Identifying the unique psychosocial perspectives and challenges. *Journal of Gerontological Social Work, 53*(5), 421−435.

Talbott, M.M. (1998). Older widows' attitudes towards men and remarriage. *Journal of Aging Studies, 12*(4), 429−449.

Watson, W.K., & Stelle, C. (2011). Dating for older women: Experiences and meanings of dating in later life. *Journal of Women & Aging, 23*(3), 263−275.

Old and desirable: older women's accounts of ageing bodies in intimate relationships

Rachel Thorpe[a], Bianca Fileborn[a], Gail Hawkes[b], Marian Pitts[a] and Victor Minichiello[a]

[a]Australian Research Centre in Sex, Health and Society, La Trobe University, Melbourne, Australia; [b]School of Behavioural and Cognitive Sciences, University of New England, Armidale, Australia

Despite the body being central to the experience of ageing, little attention has been paid to how relationships may mediate the experience of ageing bodies. This article considers older Australian women's accounts of their bodies and of embodied experiences in the context of both long-term and newly formed intimate relationships. Drawn from a broader study of ageing and sexuality, our analyses of semi-structured interviews with 20 women aged 55 to 72 revealed that while women were frequently unhappy with their appearance, this was less important to them in relationships. During sexual intimacy, embodied experience and the capacity for bodies to be sites of pleasure were emphasised. Overall, participants experienced their bodies as sites of negotiation between socially constructed meanings of older bodies and subjectively produced ones, in complex and sometimes contradictory ways that fell outside simple distinctions between social and individual.

Introduction

Ageing bodies are considered to constitute the antithesis of beauty and desirability. Youth and beauty in this sense cannot be divided, a message that has, over centuries of repetition in both popular and high culture, become naturalised (Bellamy, Gott, Hinchliff, & Nicholson, 2011; Bytheway & Johnson, 1998; Gott & Hinchliff, 2003; Holstein, 2001; Sandberg, 2013; Vares, 2009). The body is therefore an important site for understanding ageing (Calasanti & Slevin, 2001a, 2001b). Old age is often positioned as being more problematic for women than for men, as women's assets are assumed to lessen with age, as their bodies become further differentiated from youthful norms, while age may actually increase a man's attractiveness, although with greater equality between the sexes this may be less true now than previously (Calasanti & Slevin, 2001a; Krekula, 2007; Oberg & Tornstam, 1999; Tunaley, Walsh, & Nicolson, 1999; Vares, 2009). For women ageing is assumed to be experienced as loss – of youth; of sexual attraction; of skin elasticity; of identity; even of social visibility (Calasanti, 2003, 2004; Loe, 2004; Sandberg, 2013; Sontag, 1979). This assumption is based upon the "double jeopardy" theory that women are doubly disadvantaged in later life because of the intersection of ageism with sexism (Calasanti & Slevin, 2001a; Fairhurst, 1988; Gilleard & Higgs, 2000; Oberg & Tornstam, 1999; Tunaley et al., 1999). However this perspective has been criticised as an oversimplification, for taking men's experiences as the norm and assuming that the negative influences of ageism and sexism are necessarily additive (Calasanti & Slevin, 2001b; Krekula, 2007). Furthermore, this perspective privileges bodily appearance and does not allow for any resistance or re-conceptualisation of ageing bodies by individuals. Recent qualitative research indicates that older women are able to resist youthful norms and conceptualise their bodies in other ways (Hurd Clarke, 2002; Krekula, 2007; Vares, 2009).

Older bodies and sexual relationships

Despite the importance of the body for understanding old age, very little research has focused on how older women perceive their own bodies, particularly in the context of sexually intimate relationships (Calasanti & Slevin, 2001a; Hurd, 2000; Krekula, 2007; Laz, 2003). This topic is important given that people are living longer in many Western countries, including Australia, and are therefore more likely to be in relationships for longer or to enter into new relationships in older age (Trudel, Turgeon, & Piché, 2010). Rather than assuming that old age is experienced as loss of sexual attractiveness, we need to consider how women can negotiate complex messages about ageing bodies in different contexts, including relationships. In a study of 16 women aged from 75 to 96, Krekula, found that some women expressed pride in their dressed bodies and also when their bodies offered a source of pleasure in sexual intimacies. However, they remained negative about their physical bodies (Krekula, 2007). Clarke's (2010) extended study of women experiencing their ageing bodies supports these findings and is especially striking in the detail and depth of her participants' negative scrutiny of their bodies. In Laz's (2003) earlier study of men and women aged over 50, some emphasised changes in appearance, though not all experienced these as negative. Nevertheless, negative comments reflected poor functionality rather than other less easily defined aspects. Similarly, Hurd's (2000) study found that having a healthy, functional body may be more important than appearance in older age. These studies suggest that older bodies are conceptualised quite differently when women reflect upon bodily appearance compared with their embodied recollections of everyday experiences (Krekula, 2007; Laz, 2003). Embodied accounts of ageing may emphasise the expression of identity through the body, such as through dress or during exercise or sex (Krekula, 2007; Laz, 2003; Sandberg, 2013).

This paper addresses a gap in the literature around embodied ageing in intimate relationships. The body is important both to the experience of ageing and to the sense of self as sexually desirable across the life course (Calasanti & Slevin, 2001a, 2001b; Montemurro & Gillen, 2013). Long-term relationships may provide a sense of self as continuous over time, despite the ageing of the body, while women entering newer relationships may find themselves having to negotiate current cultural messages about ageing, appearance and desire (Kaufman, 1986; Montemurro & Gillen, 2013; Oberg & Tornstam, 1999). We explore and discuss some aspects of older women's bodies in private, in public and in sexually intimate situations. We argue that while women often reflect negatively upon bodily appearance, narratives of ageing within intimate relationships suggest that older bodies are sites of negotiation of multiple and contrasting meanings, including loss, pleasure and desire.

Methods

The main aims of this study were to study the sexual subjectivities of the first post-liberation generation of Australian women and to explore how these women conceptualised and experienced their bodies in the context of contemporary ideologies on gender and ageing. This study forms part of a larger project focusing more broadly on the sexuality of older Australian women. Qualitative semi-structured interviews were employed in order to obtain first person accounts of embodied ageing, including the language that the women used to discuss position their experiences. Women born between 1925 and 1957 who lived in the state of Victoria were invited to participate in the study. Recruitment efforts involved a combination of advertisements, radio publicity and snowballing.

Twenty-eight women participated in a face-to-face interview with the first author either at the participant's house or the researcher's workplace. The interviews were between 1 and 2.5 hours in duration and all participants signed a consent form. The interview schedule included open-ended questions about ageing, sexuality and the body in everyday life and probing questions were used in order to avoid making assumptions surrounding participants' meanings. The study was approved by the La Trobe University Human Ethics Committee. The interviews were transcribed verbatim and the transcription was then checked against the audio recording. Transcripts were sent to participants for verification. All names have been changed to ensure anonymity. The data analysed in this paper are drawn from the parts of the interview in which the women discussed their perceptions of their bodies in public, in private and during sexual intimacy.

Of the 28 women who were interviewed, 20 were in relationships at the time of the interview and form the basis of this paper. These women were aged 55–72 (mean = 66 ± 5) years. One woman was in a same-sex relationship, the rest were in a heterosexual relationships. Fourteen were in a relationship (married or common law) of five or more years' duration (range = 9–48 years); six women had been with their current partners for less than five years (range = 1–4 years).

Data analysis

Data coding and analysis were conducted by the first author using a thematic analysis approach (Ryan & Bernard, 2000). Thematic codes were initially identified from the literature and refined during the process of interviewing and by reading and re-reading the interview transcripts. These were then compared against the data from the broader project to ensure consistency and agreement on the significant emerging themes and connections between themes. The researchers were particularly concerned with identifying key themes relating to participants' perceptions of their bodies, their current sexual desires and sexual activities, and the ways in which experiences of ageing shaped these perceptions. Interviews were initially coded by hand in chunks, and then entered into NVivo 10, with this approach lending itself to a thorough reading and analysis of the data. Memos were used to record theoretical concepts emerging from the coding process and relationships among themes (Bazeley, 2013). Furthermore, analysis was then conducted by the first author using a post-structuralist approach (Sondergaard, 2002a). This analytic strategy considers how subjectivities are situated within and produced by historically specific ideologies on women's bodies and ageing (Bordo, 1993; Riggs, 2012; Sondergaard, 2002a, 2002b). This paper is based upon analysis of the codes "bodies in relationships" and "body and ageing".

Results

This paper concerns interviews with women who were in relationships, either long term, or more recently formed, as this allowed us to consider how being in an intimate relationship and engaging in sexual intimacy influenced the women's perceptions of their bodies. We consider the women who were in long-term relationships separately from those who were in more newly formed relationships, as relationship length was commonly cited by the women as influencing their perceptions of their bodies. Furthermore, as will be discussed, the experience of entering into sexual intimacy with new partners in older age led these women to reflect quite differently upon their bodies. Finally, we consider how the women made sense of their bodies during sexual intimacy.

Many of the women in long-term relationships indicated that they were not concerned about their bodily appearance in the context of their relationship. For example, Carolyn, age 67, who had been married for 44 years, said, "I don't think about it". These women nominated the longevity and familiarity of the relationship as the reason for their lack of body consciousness. Long-term relationships were therefore often presented as a space in which bodies were accepted, regardless of appearance. Some of the women, such as Brigitte, associated such lack of concern about bodily appearance with ongoing mutual attraction and affection in their relationship. That is, they indicated that they received positive feedback from their partners, were comfortable showing their bodies to their partners and also found their partners' bodies attractive:

Rachel: HOW DO YOU FEEL ABOUT NUDITY IN THE HOME?

Brigitte: Perfectly alright, we're not, I'm not embarrassed and we're quite free with nudity.

Rachel: AND HOW DO YOU FEEL WHEN YOU'RE GETTING UNDRESSED IN FRONT OF YOUR HUSBAND?

Brigitte: Good yeah, he loves it when I do it, he loves it, he still loves my body. He is gorgeous, I am very lucky. (Brigitte, 67, married for 48 years)

Here, Brigitte presents a picture of an older couple who consider each other's bodies to be desirable and physically attractive in older age. Brigitte's account emphasises a mutual lack of body consciousness within the relationship. In this account, age is not presented as changing the value or meaning of their bodies which remain desirable, unproblematic and able to meet normative understandings of "attractive" bodies.

In contrast, most of the women in long-term relationships, despite stating that they were unconcerned about their appearance in their relationships, were critical more generally of their bodily appearance and discussed features that they would like to change. Some also criticised their partners' appearance. These women discussed ageing as having brought about bodily changes that contributed to decreased attractiveness, most commonly weight gain and sagging. However, most indicated that these negative appraisals were their own opinions and not those of their partners. Indeed, they often suggested that their partners did find their bodies attractive, although they found this difficult to believe:

Rachel: HOW DO YOU FEEL ABOUT YOUR BODY IN INTIMATE MOMENTS?

Joan: I am okay with my husband because, as I say, we've been together a long time. We are both getting older, we are both getting fatter and yeah that's fine.

Rachel: SO YOU FEEL COMFORTABLE?

Joan: Yeah. Yeah I mean I don't feel terrific and as I said before I don't feel like oh I am so sexy. But I mean he, he is happy so maybe he thinks I am alright. (Joan, 60, married for 37 years)

In the above quotation, Joan suggests that while she accepts her bodily appearance when she is with her husband, she does not consider either of their bodies to be attractive. Her comments indicate that she perceived ageing to be inevitably associated with ongoing bodily decline and loss of attractiveness. Furthermore, she did not consider that her appearance conformed to a wider social definition of attractiveness or that she was "sexy", however she did believe that her husband continued to find her attractive. Although Joan represents her body, and that of her husband, as embodying flaws associated with ageing, she believes that these flaws are less important, or even unimportant, within the relationship. As this quotation from Joan suggests, older bodies were perceived as both flawed and desirable, and long-term relationships discussed as providing a space for mutual acceptance of bodily flaws.

However, this acceptance was not unproblematic, as approval from partners did not negate the women's own bodily discontent. Some participants emphasised their partners' approval of their bodies, despite their own criticisms. These women, including Anke, suggested that their partners' perspective was more important than their own:

Anke: And I'm very lucky that the man I married loves me dearly and he doesn't care, he still thinks I'm the best looking female in the world.

Rachel: THAT'S GREAT

Anke: And that's great after 50 years of marriage, yeah. So no I don't like this bit myself [stomach], but I don't dwell on it. (Anke, 71)

Here, Anke emphasises that her husband's love and attraction to her transcends social norms of beauty, that is, he finds her attractive despite her own perception that ageing has had a negative effect on her physical appearance. Anke also suggests that she is fortunate that her relationship free her from the bodily insecurities that she perceives other older women are subject to. She repeats this later in the interview, commenting "Oh, no I don't like what I look like now, but I don't have to worry about it". Yet her perspective does not discount the relevance of appearance in her relationship. Rather it offers evidence for the continued dependence on external legitimating opinions – notably of her long-standing, male partner.

However, long-term partners did not always provide positive bodily feedback. Two women noted being ashamed of their bodies and avoiding showing them to their husbands. These women accounted for their bodily discomfort by discussing changes in the appearance of their own bodies and that of their husbands' which had developed over time had taken place over time. Rather than positioning bodily appearance as unproblematic and accepted within the familiar context of the relationship, these women suggested that ageing had in fact brought the body into focus:

Heather: I also don't undress in front of my husband.

Rachel: WHY NOT?

Heather: The only time I did recently was when I'd lost a bit of weight (laughing). That's sad isn't it?

Rachel: SO YOU FELT MORE COMFORTABLE THEN?

Heather: Yeah. It's really just being self-conscious about the changes. Because the changes that he has allowed to happen in his body are more obvious and we are don't seem to be as comfortable with one another as we used to be. (Heather, 61, in a relationship for 46 years)

In the above extract, Heather attributes her embarrassment about her appearance to changes that have occurred in her body and that of her husband. Although we asked women about their own bodies, partners' bodies were frequently raised as contributing to overall acceptance or embarrassment within relationships. In Heather's case, weight gain and ageing were presented as having shifted the meaning of both of their bodies in the context of the relationship, from accepted to shame inducing. These meanings were also gendered in that Heather was less embarrassed by her body when she was slimmer, yet did not discuss the possibility that her husband could lose weight or indicate that her affection for him was dependent upon his appearance. However, she did place emphasis upon her husband's weight gain as having disrupted the level of comfort and acceptance that had previously existed between them.

So far, this paper has discussed the experiences of those women who were in long-term relationships. We now focus on the six women who had entered into a relationship in the previous five years. All of these women had been married previously. In comparison to those in long-term relationships, who frequently downplayed bodily appearance, these women's accounts of entering into new relationships tended to emphasise the appearance of the older body, as the experience and memory of showing their body to their partners for the first time was recent. They also commonly drew upon comparisons between their bodies in their current relationships and in previous relationships, thereby bringing the desirability of old age and comparisons between old bodies and young bodies into focus.

In the following extract, the deep impact of the unequivocal negative construction of the ageing physical body and the lack of a reference point beyond young womanhood was demonstrated when Kay contemplated the possibility of a new sexual relationship:

I could not imagine, my stomach had fallen from here down to here, and my breasts had gone down to my navel, my memory of my body when I was fully sexual was of being proud of my body, of enjoying taking my clothes off. …I think I was avoiding intimacy even though I was longing for it because I couldn't picture it at this stage in my life. And I also couldn't picture being with a man my own age. (Kay, 75, in a relationship for 1 year)

Here, Kay describes her body by drawing upon comparisons with her appearance as a younger woman, emphasising the negative changes that have taken place. Her use of words, such as "fallen" and "gone down" produces an image of a body upon which the physiological effects of age are evident and are interpreted as a loss of which she used to be. Her account represents older bodies as incongruent with sex and as shameful, while youth symbolises sexuality, desire and bodily pride. In this re-telling of her first intimate sexual encounter with a new partner, Kay struggles to associate the appearance of old age, both that of her own body and that of her partner, with sexual desire or desirability.

Despite expressing fear of rejection, the women who had entered into new relationships in later life, including Kay, actually recalled their lovers' responses to their bodies as positive. The women expressed surprise that their lovers were attracted to them and desired what they considered to be undesirable bodies:

> When I saw him with the sheet up to the neck I just smiled. Because I thought, we are both old, we are both older. I had my hands a little bit over my wrinkled up belly and he said "oh Kay, I love your breasts, I didn't expect this". (Kay, 75)

In this quotation, Kay indicates that her partner was embarrassed by his own body and subject to the age-negative fears about what older women looked like naked but was spontaneously and pleasantly surprised. She was able to relate this encounter with amusement, for in the reality of a new sexual encounter, both engaged in reclaiming the situation through their own individual lenses. Through this, signs of age were still present, but were no longer considered incompatible with sexual attraction or pleasurable intimacy. Other women, such as Marion (63, in a relationship for 2 years), indicated that their partners praised aspects of their bodies, such as curves, that they themselves found unattractive, "He said I am Rubinesque and flatters me...and I have never, ever had that before in my life". For Marion, being older was in fact associated with receiving positive attention about her body that she had not received when she was younger. These women's accounts suggest older bodies were valued differently even within newer relationships and in ways that fell outside of the ageist/sexist stereotypes. Within relationships both partners' individual and shared relationship histories and personal life histories contributed to the overall meaning of bodies, rather than meanings being drawn directly from social norms. This did not mean that the women in relationships accepted their bodies, but rather that they believed that the negative social value that they attached to their bodies in other contexts was less important when they were with their intimate partners.

When discussing their bodies during sexual intimacy, the women emphasised embodied sensations rather than appearance, eliciting bodily accounts that were mostly positive, regardless of relationship length. For example, it was common for the women to use positive language when discussing their bodies during sex, even if they had described their appearance in the mirror using negative language. Carol (in a relationship with another woman for 9 years), who said that she "hated" to look at her body in the mirror, particularly her stomach, said:

> Carol: When we are having sex I feel great about my body. Yeah isn't that funny?...Because you are involved, you love the other person and you feel attracted to them and it's exciting, so you just, you are in the moment. So I feel good about my body then. But that's probably about the only time I do really (laughing). (Carol, aged 60)

Carol's dislike of her bodily appearance could be interpreted as contradicting the positive language that she used to describe her body during sex. Here, her account highlighted the potential for the same body to represent multiple and contrasting meanings for its inhabitant. When discussing her body during sex, Carol recalled her feelings and emotions. This was an embodied account, in which the capacity of the body to elicit pleasure and excitement, rather than the externally available image, was privileged. This echoes Kay's account (above), in which the signs of ageing were re-interpreted in an interaction with her lover. Her breasts, her "wrinkled up belly" were admired and desired within the sexual encounter. Lynette, also distinguished between bodily appearance and embodied pleasure:

Well in intimate moments that sort of goes by the wayside thank god because my flesh stills feels that lovely sense of touch, so that's all that matters. (Lynette, 55, in a relationship for 2 years)

In Lynette's reflection, the older body was valued positively for its sensual capacity – an example of embodied valuation beyond the social stereotypes. Her emphasis on the embodied value negated any concerns about appearance, as opposed to the experience of the body. Lynette expresses relief that during sexual intimacy her concerns about her body "go(es) by the wayside", reflecting the fact that concerns about appearance were significant to her. Other women also referred to the continuing sensual capacity of parts of their bodies, such as breasts. In these accounts, older bodies were recalled as continuous with sensuality and pleasure, in contrast to the often taken for granted meaning of ageing as leading to loss of identity and attractiveness. These accounts of older bodies during sexual intimacy provide further evidence for the multifaceted nature of bodily meanings in older age.

Discussion

In this paper, we have presented empirical findings that highlight the capacity for older women's bodies to represent multiple and contrasting meanings. Bodily attributes were not experienced as fixed, nor were they defined objectively. Instead, varying meanings emerged in ways dependent on subjective experiences in the moment or were produced by shared life-history experiences, especially, but not exclusively, in long-term relationships. Intimate relationships and sexual intimacy provided opportunities for older bodies to be experienced and accepted as desirable and as sources of pleasure. These meanings were identified as particularly important even when the women had been in relationships for over 40 years. Most believed that long-term partners regarded them with love and affection regardless of appearance and they attached importance to their partners' perceptions. Despite existing research and popular views that ageing is particularly difficult for women because they are judged primarily by their appearance, these data suggest that the ageing body can still deliver positive experiences and individual pleasures (Krekula, 2007; Sandberg, 2013).

However, it would be an oversimplification if we drew from these data another "either/or" – that older women's subjective experience in intimate relationships is an antidote to negative sexist and ageist stereotypes. Rather, we think that intimate relationships are an important biographical factor that may mediate the experience of body and identity in older age and throughout the life course. However, the influence of relationships on embodied meanings appears to be complex.

First, despite suggestions in the literature that older age may release women from social expectations to conform to cultural norms of femininity, appearance remained important to our participants' conceptions of themselves (Calasanti & Slevin, 2001a). They all compared their bodies to social norms of feminine appearance and most believed that they did not conform to these standards. Even those who did not criticise their own appearance drew upon prevailing popular views that the ageing body is unattractive, reflecting the cultural prominence of ageist discourses. Furthermore, the women's accounts of their bodies were often gendered, in that they drew upon assumptions that men would not find older women's bodies attractive and emphasised their husbands' opinions rather than their own (Vares, 2009). The women's comments about the effects of age on their male partners' appearance also suggested that male bodies were compared against, and often considered to fall short of youthful standards and that these changes contributed to mutual bodily discomfort in the relationship.

Bodily appearance for these women is less important for those in long-term relationships than for those entering new relationships. The women who had recently entered into new relationships did offer bodily appearance as a major concern. In expressing these misgivings, our participants drew directly on the only discourse available to them to express their feelings about their ageing bodies – that equated age changes with ugliness – highlighting the gap between their own bodies and youthful norms of sexual attractiveness (Sontag, 1979; Tunaley et al., 1999; Vares, 2009). Revealing another layer of the complexity of ageing and subjectivity, these women indicated that their partners considered them to be attractive regardless of bodily changes associated with age and regardless of the length of the relationship. Although this appeared to mediate their age-negativity, such "active approval" was not sufficient to prevent the self-deprecating descriptions of changes associated with ageing. How these women experienced their ageing bodies was derived from experience and life history as well as from social and cultural norms. They drew upon their own personal histories in associating sexual intimacy with their youthful bodies in previous relationships, rather than their older bodies. Therefore, the meanings of older bodies in newer relationships were also derived both from embodied experiences and social meanings and these influences were represented in more complex ways than the notion that ageing is necessarily difficult for women, or that being in a relationship is always a positive influence.

A striking feature of our findings was that many women struggled to associate the image of older bodies with sexual desirability. This seems to indicate a lack of broader cultural reference points for ageing and sexuality, particularly for women (Bellamy et al., 2011; Holstein, 2006; Plummer, 2010; Shilling, 2012). However, when recalling embodied sensations and emotions during encounters of sex and intimacy, older bodies were represented as inseparable from their sensuality and from the delights of the encounter. In particular, when discussing sexual intimacy, the women placed emphasis upon physical sensations such as touch. Subjective embodiment, rather than appearance defined these accounts. The pleasures of intimate touch remain unaddressed by any age-negative presentations of older sexuality – despite its status as the first primal sense to develop and the last to disappear in humans. Through touch, women's bodies remained a site of physical pleasure that did not diminish with age. For these women, drawing on the embodied value negated any concerns about the appearance, as opposed to the experience of the body. Our data support the notion that becoming older does not necessarily change women's experiences of sensuality and pleasure (Krekula, 2007).

We suggest that the contradictions within subjective accounts of ageing raise an important point that while older bodies can be desirable and desiring, these qualities are often overlooked or de-emphasised. Our culture's emphasis upon youth and beauty is reproduced by older people who position their appearance in comparison with these norms as unattractive or lacking. However, in focusing on narratives of embodied pleasure, we can see that older women's bodies are sites for negotiating multiple and contrasting meanings, including loss, continuation and change.

This study began with the proposition that a unique cohort of women, who may have been influenced by the body positivity and freedoms of expression encouraged during the "swinging sixties", was entering into old age. In the current youth-obsessed social settings we wished to explore whether these early (if conditional) liberations encouraged a more age-positive discourse within which these women and those who will follow could embrace and value the process of ageing. Our findings complicate rather than clarify this research question. It is clear from our data that old ideas have been deeply entrenched, notably the direct association of age with unattractiveness. At the same time, the experiential accounts of our participants indicate that it is possible for older women to conceive of their bodies as being both old and wrinkled and desirable.

Acknowledgements

The authors wish to thank all the women who participated in the study for their time and personal reflections. The authors also wish to thank the editors for their helpful comments on an earlier version of the paper.

Funding

This work was supported by the Australian Research Council [grant number DP110101199]. Rachel Thorpe was supported by a La Trobe University Ph.D. scholarship.

References

Bazeley, P. (2013). *Qualitative data analysis: Practical strategies*. London: Sage.

Bellamy, G., Gott, M., Hinchliff, S., & Nicholson, P. (2011). Contemporary women's understandings of female sexuality. *Sexual and Relationship Therapy, 26*(1), 84–95.

Bordo, S. (1993). *Unbearable weight: Feminism, western culture and the body*. Berkeley: University of California Press.

Bytheway, B., & Johnson, J. (1998). The sight of age. In S. Nettleton & J. Watson (Eds.), *The body in everyday life* (pp. 243–257). London: Routledge.

Calasanti, T. (2003). Theorising age relations. In S. Biggs, A. Lowenstein, & J. Hendricks (Eds.), *The need for theory: Critical approaches to social gerontology* (pp. 199–218). Amityville, NY: Baywood.

Calasanti, T. (2004). New directions in feminist gerontology: An introduction. *Journal of Aging Studies, 18*(1), 1–8. doi: 10.1016/j.jaging.2003.09.002

Calasanti, T., & Slevin, K. (2001a). Bodies in old age. In T.M. Calasanti & K.F. Slevin (Eds.), *Gender, social inequalities and aging* (pp. 51–71). Walnut Creek, CA: AltaMira.

Calasanti, T., & Slevin, K. (2001b). A gender lens on old age. In T. Calasanti & K. Slevin (Eds.), *Gender, social inequalities and aging* (pp. 13–28). Walnut Creek, CA: AltaMira.

Fairhurst, E. (1988). 'Growing old gracefully' as opposed to 'mutton dressed as lamb': The social construction of recognising older women. In S. Nettleton & J. Watson (Eds.), *The body in everyday life* (pp. 258–275). London: Routledge.

Gilleard, C., & Higgs, P. (2000). *Cultures of ageing*. London: Prentice Hall.

Gott, M., & Hinchliff, S. (2003). Sex and ageing: A gendered issue. In S. Arber, K. Davidson, & J. Ginn (Eds.), *Gender and ageing: Changing roles and relationships* (pp. 63–78). Maidenhead: Open University Press.

Holstein, M.B. (2001). A feminist perspective on anti-aging medicine. *Generations – Journal of the American Society on Aging, 25*(4), 38–43.

Holstein, M.B. (2006). On being an ageing woman. In T.M. Calasanti & K.F. Slevin (Eds.), *Age matters. Realigning feminist thinking*. New York, NY: Routledge.

Hurd, L.C. (2000). Older women's body image and embodied experience: An exploration. *Journal of Women & Aging, 12*(3–4), 77–97.

Hurd Clarke, L. (2002). Beauty in later-life: Older women's perceptions of physical attractiveness. *Canadian Journal on Aging, 21*(3), 429–442.

Hurd Clarke, L. (2010). *Facing age: Women growing older in anti-aging culture*. Toronto: Rowman and Littlefield.

Kaufman, S.R. (1986). *The ageless self: Sources of meaning in later life*. Wisconsin: University of Wisconsin Press.

Krekula, C. (2007). The intersection of age and gender: Reworking gender theory and social gerontology. *Current Sociology, 55*(2), 155–171.

Laz, C. (2003). Age embodied. *Journal of Aging Studies, 17*(4), 503–519.

Loe, M. (2004). Sex and the senior woman: Pleasure and danger in the Viagra era. *Sexualities, 7*(3), 303–326.

Montemurro, B., & Gillen, M.M. (2013). Wrinkles and sagging flesh: Exploring transformations in women's sexual body image. *Journal of Women and Aging, 25*, 3–23.

Oberg, P., & Tornstam, L. (1999). Body images among men and women of different ages. *Ageing and Society, 19*, 629–644.

Plummer, K. (2010). Generational sexualities, subterranean traditions, and the hauntings of the sexual world: Some preliminary remarks. *Symbolic Interaction, 33*(2), 163–190.

Riggs, D. (2012). Subjectivity in sexology practice and research. *Sexual and Relationship Therapy, 27*(1), 1–2.

Ryan, G.W., & Bernard, H.R. (2000). Data management and analysis methods. In N.K. Denzin & Y.S. Lincoln (Eds.), *Handbook of qualitative research* (2nd ed., pp. 769–802). Thousand Oaks, CA: Sage.

Sandberg, L. (2013). Affirmative old age – the ageing body and feminist theories on difference. *International Journal of Aging and Later Life, 8*(1), 11–40.

Shilling, C. (2012). *The body and social theory*. London: Sage.

Sondergaard, D.M. (2002a). Poststructuralist approaches to empirical analysis. *Qualitative Studies in Education, 15*(2), 187–204.

Sondergaard, D.M. (2002b). Theorising subjectivity: Contesting the monopoly of Psychoanalysis. *Feminism and Psychology, 12*(4), 445–454.

Sontag, S. (1979). The double standard of aging. In V. Carver & P. Liddiard (Eds.), *An ageing population* (pp. 72–80). Milton Keynes: Open University.

Trudel, G., Turgeon, L., & Piché, L. (2010). Marital and sexual aspects of old age. *Sexual and Relationship Therapy, 25*, 316–341.

Tunaley, J.R., Walsh, S., & Nicolson, P. (1999). 'I'm not bad for my age': The meaning of body size and eating in the lives of older women. *Ageing & Society, 19*, 741–759.

Vares, T. (2009). Reading the 'sexy oldie': Gender, age(ing) and embodiment. *Sexualities, 12*(4), 503–524.

Midlife menopause: male partners talking

Lih-Mei Liao[a], Sarah Lunn[b] and Martyn Baker[c]

[a]Institute for Women's Health, University College London, London, UK; [b]Camden & Islington NHS Foundation Trust, Clinical Health Psychology Services, London, UK; [c]Department of Psychology, University of East London, London, UK

Psychological research on menopause has focused upon women's ideas and experiences. This qualitative study explored heterosexual male partners' perspectives of midlife menopause. In-depth interviews were conducted with eight men currently in a long-term relationship with a woman aged between 45 and 55 years and experiencing menstrual changes associated with menopause. The male partners alluded to emotional instability in the women who had been propelled by menopause into a trajectory of loss. Experiences and outcomes were believed to be variable, depending on the strengths of the individual. The female sexuality spoiled by menopause was expressed as a shared loss that had to be actively managed within the relationship. Discussion however was prohibited by a social etiquette that protected both partners from exposure and also contributed to a male "ignorance". A more positive story of the menopause transition was also alluded to if inconsistently, whereby the challenges of living with menopause could be laudably met and benefits were potentially available to both parties. The interviewees saw knowledge about menopause as a remedy not just for their ignorance but as a way towards a future (better) society that is less constrained by the taboo.

Introduction

The word "menopause" literally means cessation of the monthly cycles. In industrialised societies, on average, the final menstrual period occurs between ages 50 and 51. In the medical world, menopause is defined retrospectively by 12 months of absence of menstrual bleeding without identifiable medical reasons (World Health Organisation, 1996). The lead up to menopause, referred to as perimenopause, typically spans several years and begins in mid-forties. The transition is only considered "abnormal" or "premature" if it occurs before the age of 40. To lay people, menopause is generally referred to as "change of life" or "the change", an imprecise but culturally shared concept that denotes midlife, aging and the gradual end to fertility potential in a woman.

Bodily changes give rise to subjective experiences that are influenced by and contribute to shared meanings. In terms of physical and psychological well-being, there is broad agreement from quantitative and qualitative research that patterns of symptom reporting and medical help seeking vary between social groups and along cultural and temporal dimensions, rendering it difficult to insist upon an exclusively essentialist framework for understanding women's experiences. Behavioural and social scientists have contributed to clinical research that aimed to debunk some of the pathologising myths of menopause, in particular the social construction of the "menopausal syndrome" (Avis et al., 2001). However, for women living in contemporary Westernised societies, hot flushes, night sweats and attendant effects on health (e.g. sleep deprivation) are recognised as common during the menopause transition, as is vaginal dryness (Freeman et al., 2007). These physical symptoms are reliably improved by hormone replacement therapy (HRT). In addition, a significant minority of women report compromised psychological and sexual wellness associated with menopause.

Competing explanations of the more negative or distressing experiences of menopause are based on essentialist and discursive standpoints. In a number of societies for example, menopause is experienced as a positive and augmenting time of life for women, where social privileges become more accessible. In some communities for example, new vocations and social roles such as name givers and healers become available to women who have reached menopause; the same is true for the respect for and the special status of "wise women" (Hall, Callister, Berry, & Matsumura, 2007). However, in many societies, ageing is devaluing especially for women, such that menopause may be experienced as a social stigma. In Western societies in particular, representations of women as "weakened" in significant ways by menopause have lent themselves to the project of medicalisation (Wilson, 1968), a project not entirely unfounded on some very major partisan financial interests. Thus, the popular cultural and the master medical narratives (Jones, 1994) intersect with consumerist interests to universalise menopause as a disease and the affected woman as a patient in need of treatment in order to hold grimly to feminine integrity.

These meanings can be expected to inform women's experiences and expressions in relation to menopause, not just the hormonal changes (Daly, 1995). Some studies have demonstrated predictive statistical relationships between negative attitudes to menopause and greater levels of symptom reporting and medical help seeking (e.g. Bloch, 2002). The most recent psychological studies have identified negative attitudes to menopause in women and men but especially in younger women (Smith, Mann, Mirza, & Hunter, 2011) and, furthermore, women who hold negative attitudes towards menopause report more symptoms associated with menopause (Ayers, Forshaw, & Hunter, 2010).

Relative to the scale of the literatures, there has been negligible interest in male perspectives of menopause, even though earlier (albeit methodologically limited) studies suggested potentially interesting differences between men and women's beliefs about different aspects of menopause (Dege & Gretzinger, 1982; Kahana, Kiyak, & Liang, 1980; Neugarten & Kraines, 1965). In a more recent study that examined attitudes to HRT among 500 women and men (Lomranz, Becker, Eyal, Pines, & Mester, 2000), women were reported to be even more likely than men to consider menopause a medical problem rather than a developmental process. Embodied experiences are relational not just at cultural and subcultural but familial levels. Thus, the ideas and behaviours of male partners could be an additional interesting line of inquiry. Kowalczyk, Nowosielski, Folwarczny, Szpak, and Skrzypulec (2008), for example, asked women about how they perceived the impact of their partner's behaviour on their menstrual problems. All of the women reported that none of their male partners spoke about issues of menopause; they did not experience support from their male partners during what they considered to be a significant time of life for them.

The cultural context within which heterosexual men formulate and express their psychological opinions has undergone considerable changes since the earlier studies were carried out. The concept of "the new man" has especially opened up new discourses about (heterosexual) men (Peterson, 1998). Self-help books such as Dick Roth's (1999) *A Husband's Guide to Understanding the Menopause* signal a change in social expectations.

The supposed softening of hegemonic masculinity may have implications for the way in which male partners respond to what is conventionally seen as "women's trouble".

Rationale for the current study

The need for exploration of male partners' perspectives was identified by the first author in her work in psychological counselling with women presenting physical and psychological problems attributed to menopause. When inquiries were made about social support, the women, almost without exception, would report being unaware of their male partner's knowledge of or level of interest in the topic. The current study was an attempt to explore male partners' views of menopause. Given the relative absence of investigations in our topic of interest, qualitative analysis was felt to be particularly appropriate for this preliminary work (Murphy, Dingwall, Greatbatch, Parker, & Watson, 1998). Although the goal was not to restrict the men's talk, the focus of this preliminary work was on what the men might say about the effects of menopause on their partners, themselves and their relationships.

Method

Recruitment

All participants had to be in a long-term relationship with a woman of menopausal age (aged between 45 and 55 years)[1]. Men whose relationship with their partner had begun less than five years ago, or whose partner had reached menopause as a result of medical problems or interventions (e.g. chemotherapy, surgery), or who held a professional perspective on menopause (e.g. physicians, nurses) were excluded at recruitment stage. Of the eight study participants, seven were contacted through work colleagues, friends and acquaintances. One participant was recruited through an advertisement in a local leisure magazine. None of the men were known to the interviewer prior to the study.

Participants

All of the men were aged between 42 and 62 years (mean = 51.5 years). Two identified themselves as British, two Irish, two American, one Trinidadian and one South African. The sample comprised professional and semi-skilled manual workers, seven of whom were currently employed. Respondents reported a median 16 years of formal education for themselves and 15.5 years for their partners. Their female partners were aged between 45 and 55 years with a mean age of 51 years; the duration of the relationship ranged from 8 to 40 years with a mean duration of 23 years. Five of the couples had one or two children and three of the couples did not have children. Five of the partners were described as no longer menstruating and three as still menstruating but had experienced menstrual changes. All of the men reported that they had their partners' approval for their participation.

Procedure

Ethical approval had been granted by the University of East London Ethics Committee. Recruitment was carried out by two female psychologists in their early thirties and early forties. The interviews were conducted by the white female psychologist in her early thirties. A brief telephone conversation was carried out with all interested respondents in order to explain the nature of the study and offer the opportunity for them to discuss with their partners about participation and to ask further questions. Consent was then obtained (in word and writing) from each participant. An in-depth interview was then carried out either at the participant's home or the interviewer's workplace. The interviews lasted between $1\frac{1}{4}$ to 2 hours, broadly guided by an interview schedule developed by all of the authors. Whilst the schedule ensured that the three broad topic areas were covered (i.e. understanding, communication, perceived impact), there was also a definite attempt to ask open questions as far as possible. An interview guide was put together to balance the opportunity for participants to give their own accounts and a loose structure imposed by us to explore our focus of interest. The final interview guide had taken into account comments and feedback from work colleagues.

Analysis

Each interview was audio-taped and transcribed verbatim. In an attempt to further capture the meaning of each communication, additional verbal utterances such as laughter and sighing as well as pauses were also recorded. The transcripts were subjected to an initial thematic analysis (TA) as outlined in Braun and Clarke (2006). Although different types of qualitative analysis ask different questions of and make different assumptions about the data, there is much procedural overlap because all analyses share the goal of observing patterns in accounts of events or experiences. We were drawn to the argument that TA "offers an accessible and theoretically-flexible approach to analysing qualitative data" (Braun & Clarke, 2006, p. 77). Having approached this research from clinical practice, and having found very little empirical research with men, we were curious and excited about what our informants might offer. TA enabled us to meet our goal of an initial exploration of patterns of coherence and contradictions in male partners' accounts without being caught up in the essentialist-discursive polarity in the literature on menopause.

Our curiosity had been piqued when our mid-aged female clients talked about the impact of "the change" and their male partners' disengagement with it. We approached this particular piece of research hopeful for new talk and emergent ideas and were less interested in elucidating the "fine-grained functionality" (Braun & Clarke, 2006) of the talk, even though this could not be entirely suspended in our reading of the textual data.

Results and discussion

This section focuses on the way in which the eight participants anticipated, perceived, interpreted and responded to "menopause". Where possible our observations are linked to ideas about menopause in the literature and popular culture. Direct quotes from the participants (in italics) are selected for being typical or poignant for each theme. The seven key themes are presented under three distinct headings to express our interpretation of the meanings: "female transformation", "shared process" and "sex taboo".

A female transformation

This section refers to the participants' descriptions of what menopause might entail, what it meant for women, and how women might manage the process. Menopause was described as something to be entered into and completed within a defined time frame, i.e. a journey. The woman emerged, at some point, as an altered person (for the better or worse) or relatively unscathed,

> I imagine that a lot of men are going to think 'What's going to happen at the end of this?__[2] is she still going to be like why I married her?' (1:445)[3]

Badness, madness and losses

The process of transformation was described as potentially hazardous if "natural" and inevitable. Variability was acknowledged, but the menopausing woman was frequently described as emotionally charged,

> ...the flash-point is high. The temper is very very short. You know they can jump up very very easily on a situation whereas before it wouldn't be. (8:123)

There were two characteristics to this transformation. First, women were viewed as capable of controlling their outbursts (via hormone treatment) and thus were responsible for being "bad",

> ...she can turn and be a right nasty bitch and you just don't know. (4:318)

> She turns into some kind of mad woman who won't let me near her... (3:560)

The alternative view, whereby the bad behaviour was seen as out of character, positioned the woman as helpless in the face of her "raging hormones" that drove her to the "madness":

> She doesn't want it. She's fighting it herself. But sometimes she can't help it. She just gets stroppy. (4:453)

The male partners typically presented these contradictory facets simultaneously, both of which drew on notions of hormonally induced psychical instability and deterioration. These notions are strongly reminiscent of both scientific and folk discourses, whereby women are either positioned as culpable for their psychological deviation (Dryden, 1999) or categorised as unwittingly at the mercy of untameable female biology (Ussher, 1992).

The participants drew on popular discourses whereby multiple losses are envisaged at menopause – a time when fertility ends and women are believed to leave behind their youth, femininity and sexuality (Gannon, 1994).

> (It is as if they were wearing)[4] menopause blue raincoats___(i.e.) these women were resigning themselves to some kind of loss__the raincoat was determined to be a particularly asexual character__the woman feels ashamed and therefore shrinks from the scene... (5:232)

There was also a level of awareness, if much less salient, of the risk of indiscriminately attributing a rather wide range of ordinary problems to menopause,

> I mean she may just have the hump about something and people put it down to the fact that she's going through menopause. (1:203)

Potential for female growth

Some men identified mitigating factors such as an active working life or personal resilience to potential variable outcomes,

> ...the individual has a lot to do with it and strength of character and if you're going to let something like that get you down then it will. (1:328)

One potential implication is that women who experience more difficulties at menopause may be personally lacking in some way. The tendency to individualise female difficulties has been identified by critics as a fundamental limitation of the "master" medical narrative (Jones, 1994) that conveniently de-contextualises mid-aged women's expressions.

In discussing factors that could mitigate outcome, menopause was thought to be potentially beneficial. It was viewed as potentially energising and capable of enhancing a woman's libido. Although such optimism was generally expressed in parallel to the co-existing fear that her sexuality might rapidly fade, women were described as entering a new liberating life stage where they were able to expand and develop into more mature, enriched and self-accepting individuals,

> Drawing from it rather than it drawing from you...[5] you (women) come out (of menopause) thinking I'm a bit more than a woman, you know, just that little bit extra... (1:432)

This more positive outlook echoes the alternative and wider perspective of menopause, chiefly in feminist and social science literatures (Greer, 1991; Hunter & O'Dea, 1997; Palmund, 1997), whereby menopause is said to represent a time of renewal, wisdom and the opportunity to create new meanings for life. In contrast to the traditional construction of menopause as an undesirable condition requiring treatment, this alternative account described a relatively unproblematic and potentially life-enhancing transition.

A shared process

This section discusses the way in which the interviewees expressed how they were affected by their partners' menopause transition, either through their observed effects on the partner or through the anticipated implications for their joint and separate lives. They alluded to a shared transition and recognition of being propelled into a different phase in their relationship.

> I think the nature of the beast has to be of the couple__at the end of the day it's something that people have to deal with together. (3:512)

Male helplessness

Women's transformation was seen to pull ill prepared male partners into their own unwanted journey and unknown territory,

> ...I'm in a forest at the moment and I can't see the light. (8:438)

> ...the last few months I don't know whether I'm coming or going. (4:352)

Men's involvement was conceptualised in a number of ways. Most of the participants presented themselves as "supporters" by highlighting the importance of sympathy, understanding and tolerance. The impression here was of a joint endeavour where the woman's well-being was prioritised. This approach fits with the recently developed notion of "the new man" whereby qualities such as sensitivity, thoughtfulness and a willingness to help others are actively condoned (Duncan & Dowsett, 2010; Frosh, 1995). As an adverse consequence of this more caring approach, however, the men were often left feeling helpless and redundant due to a perceived inability to adequately provide this desired support,

...I feel impotent because you're not able to fulfil the role that you should be able to. (3:198)

This experienced "impotence" may be exacerbated by co-existing discursive constructions of the "real man" who is instrumental and capable of protecting "their woman" from adversity (Peterson, 1998). A further sense of "emasculation" was conveyed in men's presentation (or anticipation) of themselves as suffering at the hands of their menopausal partner – either directly through unprovoked attack:

I can't do anything right in this house... (2:94)

or indirectly through the vicarious effects upon their relationship or a fear of the unknown. Adopting an additional perspective, several men presented themselves ultimately as "acceptors of the inevitable",

...it's a bit like death isn't it, it's going to arrive one day and then you've just got to deal with it. (3:127)

Sexual losses, gains and sameness

The psychological significance of the end of female fertility and therefore shared reproductive years was mentioned by a number of men, who alluded to both positive and negative effects on female sexuality and the couple's sexual relationship.

It is one of the most visceral aspects of our identities as sexual beings... the point at which women can no longer biologically procreate is very very fundamental. (1:364)

...sexual attraction is reduced because there's some part of the subconscious which associates sex with procreation. In my mind there is an element of slightly diminished sexual potency associated with menopause. (5:407)

Anxiety about a detrimental impact of menopause upon the couple's sexual relationship was common. Fantasies of women's unmatchable or totally absent libido associated with waning sex appeal were expressed. This range of varied sexual effects were attributed to the physical and psychological effects of menopause,

I'm not immune to the fears of women running around totally free and unconstrained and so the notion of women being liberated by menopause raises anxieties in me. (5:242)

...not so much that I'm not going to find her attractive but more that I'm going to be less desirable to her, that she'll lose interest in... I guess that's my worry._I would be left desiring but not desired. (3:410)

On the other hand, the participants also expressed the view that menopause (and even female ageing) is insignificant in terms of a woman's sexual desirability, and some even identified a number of benefits relating to their partner's menopause including a deepening of the relationship, liberation from the constraints of contraception and an enhanced sexual rapport,

> ...you've got someone who knows what it's all about and who's been around the block a few times and who knows what the score is, and on the whole that is more attractive... (1:335)

> I keep saying to (partner), 'This should be the summer of your life. You know you're not going to get pregnant again. I'm not going to need to use condoms so we should have fun.' (8:567)

Anticipation of stability in the couple's sexual relationship was also expressed:

> For the majority it's not a big issue__it's just a change in her but not significant in anything to do with their relationship__She's going to go on having her normal sexuality... her desires... (7:516)

These "alternative" views contrast sharply with negative social stereotypes and have rarely been documented in men. They appear to reflect more recent expressions that highlight previously overlooked benefits accompanying the menopausal years (e.g. Greer, 1991). On the whole, however, the more positive ideas about the relationship between menopause and female sexuality seemed fragile in the interviewees' accounts and were generally less salient than the rival theme of menopause as an event that spoils sexuality.

An ageing couple

The association between menopause and ageing was strong but not frequently directly alluded to. It emerged more as an undercurrent in many of the quotes relating to sexuality in the next section.

> Menopause isn't the issue, the issue's ageing... (5:481)

> There's this feeling about menopause__that it's the beginning of old age... (7:491)

Ageing was acknowledged as more an issue for women than for men, for example,

> I wouldn't necessarily wake up in the morning and think 'God, I've got a crease there. (8:434)

However, ageing in the woman clearly had meanings for the stage/phase of the couple's relationship and therefore male ageing,

> You're suddenly brought up against the fact that you've reached an age which you associate with your parents and you don't think of yourself as. (8:434)

> It's like growing up, getting married...another part of lie. (2:77)

A sex taboo

Throughout the accounts, menopause was consistently referred to as a taboo topic – "Everyone knows it's going on but it's unmentionable" (3:164), largely because of its link to sex and sexuality. The section relates to the nature of the taboo and the implications of this for both men and women. The nature of the taboo resonates with Laws' (1990) idea that men tend to regard menstruation as a sexual matter, "principally because (men) see women as sexual beings above all else, and also because they define anything which comes from the female genitals as sexual" (Laws, 1990, p. 131).

> ...I think it's any subject that...has to do with raw sexuality, and menopause would be one of them. The others being menstruation, intercourse, seduction. (5:379)

> ...like a lot of things that have to do with sex and ageing__ they seem to have a little taboo label to it... (6:490)

Putting the lid on a spoiled sexuality

Overall, menopause more consistently signified diminished female sexuality, conversation of which was expressed as outside social etiquette. Inhibition was felt to be insidious by most of the interviewees:

> I think it's a very private thing between a man and a woman and a couple and uh...it doesn't tend to stray out too much. (7:303)

> ...men don't talk about it because it's an unexplored area that could potentially erupt and destabilises the sexual relations. (3:374)

Even within their own partnership, most interviewees felt intimidated by the (sexually) intimate nature of this topic. Varying levels of discomfort and embarrassment were expressed at the idea of discussing menopause and related experiences openly with their partner,

> I don't sit down and talk about it with her because... I can't say it's private... but it is private. (4:54)

> ...I feel the sex barrier... It would have to be a very close relationship. (2:74)

The etiquette was partially based upon a sense of loyalty to the woman, i.e. respect for her privacy, although it clearly also protected the interviewees:

> I didn't want to talk about it really as it would upset her. She'd say 'Mind your own business. __Don't you talk about it.' (4:149)

> I'm curious about it but it's not a subject I feel comfortable discussing. (5:318)

Most of the interviewees believed that women intentionally restricted discussion and speculated about female motives:

> Women don't talk about it because there's an element of shame... (8:372)

I was told [by mother] 'You don't have to worry about it, you're a man', so end of subject. (3:393)

Laws (1990) discussed the etiquette surrounding talk on menstruation. According to her findings, men were permitted to openly jest and deride the menstruating female whilst women were bound by etiquette to remain silent on matters relating to menstruation and menopause. However, it would seem that our interviewees felt equally bound by the "menopause etiquette" to remain silent.

As engagement with the topic felt impossible within confiding relationships, it was thought to be absolutely inappropriate within male groups and between acquaintances (where flippancy and humour were felt to be necessary strategies for deflecting unease in social inter-action). On rare occasions when the topic was broached, participants reported that it was rarely followed through in any depth and often swiftly discarded in favour of safer topics.

Fundamentally, however, inhibition was linked to the subtext that disclosure of one's partner's menopause could be too revealing – of a sexual failing within the relationship. There was a risk of the male partner being socially positioned as sexually deprived, due to his partner's deflated sexuality (and possibly also his own). This was such a threat that all efforts at silence had to be made to preserve the "macho mask":

> ...we just can't talk about it. I think it's probably because it's difficult to deal with.__ If sud-denly you're not getting any nooky and you want some then I guess that's a bit of a stress. (3:139)

> ...I suppose what I risk exposing is revealing who I am... (5:348)

The threat of opening up dialogue about menopause was emphasised by several of the participants:

> ...it would be sticking a stick into a very sensitive area... and something volatile or unpleas-ant could emerge... (5:188)

The interviewees' concerns are understandable. Hegemonic masculinity requires "real men" to be driven by lustful urges that demand instant gratification (Edley & Wetherell, 1995). According to prevailing social discourses, any inability to evoke desire or sexually satisfy the woman represents a failure of masculine domination that could destabilise het-erosexual male identity (Frosh, 1995).

Meeting the challenge with knowledge

During the interviews, although all of the men were familiar with the term menopause, none appeared entirely confident as to what it refers to. There was strong agreement that the lack of "general basic knowledge" (1:27) was widespread amongst men due to very limited talk amongst men and between couples. Menopause was referred as "nebulous" (1:64) and "a whole grey area that everyone seems to understand but they don't" (1:67):

> ...you sort of know about it but don't know about it ... (6:491)

> ...it's a situation which I find that I'm lonesome in for the simple reason that men just don't talk about it. (8:151)

Where talk occurs it tends to focus on problems for which discursive resources existed, and the problem talk enabled menopause to be included in conversation between men:

> ...there's some point in the proceedings when you're all going to have a moan about your girlfriends or your wife or whatever and it's like a male domain, like 'so and so last night', 'oh yer that was me last week...' (1:252)

Lack of male interest was also put forward as a culprit for male "ignorance", with menopause continued to be positioned as a "woman topic" in society:

> For selfish reasons, or they (male partners) just don't want to know about it, or they don't think it's necessary because they're not bothered. (1:219)

Most participants declared a wish (and sense of obligation) to acquire more information about menopause. Knowledge was regarded as advantageous for men and women, because sensible advice could enhance clarification and understanding, thereby enabling the men to be less helpless in the face of their partners' physical and psychological transformation,

> I just want to get some information to help me cope... (4:288)

> ...if you knew about it you could help. (8:647)

Some interviewees suggested ways in which the obstacles to improve knowledge could be overcome, and some claimed they had made active attempts to extract information, albeit haphazardly, from different sources including television/radio programmes, magazines/newspapers, information conversations and academic journals:

> ...I've not read great medical books, just little silly things...like I always read the 'Daily Mail' and I've been looking for things on that. (4:153)

> I think it (information) would have to come through mainstream media... catch us unaware... rather than a conscious decision to go and learn about it... because most of us won't... till it's too late. (3:497)

Despite the men's professed active search for and passive receptiveness to information about menopause, they regarded themselves as ignorant on the topic. Considerable interest in the personal experiences of other men and couples could be identified,

> I'd like to read the experiences of another man for instance and the insecurities and problems that they have to deal with. (3:295)

> ...anecdotal evidence of what women really feel and what they find they're not getting from their partners. (6:187)

A greater openness on a societal level was advocated by most participants, e.g. greater information distribution (via formal or informal sources). Acquiring "permission" from women to become involved in this aspect of their lives was also considered an important factor. Whilst some predicted a future progression towards openness and inclusion, others felt this change had already begun.

Methodological observations

Salmon (2013) recently suggested a number of tentative criteria for estimating the quality of qualitative studies. His "template" provides us with a structure for commenting on our methodology. We had familiarised ourselves with the literature prior to the study and identified a gap and a line of inquiry, i.e. about heterosexual men's perspectives of menopause based on their experiences of how their partners' "natural" event might have affected their relationship. We have justified the relevance of the study and the reason for a qualitative exploration. A weakness of the study is that the accounts generated by our small sample of eight men may not have brought our analysis to saturation point, so that additional themes, contradictions and dilemmas may well have been missed. We see our account as a starting point and a way of opening an interesting and relevant line of inquiry regarding menopause.

The small number of volunteers within our tight time frame did not permit a choice in sampling methods. Our volunteers were clearly willing to talk about menopause, but the beliefs and assumptions of informants less inclined to discuss the topic are key to a fuller understanding. It is also possible that our volunteers had felt particularly troubled by menopause, and a balance between men who felt more or less troubled might have helped us develop a fuller appreciation of the pluralities of male perspectives. The relatively middle class and Western background of the participants prevented observations of socioeconomic and ethnic similarities and differences. A larger sample would be necessary to specifically address the potential impact of these and additional intersecting variables, such as parenthood, work, gender positioning and sexual orientation.

The perceived social categories of the interviewer can be expected to have impacted upon the men's talk. Several interviewees attempted to ask the interviewer for information about menopause. With a male interviewer, there might have been less social pressure to express the need for male partners to overcome their "ignorance" about a developmental process that affects women. The female interviewer's age – younger than the average age of the menopause transition – may have facilitated a greater openness in that the men did not have to feel concerned about offending an actual "menopausal woman". Nevertheless, a choice of male or female interviewer would have generated a wider range of interactions leading to additional perspectives.

Further reflections

Menopause is very clearly positioned as relational in our interviewees' account. Biomedical discourses that locate changes (symptoms) inside the woman (patient) could be identified in the accounts, e.g. as a participant jested, "one of the old ladies was as randy as hell. She said the best thing she'd ever done was take HRT." (8:178). However, the story of disease requiring treatment was oblique rather than prevailing.

Nevertheless, the dominant menopause story in the eight men's accounts was one of compromise for heterosexual couples. Parallel to this story however was a more positive representation of the changed woman as someone with more to offer, having been "round the block" a few more times. This however was a much less salient theme though expressed by all of the participants to an extent. During the course of the interviews, the participants continuously oscillated between competing narratives about the menopausal woman, suggestive of tension in how to position themselves along available discourses.

Within the main story of compromise that is built on denigrating representations of the ageing woman, frustrations and worries were frequently expressed but had not been openly communicated within or outside the relationship. The interviewees declared that a societal move towards greater information accessibility and disinhibited talk was necessary before an appreciative understanding of menopause could be reached. Musings of making available some information on menopause that is tailored to male partners were put forward. We noted with interest this aspect of the men's talk, which resonates with the overuse of "information" and "education" in organisations and public services to resolve what are often relational dilemmas.

Our small empirical study sought to explore an under researched area. The men's willingness to engage in dialogue and the richness in their talk suggest that there is scope for future research. The current report suggests potential themes that could serve as an additional source for conceptual comparisons in future larger scale works.

Acknowledgements

The authors thank the anonymous participants for their conversations, and Charmaine Elliott, Felicity Corser and Sureya Ali for their assistance in the preparation of this manuscript.

Notes

1. Research has shown that menopause occurs between the ages of 45 and 54 years for three quarters of women (Greendale, Lee, & Arriola, 1999).
2. In the transcript extracts marked "__" this indicates text that has not been included so to avoid relating material that is not considered relevant or material that may impinge on a participant's confidentiality.
3. Each participant was arbitrarily allocated a number between 1 and 8, which was then used to identify the origin of each quote. The second longer number refers to the line in the transcript.
4. When brackets have been inserted within a quote, this indicates any text added in by the authors to clarify the meaning of the quote.
5. In the transcript extracts marked ". . ." this refers to where participants have left a pause.

References

Avis, N., Stellato, R., Crawford, S., Bromberger, J., Gan, P., Cain, V., & Kawaga-Singer, M. (2010). Is there a menopausal syndrome? Menopausal status and symptoms across racial/ethnic groups. *Social Science & Medicine, 52*, 345–356.

Ayers, B., Forshaw, M., & Hunter, M.S. (2010). The impact of attitudes towards the menopause on women's symptom experience: A systematic review. *Maturitas, 65*, 28–36.

Bloch, A. (2002). Self-awareness during the menopause. *Maturitas, 41*, 61–68.

Braun, V., & Clarke, V. (2006). Using thematic analysis in psychology. *Qualitative Research in Psychology, 3*(2), 77–101.

Daly, J. (1995). Caught in the web: The social construction of menopause as disease. *Journal of Reproductive and Infant Psychology, 13*, 115–126.

Dege, K., & Gretzinger, J. (1982). Attitudes of families toward menopause. In A.M. Voda, M. Dinnerstein, & S. O'Donnell (Eds.), *Changing perspectives on menopause* (pp. 60–69). Austin, TX: University of Texas Press.

Dryden, C. (1999). *Being married, doing gender: A critical analysis of gender relationships in marriage*. London: Routledge.

Duncan, D., & Dowsett, G.W. (2010). "There's no teleology to it; it's just about the spirit of play": Men, intimacy, and "late" modernity. *Journal of Men's Studies, 18*, 45–62.

Edley, N., & Wetherell, M. (1995). *Men in perspective: Practice, power and identity*. London: Harvester Wheatsheaf.

Freeman, E., Sammel, M., Lin, H., Gracia, C., Pien, G., Nelson, D., & Sheng, L. (2007). Symptoms associated with menopausal transition and reproductive hormones in midlife women. *Obstetrics & Gynecology, 110*, 230–240.

Frosh, S. (1995). Unpacking masculinity. In C. Burch & B. Speed (Eds.), *Gender, power and relationships* (pp. 218–231). London: Routledge.

Gannon, L. (1994). Sexuality and the menopause. In P.Y.L. Choi & P. Nicolson (Eds.), *Female sexuality* (pp. 100–124). London: Harvester Wheatsheaf.

Greendale, G.A., Lee, N.P., & Arriola, E.R. (1999). Menopause. *The Lancet, 353*, 571–578.

Greer, G. (1991). *The change: Women, ageing and the menopause*. London: Hamish Hamilton.

Hall, L., Callister, L., Berry, J., & Matsumira, G. (2007). Meanings of menopause: Cultural influences on perception and management of menopause. *Journal of Holistic Nursing, 25*, 106–118.

Hunter, M.S., & O'Dea, I. (1997). Menopause: Bodily changes and multiple meanings. In J. Ussher (Ed.), *Body talk: Material and discursive regulation of sexuality, madness and reproduction* (pp. 199–223). London: Routledge.

Jones, J. (1994). Embodied meaning: menopause and the change of life. *Social Work in Health Care, 19*, 43–65.

Kahana, E., Kiyak, A., & Liang, J. (1980). Menopause in the context of other life events. In A. Dan & C. Beecher (Eds.), *The menstrual cycle* (pp. 167–179). New York, NY: Springer.

Kowalczyk, R., Nowosielski, K., Folwarczny, W., Szpak, R., & Skrzypulec, V. (2008). Influence of partner on alleviation of menopause symptoms in women – preliminary questionnaire study. *Sexologies, T-10-P-07*, 151.

Laws, S. (1990). *Issues of blood: The politics of menstruation*. London: MacMillan Press.

Lomranz, J., Becker, D., Eyal, N., Pines, A., & Mester, R. (2000). Attitudes towards hormone replacement therapy among middle-aged women and men. *European Journal of Obstetrics, Gynecology and Reproductive Biology, 93*, 199–203.

Murphy, E., Dingwall, R., Greatbatch, D., Parker, S., & Watson, P. (1998). Qualitative research methods in health technology assessment: A review of the literature. *Health Technology Assessment, 2*, 58–63.

Neugarten, B.L., & Kraines, R.J. (1965). "Menopausal symptoms" in women of various ages. *Psychosomatic Medicine, 27*, 266–273.

Palmund, I. (1997). The social construction of menopause at risk. *Journal of Psychosomatic Obstetrics and Gyneacology, 18*, 87–94.

Peterson, A. (1998). *Unmasking the masculine: "Men" and "identity" in a sceptical age*. London: Sage.

Roth, D. (1999). *"No, it's not hot in here". A husband's guide to understanding the menopause*. Hadley, MA: North Star Publications.

Salmon, P. (2013). Assessing the quality of qualitative research. *Patient Education and Counseling, 90*, 1–3.

Smith, M., Mann, E., Mirza, A., & Hunter, M. (2011). Men and women's perceptions of hot flushes within social situations: Are menopausal women's negative beliefs valid? *Maturitas, 69*, 57–62.

Ussher, J. (1992). Reproductive rhetoric and the blaming of the body. In P. Nicolson & J. Ussher (Eds.), *The psychology of women's health and health care* (pp. 31–61). London: MacMillan Press Ltd.

Wilson, R.A. (1968). *Feminine forever*. Lanham, MD: M Evans & Co.

World Health Organisation Scientific Group (1996). *Research on the menopause in the 1990s, WHO technical report series 866*. Geneva: Author.

Index